# Learning, Curriculum and Employability in Higher Education

## How can universities ensure that they are preparing their students for today's competitive job market?

The rapid growth of Higher Education over the past fifty years has seen expectations increasing, and governments seeking to widen participation. There is now an urgent need for the government and higher education institutions to address the issue of graduate employability.

With insight and clarity, the authors of this timely and insightful book encourage a pro-active stance to this topic by offering a ground-breaking model that can be easily implemented in institutions to make low-cost, high-gain improvements to students' employability. They discuss how an employability-friendly curriculum can be developed, even in subjects that might not be characterised as vocational and cover a range of topics covered including:

- the challenge of employability;
- case studies from four disciplinary areas;
- the enhancement of practice;
- assessing for employability;
- the Skills *plus* project.

This book draws on a set of over 200 in-depth interviews with graduates in employment, and includes a unique account of the meanings of employability in the workplace. Anyone with a responsibility for curriculum development or policy making within higher education, who wants to advance learning *and* promote student employability, will find this book essential reading.

**Peter Knight** is a Senior Lecturer at the Open University. **Mantz Yorke** is Professor of Higher Education at Liverpool John Moores University.

# Learning, Curriculum and Employability in Higher Education

Peter Knight and
Mantz Yorke

RoutledgeFalmer
Taylor & Francis Group

LONDON AND NEW YORK

First published 2004
by RoutledgeFalmer
11 New Fetter Lane, London EC4P 4EE

Simultaneously published in the USA and Canada
by RoutledgeFalmer
29 West 35th Street, New York, NY 10001

*RoutledgeFalmer is an imprint of the Taylor & Francis Group*

© 2004 Peter Knight and Mantz Yorke

Typeset in Times by
HWA Text and Data Management, Tunbridge Wells
Printed and bound in Great Britain by
The Cromwell Press, Trowbridge, Wiltshire

*British Library Cataloguing in Publication Data*
A catalogue record for this book is available from the British Library

*Library of Congress Cataloging in Publication Data*
A catalog record for this book has been requested

ISBN 0–415–30342–7 (hb)
ISBN 0–415–30343–5 (pb)

# Contents

# Illustrations

## Figures

## Tables

## Boxes

# Contributors

**Margaret Edwards** is the Director of the School of Social Science at Liverpool John Moores University. Her academic background is in Sociology which she has taught for a number of years (and continues to teach) at the university. Her teaching experience also includes work in FE and with the Open University. Dr Edwards's research interests include HE management, including change management, and HE curricular issues, such as employability, assessment, and the widening of participation in HE. She currently holds advisory roles, especially in learning and teaching developments, with Merseyside FE/HE consortia and within the university.

**Jane Gawthrope** is Manager of the Learning Teaching Support Network English Subject Centre (whose role is to serve and support teaching and learning in the discipline across UK higher education), and is responsible for planning, operations and financial control. She also takes the lead on employability projects within the Subject Centre. Jane completed a first degree in Management Sciences and then an MA in Librarianship, before embarking on a career in academic libraries. She was formerly Deputy Head of Library Services at Brunel University.

**Peter Knight** works in the Open University where he advises on the development of curricula and assessment strategies. He has a long-standing interest in curriculum, especially in learning, teaching and assessment. Lately, this interest has mainly been expressed through work on higher education. His role in the Higher Education Funding Council for England's Enhancing Student Employ-ability Co-ordination Team has given him a unique opportunity to extend this work.

**Geraldine Lyte** is Lecturer in Nursing at the School of Nursing, Midwifery and Health Visiting at the University of Manchester, UK. For more than ten years she has been developing a profile of research and development to promote the application of clinical assessment and situation/problem-solving in under-graduate nursing curricula, using problem-based learning. Since 2001 Geraldine has been co-ordinating the introduction of problem-based learning in under-graduate programmes at Manchester. She also has an established profile of research in children's nursing, her clinical specialty.

**Philip Martin** is Dean of Humanities at De Montfort University. Until March 2003 he was Director of the Learning Teaching Support Network English Subject Centre, Royal Holloway, University of London, and he has also held posts at the University of Gloucestershire, King Alfred's, Winchester, and the University of Exeter. He is the author of three books and numerous articles on Romantic Literature, and he has also published on the teaching of the Humanities. He is editor of the journal, *Literature & History*, a past President of the British Association for Romantic Studies, and the current chair of the Council for College and University English.

**Chris McGoldrick** has wide-ranging teaching and research experience. She teaches Geography at Liverpool John Moores University, with an emphasis on socio-economic issues. Her current research and consultancy interests include the higher education curriculum, policies for disadvantaged people, and minority ethnic business development.

**Aled Williams**, of the School of Construction and Property Management at the University of Salford, is Subject Co-ordinator for Construction, Surveying and Real Estate in the UK Learning and Teaching Support Network's Centre for Education in the Built Environment. He spent over eight years as a Lecturer in the School of the Built Environment at Liverpool John Moores University, where his duties included leading the BSc (Hons) programme in Property Management. He was instrumental in mapping the Skills *plus* project onto the Construction Management curricula.

**Mantz Yorke** is Professor of Higher Education at Liverpool John Moores University. His early career was in teaching and teacher education, after which he turned to staff development and educational research at Manchester Polytechnic. He then spent six years as a senior manager at Liverpool Polytechnic followed by two years on secondment as Director of Quality Enhancement at the Higher Education Quality Council. Since returning to his institution he has researched and reflected on various aspects of the student experience, including employability. He is a member of the Enhancing Student Employability Co-ordination Team funded by the Higher Education Funding Council for England.

# Introduction

## Employability: a theme of contemporary international significance

'Employability' may be a British term, but the concern with higher education's contribution to the graduate labour market is international. The case we develop here has significant implications for higher education practices across the world, although our examples are mainly from the UK; however, our set of references shows that we have been informed by work published elsewhere. Although we appreciate the danger of over-generalizing from distinctive UK concerns and its unique higher education system, we do consider that our arguments transcend the examples. We invite readers to appraise what we have to say in the light of their own particular situations.

### Employability: concern and action

We find no shortage of projects to help students develop the 'assets' that employers value, to identify suitable job opportunities and to present themselves to best advantage. There is a sense, though, that these activities, valuable though they are, occupy the margins of higher education. Consider an unpublished analysis of the ways in which the UK Learning and Teaching Support Network's 24 subject centres stood in regard to employability early in 2002: about half the centres claimed that employability was on their agenda but it was found that 'the level of activity reported did not appear to reflect this ... the actual level of interest and work related to employability across the centres can only be described as low'.

### Employability and academic values

One explanation for a low level of engagement with employability might be that, in the absence of a common definition of employability, higher education teachers interpret it as an intrusion on the proper concerns of academic life. In contrast, our central claim is that a concern for employability aligns with a concern for academic values and the promotion of good learning. We do not mean this in a trivial sense but argue that promoting employability means highlighting and then taking seriously goals of higher education that have often been left to look after themselves. For example, it is often said that higher education develops learner autonomy, but it is not always clear what autonomy amounts to nor how it is fostered. Again, higher education often claims to develop self-management, although there are problems in reconciling this with the carefully-structured arrangements that many programmes have developed to support students and maximize achievement. Enhancing employability means, then, taking seriously many of the long-established goals of higher education and devising arrangements likely to help most students to make stronger, convincing claims to achievement in respect of them. This, we shall argue, involves looking at the design of academic *programmes*,[1] while being necessarily sensitive to module or course design and appreciative of the enrichment provided by elective courses, curriculum enhancements, optional internships, placements and other work experience, as well as the contributions of careers advisers and other student support and guidance services. It is a complicated and ambitious approach to a complex and ambitious goal, for enhancing employability implies enhancing the quality of learning, teaching and assessment.

### *Employability and subsidiarity*

Weick (1976) distinguished between tight-coupled organizations, like a factory, in which inputs are turned into predictable outputs through closely-linked and exact processes, and loose-coupled ones in which inputs, processes and outputs are characterized by degrees of uncertainty. Universities tend towards the loose-coupled end: inputs (students, for example) vary, the processes that affect them (teaching, for instance) are not standardized and the outcomes tend to be unpredictable, especially if we look beyond grade point averages or degree classes. Universities are not wholly loose-coupled, for there are elements of tight-coupling – rules, expectations, systems and, to some extent, shared values. At best they are tight on principles and core purposes and more permissive, or loose-coupled, when it comes to the means of fulfilling them.

Our analysis of the development in students of employability is best expressed in terms of subsidiarity, which is a concept used in the European Union to demarcate between central and national powers. Decisions taken by the EU are to be implemented at the lowest possible level in ways that are both faithful to the directive or legislation and appropriate to local circumstances. The concept resembles 'loose-tight coupling' (Morgan, 1997), which refers to organizations that set values and priorities centrally and insist that the whole organization adhere to them while leaving questions of implementation to the discretion of workers and workgroups. So, too, with employability in higher education. We argue that complex outcomes of learning, such as those covered by 'employability' need to be seen as programme-level achievements and that arrangements to foster them need to be seen as *programme-level* concerns. Although learning intentions need to be set at programme level and although programme teams need to make sure that the teaching, learning and assessment arrangements in the component parts come together sufficiently to make the learning intentions realistic, creativity and academic freedom need not be stifled in the process. Following the principle of subsidiarity, teachers are free to engage learners with important subject matter in ways that are consistent with the programme goals and with the demands of the material itself. Plainly, there would need to be some degree of negotiation to make sure that the modules in a programme form a coherent set, but within this framework teachers would have considerable freedom.

## Audience

We address the concerns of colleagues at a number of levels within the higher education system. Readers are most likely to be those who have an active engagement in curriculum design and implementation, since they are likely to need to follow through our argument in a fair degree of detail. Some of these readers will be programme or departmental leaders, careers officers, educational development staff or other change agents; some will be responsible for course components, such as modules; and others will be engaged in reflection on their practice as individual teachers, perhaps as part of their work towards a qualification as a teacher in higher education.

## Navigating this book

We anticipate that readers will want to engage with the issue of employability in a variety of ways, depending on where they stand. Some, such as Pro-Vice-Chancellors with institutional responsibilities for curriculum matters, may want to concentrate their attention on the general background to employability covered in Chapters 1–3 and on the strategic considerations discussed in Chapters 12 and 13, whilst dipping into other chapters for 'infill' detail. Those who are faced more directly with the development and implementation of curricula will probably feel the need to read more extensively in the book in order to marry the theoretical arguments of the early chapters with the more practical evidence and suggestions that are to be found particularly in Chapters 6–8 and 12. Chapters 5 and 9–11 contain accounts from colleagues who have grappled in different ways with the issue of employability, and illustrate a number of points made elsewhere in the text. For those who have an interest in a workplace perspective on employability that does not emanate from the rarefied heights of the human resources manager in a large organization, Chapter 4 provides some evidence from newly-appointed graduates and from their work colleagues of longer-standing experience.

## Note

1   We distinguish between 'programmes' that lead to named awards, such as an honours degree or a higher national diploma, and components of programmes which are often termed 'modules' or 'courses'.

# Part I

# Employability

The first five chapters share a common concern to describe what is commonly being done to enhance employability while also developing an account of it that has some conceptual and empirical weight behind it.

There is nothing remarkable about the actions being taken in England to enhance employability – they are to be found in the curriculum and co-curriculum in many countries. Only in England, though, has a major government agency, in this case the Higher Education Funding Council for England, sponsored national work to raise awareness of what higher education institutions might do to enhance student employability, which means that English innovations are relatively well documented. Our choice of English examples to illustrate developments that can be identified around the world is one of convenience and not a claim that only in England is employability a concern.

Indeed, the account of employability that we develop, particularly in Chapters 2 and 3, emphasizes that this is an international concern. We argue that many of the outcomes and processes that are often reckoned to be characteristic of good higher education are highly conducive to strong claims to employability. So far from a care for employability being toxic to academic values, as is vulgarly often supposed, we see considerable overlap between what employers say they value in new graduate hires and what are regarded as hallmarks of good higher education. We say that insofar as there is some international agreement about the outcomes and processes associated with good higher education, then there is also, in practice, a concern for those things widely valued by employers. In short, higher education, at its best, contributes powerfully to well-based claims to employability because it proceeds by those processes and promotes those outcomes that researchers across the world have found to be valued in the graduate labour markets.

In Part I we describe practices that enrich these contributions, paying particular attention to the role played by the co-curriculum – by voluntary, elective and extra-curricular activities. However, we argue that valuable though good co-curricular arrangements are, good mainstream curricula have the greater potential. We rest our view of 'good higher education' and 'good mainstream curricula' on educational and psychological research sources that are seldom used in discussions of employability, which are often so under-theorized as to be quite vulnerable to challenge.

# Chapter 1

# The challenge of employability

## Where's the problem?

In England, where government figures show that almost all higher education institutions see over 90 per cent of new graduates in employment or taking further courses six months after graduation, academic staff are likely to wonder why anything needs to be done about employability. The 2003 White Paper (DfES, 2003) also notes that graduates in England have enjoyed a substantial lifetime wage premium. Elsewhere in the world premiums may be smaller and there may be greater concern about graduate employment rates, but it still seems necessary to explain what the problem is.

Three responses are as follows:

1   Many policy-makers believe that post-industrial countries will flourish according to their success in competing with other 'knowledge economies': the EC envisages Europe becoming the world's leading knowledge economy by 2010 (Bourgeois, 2002), which depends upon new graduates being highly employable. It is not enough that they can find some work – it needs to be work that adds to the knowledge economy (Leadbeater, 2000; Reich, 2002). Governments, employers and other stakeholders have come to expect higher education to contribute to the development of a variety of complex 'skills'[1] as well as ensuring an advanced command of worthwhile subjects. They tend to say that this enhances the stock of human capital and makes for national economic well-being; the idea is that educational success is an engine of wealth creation, especially in the knowledge economies of successful capitalism. In the words of a UK Government report:

Human capital directly increases productivity by raising the productive potential of employees. [...] Improving skills and human capital is important in promoting growth, both as an input to production and by aiding technological progress. This has been recognized both in endogenous growth theory and also in empirical studies comparing growth in different countries.

(HM Treasury, 2000: 26, 32)

Higher education institutions (HEIs) in the UK are now charged with promoting graduate employability – contributing directly to the stock of human capital – and their performances are monitored. Although no other country has acted as decisively as this, there is a concern in the states and provinces of the USA, Australia and Canada that higher education should give value for money by contributing highly-employable graduates to their economies.

2    Many governments are concerned to get high participation rates in higher education. However, strategies for widening participation need to be complemented by strategies for enhancing employability, not least because if new graduates fail to find jobs they consider worthy of their achievements, then there is a disincentive to others to participate. In England there are some signs that the lifetime earnings premium for a first degree is declining as the number of graduates entering the labour force increases.

3    What we commend as employability-enhancing practices are also practices that should be attractive to universities and colleges committed to enhancing the quality of learning, teaching and assessment: the principles of good learning and those for enhancing employability tend to be congruent.

The first two lines of argument are common, although vulnerable to claims that there is a demand-side problem with the notion of employability. Coleman and Keep (2001) argue that advanced Anglo-Saxon economies are too reliant on low-skill enterprises and that while employers may say they want graduates they often do not (Wolf, 2002) or cannot use them fully. The argument that there are skills gaps and shortages is often heard, as in this case:

> According to the Conference Board of Canada ..., 8 out of 10 organizations said that graduates should have better interpersonal skills, writing, presentation, listening and teamwork skills. A recent federal report card on the knowledge economy concluded, 'Canadians have outstanding technical skills, but can't work in teams, solve "real world" business problems and need to work on expressing themselves clearly'.
>
> (Knowledge House, 2000: 3)

As an economic strategy, supply-side interventions to enhance graduate employability may promise more than can be delivered when the demand side is weak and when, whatever they say, enterprises do not capitalize upon the graduates they recruit. We do not need to take sides because we consider the third point persuasive by itself. Together the three points constitute a claim that the sorts of attainments valued by employers actually align quite well with educational values and admired practices. Despite the name, 'employability' can be understood as a concern with learning that has benefits for citizenship, continued learning and life in general. This position is endorsed by the Work Experience Group (2002: 9): 'Many of the skills required for success in work are the same as those needed for success in life more generally'.

Consequently, we follow the description of employability used by the Generic Centre of the UK Learning and Teaching Support Network (LTSN)[2] and its associated Enhancing Student Employability Co-ordination Team (ESECT).[3] They see employability as a set of achievements, understandings and personal attributes that make individuals more likely to gain employment and be successful in their chosen occupations.

In later chapters we shall be developing the theme that good higher education practices make for strong claims to employability. First, we need to distinguish between employability and employment.

## Employment and employability are different concepts

Employability, understood as suitability for graduate employment, is clearly not the same as graduate employment rates. In the UK, data are collected on whether graduates are employed six months after graduation (see HEFCE, 2002: 115ff). Although these data identify universities, colleges and subject areas associated with unusually low employment rates, and although there is a temptation to assume that low rates are evidence of poor institutional performance, we resist the inference that employment rates six months after graduation are valid indicators of employability. For example, researchers on the *Access to What?* project comment that:

> In general, the findings support other studies which indicate that success in the labour market is to some extent associated with the background characteristics of the graduates. However, there are differences according to the various dimensions of employment success. There are also gender differences in the effects of background characteristics.

> In the case of lower socio-economic background (as measured by parental occupation and parental education), both men and women graduates from lower socio-economic backgrounds received lower average salaries than graduates from more advantaged social backgrounds ... In addition, male graduates from these backgrounds were more likely to have experienced a period of unemployment and were less likely to be in managerial and professional jobs than their middle-class counterparts ...

> ... Asian men were less likely than other male graduates to characterise their jobs as ones which provided good opportunities to use their knowledge and skills. This was not the case, however, for Asian women who were also more likely to have a graduate job and to find their work challenging. Asian graduates of both genders were more likely than other graduates to be in managerial or professional jobs although these positive employment outcomes were not reflected in higher salaries or greater job satisfaction. In general, Higher Education Statistics Agency (HESA) data indicated that graduates from ethnic

minorities face greater difficulties in obtaining an initial job but are not less likely than other graduates to be in graduate level jobs. Substantially higher proportions of graduates among each black minority group and among both Indian and Pakistani groups were still seeking employment or training (without having any other main activity) six months after graduation. The same was true for Bangladeshi men. However, unemployment levels were only slightly above those of white graduates for Chinese and other Asian groups, and among Bangladeshi women.

(CHERI, 2002: 1, 2)

Harvey (2001: 103) develops these points, with Little (2001: 126) observing that '… the impact of social and cultural capital (independent of education) on the operation of the labour market varies by country'. Rhem (1998) says that working class students in the USA, rather like their English counterparts, are more likely to lack self-confidence as students, have fewer academic skills and not know how to 'work the system'.

This is an important reason why we distinguish between 'employability', which refers to fitness, and employment rates, which reflect the operation of labour markets (Linke, 1991) that tend to compound the disadvantage experienced by certain groups of graduates. Nor do labour markets place all employable graduates in graduate jobs:[4] 'employability' may improve graduates' chances of getting graduate jobs but it does not assure them. There is the question of demand for graduate labour to consider as well. For example we will shortly address claims that Anglo-Saxon economies tend to rely on low skills, low profit enterprises and that there might be less of an employability problem than of an employment problem. Our reading of Maharasoa and Hay (2001) is that this is recognizable in South Africa, especially for Arts and Humanities graduates.

The question that dominates this book is how achievements appropriate to graduate jobs may be promoted. In the next section we offer an answer in terms of learning to make transitions, and translations, which implies some transformation of students during their undergraduate years. We will extend this rather high-level analysis with more concrete suggestions in later chapters.

## Transitions, translations and transformations

Our analysis implies that many higher education institutions will need to change. We will not develop the organizational side here, concentrating instead on the implications for students. Nevertheless, we insist that many departments, universities and colleges will need to re-form themselves, in some cases to transform themselves, if they are to provide the *programmes* and undergraduate experiences that make for employability; they have transitions to make from being concerned only with academic practices into being organizations concerned to promote a range of achievements *through* good academic practices; and they need to translate their goals and contributions to 'the knowledge economy' into terms that are readily understood by participants (students and teachers) and consumers (employers, graduate schools and funders). And, as we shall argue in the next section, each of these three processes is complex or supercomplex, resistant to the application of the rational planning practices that are appropriate to more determinate, less dynamic and smaller-scale projects. We hint here, then, at the desirability of breaking from some of the more formulaic thinking about higher education that has, internationally, seeped into the sector in the past couple of decades.

That said, we turn to the ways in which these processes relate to students' planned undergraduate experiences.

### Transitions

Employer organizations often criticize the standard of new graduates, saying that they leave higher education without enough business sense, understanding of the real world and readiness for work.[5] Is this evidence of a failing in higher education?

Teachers in higher education often complain about the standard of new students, saying that they lack 'the basics', are accustomed to being spoon-fed and are not used to thinking hard enough. Is this evidence of a failing in schools and colleges?

Of course, the teachers who complain about new students seem to be proud of their graduates and defensive when criticized by employers. And interviews we did in the Skills *plus* project (which is summarized in Box 1.1) found employers of recent graduates to be quite satisfied with them once they had six months or so to their credit. One interpretation is that the impact of employability development in the undergraduate years may be greatest in the first few months of graduates' careers, smoothing them through the transition.

Transitions are hard. In developmental psychology, we know that transition from one 'stage' to a higher one is often preceded by a drop in performance (van Geert, 1994). But the mechanisms van Geert uses to explain developmental transitions[6] do not explain the difficulty of transition from school to college or from college to higher education. Our explanation uses the concept of 'practical intelligence', as developed by Sternberg and colleagues (2000) who

> ... present a number of studies showing dissociations between academic and practical intelligence ... our argument is that academic intelligence is not enough and that successful prediction and, more importantly, understanding of performance in the everyday world require assessment of practical as well as academic intelligence.
>
> (Sternberg *et al.*, 2000: xiii)

Central to practical intelligence is tacit knowledge. Sternberg's team 'found that individuals who exhibit the ability to acquire and use tacit knowledge are more effective in their respective performance domains' (p. 223). By 'tacit knowledge' they mean

*Box 1.1*  The Skills *plus* project, 2000–2

The project had two main streams of activity. The research side used qualitative methods to explore what employability meant to 97 recent graduates and 117 of their supervisors, mentors and co-workers. Chapter 4 summarizes the findings. There was also a survey of first and final year students' efficacy beliefs and a pilot study of employability as seen through the eyes of ten recent graduates who had failed to find jobs six months after graduation (Knight and Knight, 2002).

The development side involved work with 17 departments representing subjects from Pharmacology, through Environmental Science to History, drawn from two research universities and two post-1992 universities. This work was underpinned by:

- The USEM account of employability (see Chapter 3), which had been constructed by the project principals as a description that was consistent with research literatures and expansive enough to envelop non-cognitive elements as well as understanding and skilful practices.
- A conviction that whatever the strengths of other approaches to enhancing employability, it needed to be understood as a curriculum issue.
- The belief that employability could be honestly presented as something that could be legitimately fostered in any programme in any university.

This position was set out in the project's first paper, *Tuning the Undergraduate Curriculum.*[7] It described teaching, learning and assessment practices that were suited to the sorts of learning described by USEM and set out a low cost, high gain approach to existing curricula that should considerably enhance their contribution to employability. Relying on series of audits, 'tuning' and negotiation, this approach was refined and developed by 16 of the 17 departments. Some of the outcomes are described in Chapters 9, 10 and 11.

Assessment issues had to be addressed, which led to the development of a differentiated account of programme assessment systems (see Knight and Yorke, 2003b and Chapter 8).[8]

The project also showed how important it was that students understood that the goals of a programme were wider than academic achievement alone and appreciated the ways in which the work they did could lead to strong claims to employability. In the words of the project, students needed to be 'knowing students'.

The procedural knowledge one learns in everyday life that is usually not taught[9] and often is not even verbalized. Tacit knowledge includes things like knowing what to say to whom, knowing when to say it, and knowing how to say it for maximum effect.

(Sternberg et al., 2000: ix)

They add that 'tacit knowledge is needed to successfully adapt to, select, or shape real-world environments' (p. 104), noting that 'experience in a particular domain is important in the acquisition of tacit knowledge' (p. 223). They note that

[Researchers] found evidence that older managers who performed at the highest levels on average had high levels of tacit knowledge, even though on average they had relatively low scores on psychometric reasoning measures.

(Sternberg et al., 2000: 44)

The significance of knowledge of the specific can be seen in their analysis of problem-solving in which familiarity with the setting is important, partly because problem definition has to be contexted (the way the problem is understood has to relate to a particular circumstance) as do the strategies chosen to address it. So, too, in their analysis of wisdom, which they saw as 'a higher-level outgrowth of practical intelligence' (p. 59). Their analysis uses a distinction between fluid abilities (those required to deal with novelty) and crystallized ones (situated and based on accumulated knowledge). They then claim that wisdom, 'seems to behave more like crystallized than like fluid intelligence in its development over the life course' (p. 59). Their analysis of the five components of wisdom recognizes the importance of the general: 'life-span contextualism ... knowledge about differences in values, goals and priorities ... knowledge about the relative indeterminacy and unpredictability of life and ways to manage them' (p. 59). They also emphasize 'rich factual knowledge ... rich procedural knowledge' (p. 59), both of which need a good grasp of the specifics of a role, context and time. Much of this knowledge is tacit. This is in a chapter headed 'the specificity of practical intelligence'.

There is an interesting similarity between these ideas and those developed by Bereiter and Scardamalia (1993) in their account of the development of expertise. Their case cannot be quickly and faithfully summarized but its main features include:

- An emphasis on knowledge: experts are steeped in their domain, perhaps for some 10,000 hours.
- A discussion of the limits of formal or 'book' knowledge. They say:

The obvious kinds [of knowledge] ... are procedural knowledge (skill) and formal knowledge (as in 'book learning'). Expertise also depends on a great body of less obvious knowledge ... informal knowledge, which is the expert's elaborated and specialized form of common sense, ... impressionistic knowledge [and] ... Finally there is self-regulatory knowledge – self knowledge relevant to functioning in a domain.

(Bereiter and Scardamalia, 1993: 74)

- The proposition that expertise is a process, a way of going about things.
- An insistence that problem-solving is central to expertise, but only as long as problems include those 'at the edge of competence' – 'tame' problems do not count.
- A distinction between experts and experienced non-experts. The experienced non-experts lack the commitment to learning and lack the flexibility and creativity that come from non-routine problem-solving.
- The idea that experts have expert careers, which is to say they remain committed to learning and problem-solving.

... we have found it more useful to think of expertise as a characteristic of careers rather than as a characteristic of people. The problem then is how to get people to pursue expert careers and to sustain them in those careers.

(Bereiter and Scardamalia, 1993: 18)

- A claim that expertise is a social achievement as well as an individual one. It may also be promoted by the quality of the social environment.

We suggest that this account of practical intelligence, which puts a lot of weight on knowing the rules of *the* game (rather than of games in general), illuminates the transition to work in two ways. First, by implying that most people will have a period of non-competence in their first job because they will lack explicit and – especially – tacit knowledge of 'what we do around here': they will be culturally naïve, reliant on any explicit and formal declarations they can find, whereas the reality of communities of practice is one of tacit knowledge, 'work-arounds' and local practices (Dreyfus and Dreyfus, 1986; Wenger, 1998; Brown and Duguid, 2000). Second, because the formal, negotiable and de-contexted knowledge (Bereiter and Scardamalia, 1993) typically rewarded by higher education is quite different from the practical intelligence, or expert-like behaviour, that is likely to be more significant in the workplace. The work on expertise points in similar directions. Both lines of research suggest that expertise and practical intelligence will transfer to the extent that they are learned dispositions with accompanying heuristics and that there will be difficulties – workgroups may be dominated by experienced non-experts, there is fresh tacit knowledge to acquire, there is a flood of temporarily-novel problems to cope with and new rules of the game to be learnt.

A similar analysis can be done for the transition into higher education, recognizing that it will be particularly disconcerting for students whose experiences are quite different from the cultures that predominate in higher education. These students may have social, intellectual and cultural capital aplenty but their capitals may not be the ones dominating a particular subject, university or college. Fair access – making higher education *really* open to all who can benefit from it – does not guarantee the kinds of experiences in higher education that help those who are short of it to acquire the cultural capital that enhances employment and the chances of getting it. Hodkinson and Bloomer (2003) have suggested that shortages of appropriate cultural capital can powerfully interact with circumstances and choices to limit career trajectories. However, the significance of cultural capital is, they suggest, often unrecognized.

There are significant implications here for employability. We do not claim that transitions can be made Teflon-smooth, nor do we expect to stop employers complaining because new graduates hit the ground limping rather than running. We do believe that higher education can help students to prepare for transition to the workplace. For instance, Sternberg and colleagues argue that people can learn strategies to help them acquire tacit knowledge more effectively, arguing that it helps to learn from stories, as in the study of cases and with role-playing and simulations, where they emphasize the importance of giving plentiful feedback to participants. We hear echoes of metacognition in their proposal that

> Individuals can be asked to evaluate the case studies individually or in groups. They can assess the situation, evaluate the course of action taken and assess the consequences of action. They can consider what they might have done differently in the situation and what alternative outcomes might have resulted.
> (Sternberg *et al.*, 2000: 214)

Transitions may also be easier when students have followed programmes[10] that help them to develop what has been called 'the skill of transfer' (Bridges, 1993).

### Translation

There is also a task of translation to be done. Students on well-conceived programmes often have many striking achievements but unless they can translate achievements into a language that resonates with employers, then their intellectual, social and cultural capital may be unrealized. For example, it is widely appreciated that work experience – as an intern, term-time employee in the retail sector, voluntary worker, or on a work placement – is attractive to employers. The mistake is to assume that the experience is intrinsically attractive. Employers are interested in the learning and achievements associated with the experience. Successful students translate the experience into the language of achievement ('I showed creativity by ...') and of learning ('I learnt how to work with older people who were less educated and was able to ...'). Or take the degree itself: a small study of unemployed recent graduates (Knight and Knight, 2002) said that

> These graduates' answers almost all seem to convey the view that their qualification bears some kind of objective worth that, significantly, employers

will clearly recognise. Only two [of the ten] graduates suggested that at least some of the burden of proving their degree could form a good match with the demands of a specific job lay with them. Arguably, in terms of employment, a degree is little more than a label for an often ambiguous skill set that the holder must aim to present as effectively as possible. By failing to recognise this, it is possible that many of these graduates are not doing all they could to show employers that their qualification holds practical value.

(Knight and Knight, 2002: 4)

In other words, the award itself needs to be translated into terms that employers recognize and value. In Chapter 8 we shall argue that claims-making, primarily through a personal development planning process, is a way of helping students to translate what they do during their undergraduate years into a language that appeals to employers. Without good translation and the fluent presentation that goes with it, transitions are less likely to happen, never mind be smooth.

### Transformation

In the account of employability set out in Chapters 2 and 3 we shall argue that it is a complex set of diverse achievements and qualities that goes far beyond mainstream academic achievement. 'Soft' skills, personal qualities, dispositions and other achievements are valued. An implication is that the undergraduate years need to be years of transformation (Harvey and Knight, 1996). This is not saying that new students are bereft of 'soft' skills, lacking autonomy, short on creativity or prone to idleness. It is saying that:

- Students should be transformed academically, by becoming expert-like (Bereiter and Scardamalia, 1993) in a subject area; distinctly developing a set of academic practices; and becoming poised in working with advanced concepts.
- They should be transformed by recognizing that academic achievements are not the only ones that matter. Others are legitimate and necessary – 'soft' skills, for example.
- They should be transformed in their ability to represent the range of their achievements which will often imply that they will be adding achievements to their roster – teamwork, working autonomously, self-management, confidence in enacting a graduate identity, metacognition, for example.

For some, coming from backgrounds where the practices and values of higher education are not paramount, these transformations will be threatening and their undergraduate careers may be short. For others, it would be better to speak of consolidation of the high levels of social, intellectual and cultural capital they brought with them to university. We need not haver about the transformation: consolidation ratio since our point is that the curriculum needs to be designed to support transformation which will, in turn, support consolidation as well. This, as we argue in Chapter 12, certainly means that the curriculum should have a good range of learning intentions and be accompanied by tasks, teaching and assessment arrangements that are likely to advance them. It also implies that there is progression – arrangements to build in the second year or level on the achievements of the first, and so on. Practice is also necessary because transformations take time.

## (Super)complexity

Suppose that our analysis is persuasive. What might we do? The assumption is, of course, that this is an area in which actions can be chosen in some certainty that they will have known and desired effects. Yet Barnett (2000) has characterized this as an age of 'supercomplexity', in which the only certainty is that there are no certainties. Although his book is largely written at the level of 'the university', the arguments can easily be extended to teaching and learning processes. Fullan, a commentator of international standing, has repeatedly argued (1999, 2001) that these are uncertain processes that resist being managed in a traditional tight-coupled way. In a similar way, Claxton (1998) says that the outcomes of learning are often uncertain, sometimes slow to emerge and frequently unpredictable. Popular interpretations of the psychological concept 'constructivism', which say that individuals create their own meanings, point in a similar direction, because we may not determine the meanings a person will construct. We do know that 'alternative conceptual frameworks' are readily constructed (Knight, 1989) along with more acceptable ones. The implications for the design of curriculum and its learning arrangements are quite important, mainly because they suggest that when it comes to developing something as complex and 'fuzzy' as 'employability', we work with complexity: loose-coupling and uncertainty are the watchwords. When we try to design good connections between learning, teaching and assessment we need to accept there is no great problem with trying *to improve the chances* that students will learn *x*: the problem is being certain that any particular student will learn *x* to order. There are, though, substantial problems in bastardizing Biggs' (2003) helpful notion of 'constructive alignment' and imagining that we can make a tight-coupled set of arrangements. In education, tight-coupling is less feasible the more indeterminate and complex the intended outcomes of learning. Here we follow Goodyear (2002) in distinguishing between tasks (which teachers set) and activities (which are what students do in response to those tasks). The two tend to be different and complex activities are particularly likely to stimulate a whole range of tasks – complex activities are liable to lead to a greater range of outcomes than simple ones. To put it another way: following an older tradition of curriculum studies, we are saying that there is a difference between the planned and created curriculum (what we teachers do) and again between the created and the understood curriculum (what students learn). Slippages are endemic.

What does this mean for curriculum design? It certainly disturbs the assumptions of rational curriculum planning and those who expect a tight-coupling between teaching, resources, tasks, learning and judgements of achievement. An alternative approach to curriculum design is suggested by Ganesan and colleagues (2002). They argue that we should think in terms of creating opportunities (or affordances) that support the sorts of learning we intend to happen. We should not assume that those intentions will be fulfilled immediately, measurably or, in some cases, at all. This, then, is a view of constructive alignment as an exercise in loose-coupling, as the creation of learning possibilities by bringing together favourable affordances – teaching, resources, tasks, and judgements of achievement.

## Is employability higher education's job?

We close this chapter by noting that some colleagues are suspicious of the idea that higher education can or should contribute to student employability, apart from qualifying them with an academic award. One concern is that this project is unrealistic. For example, Hillage and Pollard report that

> Pascale … argued that
>
> > Employability envisions an arrangement in which both parties accept that work is unlikely to be the long-term proposition it once was. In exchange for the employees' dedicated effort in the shorter-term employment relationship, the company pays higher wages and invests in employees' development. This makes them more marketable when it is time to move on.
>
> A year later Pascale was arguing that employability was 'wishful thinking masquerading as a concept'.
>
> (Hillage and Pollard, 1998: 5).

Bourgeois and colleagues (1999), writing from a pan-European perspective, are also sceptical, emphasizing, like Murphy (1995), Coleman and Keep (2001), Guile (2002) and Wolf (2002), uncertainties about the capacity of the economy to provide enough (graduate) employment:

> If, however, the [students'] quest is above all for reliable and good employment, then … In a world of global economics, a shorter half-life to much knowledge, and high systemic unemployment and insecurity, expectations placed upon the university may be unattainable, its mission impossible for many of the more conventional, let alone its new non-traditional, students.
>
> (Bourgeois et al., 1999: 162)

While more open to the project of enhancing employability, Atkins, who has advised the English Employment Department, has reservations about its feasibility, writing that

> Learning and learning how to learn in the context of disciplinary study in HE certainly seems a long way distant from learning and learning how to learn in many work contexts ... This may mean that there is a limit to the extent to which traditional academic study skills can be effectively used in employment and, conversely, a limit to the extent to which the generic process skills of employment can usefully be embedded in the traditional curriculum.
>
> (Atkins, 1999: 276)

There is also a concern, often expressed by academic staff, that the discourse of employability could jeopardize the established quest for wisdom (Barnett, 1994) and related academic values. Honeybone says that a

> ... skills agenda, to a large extent externally imposed and predominantly aimed at the application of skills outside HE is no longer the best way forward, if it ever was ... skills development as then [in the 1980s and early 1990s] was frequently viewed by academics as an unwelcome addition to the purposes of HE and a diversion from the study of the disciplines'.
>
> (Honeybone, 2002: 7)

Teichler, writing as a leading researcher into European practices, considers that

> There is widespread concern that intellectual enhancement for all and equality of opportunity is being forfeited to presumed industrial demands ... and that teaching and learning in higher education might be geared to such an extent to immediate needs that higher education will lose its function of fostering critical thinking, preparing for indeterminate vocational tasks and contributing to innovation.
>
> (Teichler, 2000: 90–1)

Another concern is that the interpersonal might be neglected, with Honeybone (2002) worried that developments in employability 'may serve to remind us that continuing work is required if Higher Education is to be a "properly balanced system" with a plurality of aims' (p. 9). He asks 'should there not be an equally strong sociability agenda to set alongside that of employability?' (p. 9).

Last of all, there is a fear, alluded to earlier in this chapter, that employability cannot be separated from the person and that patterns of disadvantage will be perpetuated – 'Employability is also a function of someone's personal circumstances (*e.g.* their age, caring responsibilities, ethnicity *etc.*)' (Hillage and Pollard, 1998: 11). Indeed, one critique of the term 'employability' argues that it shifts the

*Table 1.1* Reasons for seeing employability as a challenge to academic values

| Challenge | A response |
|---|---|
| Universities exist to promote truth, wisdom, scholarship and qualities of mind. The world of work has quite different values, values that are anti-pathetic to universities' missions. | It is easiest to understand this threat in the case of corporate universities, set up to prepare people for working in a particular company. Compared to mainland Europe, employers in the UK are often relaxed about the subject of graduates' degrees, as long as applicants are literate, articulate and have the other general achievements represented on the wish-lists.[1] |
| It means doing what employers say. | There seems to be no obvious reason to object to most of what is in these lists and there is a case for being quite enthusiastic about much of it. |
| It means giving students time to go on placements and work experience, which reduces the time for academic study. | Quite possibly. Work experiences may address programme learning intentions that are not easily addressed in the classroom. Co-operative and sandwich programmes often say this is one of their great strengths. |
| My job is to teach the material and there's already too little time to cover it. If I have to teach skills as well, things will be impossible. | This is a common complaint which is also often made when teachers are encouraged to enlarge their range of teaching techniques and displace more didactic approaches. In some subjects the problem is critical, although outsiders are prone to wonder why there is such emphasis on conveying information. Alternatives would be:<br>• The emphasis in problem-based learning on learning how to acquire, evaluate and use information.<br>• Developing an understanding of the field that makes it easier to add new information as it is needed. For example, the Engineering Professors' Council's *Output Standards* (2000) portrays Engineering as a process of enquiry and not as a body of information to be learned.<br>• Focusing on the quality, rather than the quantity, of students' learning. |
| We'll have to spend more time counselling and advising students. | See above. Besides, in England, the introduction of Progress Files is supposed to make this necessary by 2005. |

Note
1    This is not to say they have no interest in degree subjects. Brennan *et al.* (2001) show that they do have views on subject specialisms but to a lesser extent than employers in other countries.

blame for unemployment from employers and the management of the economy to individuals, potentially leading to a 'blame the victim' scenario (A. Taylor, 1998).

Table 1.1 brings together a number of these concerns. An implication of this table and other expressions of concern is that there is a major job to be done in persuading academic staff to adopt employability as a concern. Given the scope they, like staff in most loose-tight coupled organizations, have for resisting, subverting and ignoring innovations they do not like (Trowler, 1998), evidence of the intensification of academic work (Altbach, 1996), and a reluctance to take on work that is not directly concerned with teaching students or doing research (Knight and Trowler, 2000), we conclude that this will not be easy and is likely to be impossible unless they, the teachers, see a concern for employability as a benign concern. Teichler's words, above, clearly indicate that this will be a substantial task.

It is one we have taken on in this book.

## Notes

1   A distinctive feature of this book is our unease with the common term 'skills'. We shall later argue that 'skills' is a misleading term and suggest 'skilful practices' as an alternative.
2   At the time of writing the shape of quality enhancement arrangements in the UK was being discussed. The LTSN brand may or may not continue but we are confident that it and its Generic Centre will have some continuing representation in new quality enhancement arrangements.
3   ESECT is a 30 month project, funded by the Higher Education Funding Council for England until March 2005.
4   There is a question about what counts as a 'graduate job'. Harvey and colleagues (1997) argue that graduates can 'grow' non-graduate jobs into graduate ones, so any job could, in theory, potentially be a graduate job. Mason (2002) distinguishes between graduate and non-graduate jobs in the service industries and finds little evidence of graduates turning non-graduate jobs into graduate ones. One thing is clear, though: if it is possible to separate graduate from non-graduate jobs, then students in some subjects and at some universities are far more successful in getting graduate jobs than those in other subjects and institutions (Jobbins, 2003).
5   It should be appreciated that UK employers accept more responsibility for training newer graduates than do their European counterparts, who seem to expect graduates to emerge from longer degree courses prepared to slide into professional roles (Brennan, 2003).
6   His argument is that resources which would normally be used in task performance are occupied by the (tacit) processes that are creating the new structures of the next developmental stage.
7   The June 2002 revision is at http://www.open.ac.uk/cobe/pdfDocs/docs-skill%2B/ANewIntroSkills.pdf (accessed 11 July 2003).
8   And also *Assessment and Employability* at http://www.open.ac.uk/cobe/pdfDocs/docs-skill%2B/ProjPaper4.pdf (accessed 11 July 2003).
9   There is growing interest in non-formal and informal learning. For a brief summary, see Knight (2002a).
10  Another distinctive feature of this book is our insistence that much of what we recommend needs to be approached as *programme* concerns. Courses or modules are too short.

## Chapter 2

# Employability

## More than skills and wish-lists

### Are skills the issue?

In this chapter we begin to set out the thinking behind our description of employ-ability as a set of achievements, understandings and personal attributes that make individuals more likely to gain employment and be successful in their chosen occupations. First comes a description of what seems to be the international default discourse, the language of skills, followed by the claim that either it is inadequate or that the term 'skills' has to be so loosely interpreted as to render it meaningless. The chapter concludes with a summary of ways in which employers and other international stakeholders have described employability. Seeing difficulties with their accounts, we develop our own account in Chapter 3. Before criticizing skills-based accounts of employability, there are two points that need attention:

First, we insist that the outcomes that employers generally value and the learning that stimulates them are, in our view, intrinsically worthwhile. Both enhance what has been called 'capability' (Stephenson, 1998), which we understand to be an overarching construct that embraces diverse achievements that can enhance citizenship, career and life in general. It will be seen that we have no truck with 'education *or* employability' thinking and that we will keep arguing that good learning enhances career, citizenship and more besides.

Second, we need to distance ourselves from assumptions that higher education can rectify labour market problems and from easy beliefs that employers know best. To repeat a point made in Chapter 1, graduate employment rates might have little to do with higher education. If employers benefit enough to increase their share of global trade, then there may be more graduate jobs available, which is good for home graduates, unless employers decide it is better to invest overseas where graduate labour costs may be five times cheaper than in a Western economy. Although we write about the supply of highly-employable graduates, we recognize that supply without demand will not invigorate economies. The point is that

> ... a full explanation of employability is not just about what people need to get and keep a job, but should take explicit account of the level of demand for employment and the way employers articulate their demand.
>
> (Hillage and Pollard, 1998: 11)

We have also referred earlier to Coleman and Keep's work (2001). If they are right and employers talk the language of high-profit, high-skills enterprises but run low-skills, low-profit ones, then we should be careful with employer views of what the economy needs. Wolf (2002) is particularly critical of the Confederation of British Industry's contribution to educational policy, and 'how', asked the Chair at *The Learning and Skills Sector* conference at Westminster, 24 April 2003, 'do you raise demand [for skills] in parts of the economy where employers don't give a monkey's about raising skills?' Or, in words attributed to David Blunkett when English Secretary of State for Education and Employment, 'employers take everything and give nothing'.

Keep's (2003) view is that the UK, like the USA, has reached a low skills equilibrium, where a lot of employers, notably in the great retailing growth sector, neither demand nor can make best use of many highly skilled people, preferring to 'grow' through mergers and acquisitions instead of adopting high skill, high added value strategies. He adds that 'skills supply is not a good starting point for policy interventions ... skills are a fourth order issue', continuing that '... many jobs are too circumscribed for a doubling of skills levels to make a difference'.[1] Mason (2002) develops the theme with an analysis of graduate employment in service industries. Beginning with data indicative of under-employment, he uses evidence from retailing, computer services, transport and communication industries to show that 'a sizeable minority of graduates employed in retailing are in non-professional and non-managerial sales and clerical positions' (p. 444). His concluding remarks include:

- By some, though not all measures of qualification and skill requirements, a substantial number of graduates are over-educated and/or their skills are under-utilised in their jobs during the first few years after graduation ...
- ... over-educated graduates now represent a substantially larger proportion of the workforce than they did before the transition to mass HE.

(Mason: 2002: 452)

In short, supply is outstripping demand. Keep (2002: 458), saying that there is a need for policy-makers to 'be willing and able to open up the black box of the firm, and seek to create therein an environment that is both rich in its potential for learning and demands and uses high levels of skill in the productive process', considers that 'there are some signs that the demand side is starting to emerge as an issue'.

Later in this chapter we shall describe employer wish-lists and identify a number of themes to take seriously, but in the belief it is for higher education to consider how far it could respond while maintaining its essential mission. They are not, in our view, to be regarded as shibboleths, notwithstanding the tendency of governments around the world to believe that employers have privileged access to special wisdom. Morley adds that

... the employability discourse is a one-way gaze with truth claims that problematise the capital of students while leaving the cultural and social capital and employment practices of employers untouched.

(Morley, 2001: 137)

## Skills-based views of 'employability'

In Chapter 1 we offered a brief description of employability and contrasted it with 'employment', a concept with which it is often confused. Here we complicate matters by identifying other notions of employability, summarized in Table 2.1. We shall not review them one by one, concentrating instead on view 3, the widespread belief that employability is assured by the possession of skills. It is not. We make this case by showing that the language of skills is more like a babble; that there is more to employability than 'skills'; and that there are substantial theoretical objections to the idea that there are skills (save in a relatively trivial sense), as well as to the corollary that they are transferable.

### Employability as skills

As Table 2.1 indicates, skills were blessed by the Dearing report (NCIHE, 1997) and the 2003 English White Paper on higher education was produced by the Department of Education and Skills. One way of challenging this preoccupation is to see what their proponents mean by 'skills', which is done here through a series of quotations suggesting that they tend to mean different things. For example, there is a rift between those following Dearing's advocacy of 'key' skills and others, such as 'generic' and 'soft' skills. The UK Cabinet Office distinguishes

... three categories of skills:

*Generic Skills*: the transferable skills that can be used across all occupational groups. These include what have already been defined as Key Skills – communication, application of numbers, problem solving, team working, IT and improving own learning and performance ... [and] reasoning skills, work process management skills, and personal values and attitudes such as motivation, discipline, judgement, leadership and initiative.
      By '*vocational skills*' we mean the specific 'technical' skills needed to work within an occupation or occupational group ...
      ... a number of *job-specific skills* may also be included. These might include local functional skills ... or employer-wide skills ...

(PIU, 2001: 119, emphasis added)

However, teachers in higher education are not necessarily using the same language, nor referring to the same things, as Bibbings shows.

Table 2.1 Seven meanings of 'employability'

| What is employability? | Notes | Comment |
|---|---|---|
| 1 Getting a (graduate) job | Employment figures are taken as a robust indicator of employability. | No necessary connection between fitness for employment and getting a job. The labour market is not perfect and the economic cycle means that some groups of graduates find it harder to get jobs at some times – at the time of writing there appears to be a glut in the UK of supposedly-employable IT graduates. |
| 2 Possession of vocational degree | Vocational degrees are seen as passports to employment, not always rightly. | |
| 3 Possession of 'key skills' or suchlike | The Dearing Report said all students should develop four 'key skills', amongst others. It is becoming common to talk of other 'soft' or 'generic' skills. In some quarters there is scepticism about the whole 'skills' enterprise. | This assertion may help, although it is far from clear what 'skills' count as 'key' skills. Brown and Hesketh's current research on graduate recruitment led Hesketh to say emphatically that human capital – attractiveness in the labour market – does not lie in skills. |
| 4 Formal work experience | Work experience consistently correlates with success in the labour market. | Extremely important when it is used to support claims to achievement. By itself, experience is inert. The claims are what matter. |
| 5 Good use of non-formal work experience and/or voluntary work | The Student Volunteering UK and CRAC Insight Plus initiatives help students to represent these experiences in ways that are likely to attract employers. | There may be some tendency for employers to prefer work experience in business sectors that are close to theirs, which means that claims based on part-time bar work may not carry as well as claims based on formal work experience in the sector. |
| 6 Skilful career planning and interview technique | Employability is in part about knowing the rules of the job-seeking game. Most of the unemployed graduates interviewed in the Skills plus project had fallen down here. | Important and pretty empty without good claims supported by plenty of evidence and appropriate experience. Canny technique is no substitute for substance, which comes from engagements in well-designed programmes. |
| 7 A mix of cognitive and non-cognitive achievements and representations | A set of achievements, understanding and personal attributes that make individuals more likely to gain employment and be successful in their chosen occupations. | This view is developed in the next section, which lays out the USEM account of employability. |

Note: Darker shading indicates the descriptions of employability that have the greatest appeal to us.

> ... feedback from employers of students on work placement suggests that key skills are the most important elements in making students employable. If they are capable of getting their degrees then they are capable of learning the knowledge they need to be able to do their jobs well, but in order to be quickly useful in the workplace they need competence in the key skills of communication ... working independently, being able to meet deadlines and manage their time, and being able to make presentations suitable for specific audiences.
>
> (Bibbings, 2001: 13)

The Keynote Project also took to the idea of 'key' skills. For our purposes, the interesting thing about this extract from its evaluation report is that although there seemed to be agreement that key skills matter, there was a lack of agreement about what they are:

> The aim of the Keynote Project is to identify, disseminate and develop the key skills of textiles, fashion and printing students, thereby enhancing their employability whilst promoting the skills of lifelong learning ... 64 per cent of the sample [of 14 departments] had agreed definitions for key skills. Within this group, 14 per cent used the skills identified by Dearing whilst the remainder had devised lists internally ... There was a significant lack of agreement about the definition of key skills in institutions which did not use the Dearing skills list.
>
> (Keynote Project, 2002: 2, 4)

In Canada, employability is related to nine 'essential skills': reading text, document use, numeracy, writing, oral communication, working with others, computer use, continuous learning, and thinking skills (Human Resources Development Canada, 2002). For other commentators, 'transferable' skills is the term of choice, neatly ignoring the view amongst psychologists that learning is transferred with effort and not necessarily with success.

> Five years on from the Dearing Report ... the employability agenda has shifted its focus from numbers of graduates leaving university with work experience onto ... the acquisition, recognition and articulation of transferable skills.
>
> (Pownall and Rimmer, 2002: 15)

These lists are at least short, but most people trying to list the 'skills' of employability end up with long – and lengthening – lists. Box 2.1 is a list we have used as a heuristic, a set of prompts to help colleagues analyze their programmes. In a similar vein, Dickerson and Green (2002) identified 36 activities that cover the tasks carried out in a wide range of jobs. They then used factor analysis to reduce the 36 to 'a taxonomy of generic skills' (p. 8), comprising literacy skills; physical skills; number skills; technical know-how; high-level communication; planning

*Box 2.1* Aspects of employability, with elaborative comments. The acquisition of disciplinary understanding and skills is assumed: note that their application is listed at 30.[3]

### A. Personal qualities
1   Malleable self-theory: (belief that attributes [for example, intelligence] are not fixed and can be developed)
2   Self-awareness: (awareness of own strengths and weaknesses, aims and values)
3   Self-confidence: (confidence in dealing with the challenges that employment and life throw up)
4   Independence: (ability to work without supervision)
5   Emotional intelligence: (sensitivity to others' emotions and the effects that they can have)
6   Adaptability: (ability to respond positively to changing circumstances and new challenges)
7   Stress tolerance: (ability to retain effectiveness under pressure)
8   Initiative: (ability to take action unprompted)
9   Willingness to learn: (commitment to ongoing learning to meet the needs of employment and life)
10  Reflectiveness: (the disposition to reflect evaluatively on the performance of oneself and others)

### B. Core skills
11  Reading effectiveness: (the recognition and retention of key points)
12  Numeracy: (ability to use numbers at an appropriate level of accuracy)
13  Information retrieval: (ability to access different sources)
14  Language skills: (possession of more than a single language)
15  Self-management: (ability to work in an efficient and structured manner)
16  Critical analysis: (ability to 'deconstruct' a problem or situation)
17  Creativity: (ability to be original or inventive and to apply lateral thinking)
18  Listening: (focused attention in which key points are recognized)
19  Written communication: (clear reports, letters etc. written specifically for the reader)
20  Oral presentations: (clear and confident presentation of information to a group [also 21, 35])
21  Explaining: (orally and in writing [see also 20, 35])
22  Global awareness: (in terms of both cultures and economics)

### C. Process skills
23  Computer literacy: (ability to use a range of software)
24  Commercial awareness: (understanding of business issues and priorities)

continued...

> **Box 2.1  continued**
>
> 25  Political sensitivity: (appreciates how organizations actually work and acts accordingly)
> 26  Ability to work cross-culturally: (both within and beyond the UK)
> 27  Ethical sensitivity: (appreciates ethical aspects of employment and acts accordingly)
> 28  Prioritizing: (ability to rank tasks according to importance)
> 29  Planning: (setting of achievable goals and structuring action)
> 30  Applying subject understanding: (use of disciplinary understanding from the HE programme)
> 31  Acting morally: (has a moral code and acts accordingly)
> 32  Coping with ambiguity and complexity: (ability to handle ambiguous and complex situations)
> 33  Problem-solving: (selection and use of appropriate methods to find solutions)
> 34  Influencing: (convincing others of the validity of one's point of view)
> 35  Arguing for and/or justifying a point of view or a course of action: (see also 20, 21)
> 36  Resolving conflict: (both intra-personally and in relationships with others)
> 37  Decision making: (choice of the best option from a range of alternatives)
> 38  Negotiating: (discussion to achieve mutually satisfactory resolution of contentious issues)
> 39  Teamwork: (can work constructively with others on a common task)

skills; client communication; horizontal communication; problem-solving; checking skills – noticing and checking for errors.

Yet, despite the statistical apparatus, the claim that this list is taxonomic is hard to take seriously,[2] particularly as the authors point out that they could have collapsed the ten into a set of eight without doing violence to the data.

Our objection to 'skills' is not simply that, as it is used, the concept is muddled but also that it is hard to label as 'skills' many of the things that employers say they want. This is not simply a matter of semantic purity, because calling something a skill puts it in a certain class with other things which, presumably, have similar qualities, similar applications and are to be developed in similar ways. Guile (2002: 252) makes a similar point when claiming that the concept of 'generic skill is a much more complex issue than has been acknowledged and therefore presents curriculum planners with considerable problems'. However, as we shall show in the next section, the range of employability 'desirables' is so great that to call them all skills, implying that they are all of the same order, seems imprudent. Let us illustrate the point with reference to Guile's analysis of generic skills (2002). He argues that the term, as widely used, refers to:

- conceptions that see generic skill as a property of the individual;
- conceptions that see it as a relationship between an individual and a work context;
- skills that are called for when working on routine or 'tame' tasks;
- skills needed when working on 'in-the-wild' or novel tasks.

It is not obvious that these four are members of the same family, although it is clear that different learning, teaching, assessment arrangements and opportunities are needed for their development. If this is a fair analysis of generic skills – and we are rather sceptical about the notion itself, preferring to talk of generic practices – then there is all the more reason for unease at the familiar view that

*employability = skills.*

### Employability is more than 'skills'

We first make the point that employability is more than skills by way of five paragraphs that report employers looking for a series of qualities and achievements that can only be called 'skills' by turning the term into a vacuous 'hooray' word.

1  A survey by the London *Financial Times* and the Association of Graduate Recruiters showed that 'the country's top graduate employers' identified ten 'secrets of career success'. In rank order (with mean scores out of 10 in parentheses) the ten factors were: interpersonal skills (9.07); other (8.7); propensity for further training (8.45); numeracy/IT skills (7.73); appropriate work experience (6.87); type of degree (5.89); gap year (4.84); foreign language (4.61); university awarding the degree (4.53); degree studied away from home (3.59) (Kelly, 2002).

2  In Hong Kong the University Grants Committee asks employers about their satisfaction with graduates under the following headings:
   - Chinese language proficiency
   - English language proficiency
   - Numerical competency
   - Information technology literacy
   - Analytical and problem-solving abilities
   - Work attitude
   - Interpersonal skills
   - Management skills.

3  Teichler (2000: 87), reflecting on his analyses of 'the wealth of proposals made in various countries by employers, committees considering the future of higher education and the majority of researchers analysing the connections between higher education and work', concluded that employable graduates should:
   - Be flexible
   - Be able and willing to contribute to innovation and be creative

- Be able to cope with uncertainties
- Be interested in and prepared for life-long learning
- Have acquired social sensitivity and communicative skills
- Be able to work in teams
- Be willing to take on responsibilities
- Become entrepreneurial
- Prepare themselves for the internationalization of the labour market through an understanding of various cultures, and
- Be versatile in generic skills which cut across different disciplines, and be literate in areas of knowledge which form the basis for various professional skills, for example in new technologies (Teichler, 2000: 87).

4   Something of this can be seen in recruitment documents from KPMG, the accountancy and consulting firm. In the 2000–1 in-tray exercise used to select new graduate hires they were looking for evidence of the following 'competency areas': personal effectiveness, communication, teamwork, business awareness, and career motivation. Evidence in respect of a further four was valued: leadership, client orientation, task management, and problem-solving and innovation (KPMG, 2000). This set was the outcome of a job analysis questionnaire enquiry of 100 KPMG staff including partners, HR staff and graduates. 'The findings were clear' (KPMG, 2000: A-4).

5   A leading British retailer, Tesco, found leadership a scarce commodity and identified other qualities:

> Other vital attributes include self-sufficiency, innovation, team-working and brave thinking. 'We need people who have helicopter vision, who can rise above everything and see the whole picture', Ms. Aspinall said, adding that her company also looked for 'drive, empathy, adaptability, communication skills, definitely not indecision'.
>
> (Utley, 2002: 10)

The claim that the language of skills is not sufficient is concisely made by Bennett and colleagues:

> The discourse on generic skills, and all its variants, is confused, confusing and under-conceptualized ... Allied to the above is evidence of the lack of a common language of skills between higher education and employers.
>
> (Bennett et al., 2000: 175).

One reason for this may be methodological and stem from fundamental difficulties in capturing practice and then adducing categories, such as lists of skills, from those imperfect representations:

> ... workers and supervisors typically simplified and clarified the complexity of work. Accordingly, job analyses based on verbal accounts by workers or

supervisors must be approached with caution ... the concept of skills requirements ... simplified and distorted our understanding of the work that occurred on the production floor.

(Darrah, 1997: 267–8)

This hints at ideas that attach to the notion of practical intelligence, which was introduced in Chapter 1. Practical intelligence is related to specific and contexted knowledge which is often tacit and resistant to capture. One implication is that abstraction and generalization may be understandable but they invariably lose contextual and specific attachments which are significant. Another is that the task will never totally succeed because some tacit knowledge remains outside our ability to verbalize (Polanyi, 1967; Donnelly, 1999). In this view, problems with the language of skills partly stem from the assumption that we can produce useful, general and detached descriptions of competence and achievement. There are philosophical and psychological reasons for thinking that success in generalizing will always be limited and may be outweighed by failures.

Holmes (2001) refers to the significance of context when he talks about the recruitment process, arguing that

The skills agenda provides little help in understanding the complexity of post-graduation career trajectories, for it assumes that the process of gaining a job is simply a matter of matching skills required and skills possessed ... what is also needed is a way of framing ... the international processes by which a graduate and employer engage with each other ... of graduates getting in and getting on.

(Holmes, 2001: 112)

This coincides with Hesketh's summary of a study of 'blue-chip' employers' graduate recruitment – 'human capital,' he said to one of us, 'is emphatically not skills' (Knight, 2002b: 35). His work showed how much depended on the contingencies of recruitment processes and drew attention to the role of things other than skills. Cappelli, for example, points to the significance of attitudes.

... recent [US] evidence suggest that some assumptions underlying the academic skills gap are shaky ... surveys suggest that employers see the most important considerations in hiring and the biggest deficit among new workforce entrants as being the attitudes concerning work that they bring with them to their jobs.

(Cappelli, 1995: 109–10)

This quotation suggests that even if the language of skills has some value (and in Box 2.2 we argue that it does not), it needs to be supplemented, which directs us to other accounts of employability.

Box 2.2 Skills: a critique

1   *The language is overextended.* Lists of 'skills' contain qualities and achievements that are not skills. According to the *Shorter Oxford Dictionary*, a skill is '[T]he ability to do something (esp. manual or physical) well' (1993: 2,882). This is important because learning to do something well is different from learning to be a certain kind of person, for example. This complicates attempts to assess skills.

2   *Like the behavioural objectives they replace, 'skills' proliferate.* Behavioural objectives were fashionable from time to time in the twentieth century. One problem was that it seemed possible to decompose any behaviour into many component behaviours. Objectives tended to breed. So too with 'skills'. Lists burgeon and become unusable.

3   *Nouns and verbs.* To say that there is a skill of communication is to imply that there is an object called 'communication'. When people then talk of having a skill, objectification is complete. The implicit message is that there are objects – skills – to be 'had'. An alternative is to use the verb, 'communicate' and recognize it as a social practice. We do not 'have' practices but, as the word implies, we continue to work at performances that are contexted and contingent. Successful performance at one time, in one place and social setting is not a warrant of similar success elsewhere and elsewhen.

4   *Ontological and epistemological issues.* The semantic issue is a manifestation of philosophical problems. In what sense can 'skills' be thought of as real? If they are in some sense real, what sort of things are they? Are there to be agreed meanings or are 'skills' just local terms of convenience? How might we know about them? This latter question is important when it comes to thinking about assessing and developing 'skills', whatever they might be.

5   *Problems with transfer.* The semantic issue is a manifestation of psychological issues – how far is cognition, for instance, stable and general, as opposed to situated and contingent? If we follow modern developments in psychology which have shown that thinking, doing and being vary from time to time, place to place and context to context, then it is difficult to suppose that transfer is easy, or even that it is common. See for instance, Perkins and Saloman's (1989) critique of accounts that privilege *general* cognitive skills. The idea of 'transferable' skills ignores this work. Even if not prefixed with 'transferable' the notion of having a skill still implies it.

In conversation, the psychologist Kurt Fischer agreed that 'skills' is not an ideal term. He recognizes that they are dynamic, not necessarily stable, and observes that the French have no word for 'skills', using

continued...

Box 2.2   continued

'competence' in translation. Psychologists distinguish between competence (can do) and performance (does do). The French phrase invites this distinction, whereas the English talk of 'having skills', without appreciating the shortfalls that typify performance. Yet Fischer sees it as a useful word to denote a concern for action (point 3 above) and context. Whatever the intention, we feel that the contextedness of skills tends to get overlooked.

6   *Generalization: context-free statements.* If 'skills' is a poor way of referring to situated practices, then what would it need before we could generalize from here and now to future performances? How much sense would it make to produce un-contexted descriptions of performance? Earlier we doubted (footnote 2) whether it is possible to produce taxonomies, such as sets of level statements, that insist that one performance (analysis, for example) is invariably superior to another (comprehension).

## Other views of employability

Not only is there a lack of agreement about what should go in any account of employability – in a skills-centred account, for instance – but Table 2.1 also indicates that there is a range of competing accounts. Kelly (2002), for example, shows that employers in different sectors have different priorities, even when asked to rank the same set of employability factors, and the Skills *plus* project found differences between the public and private sectors which we associated with the predominance of people/care work in the sample of public sector employers. Before trying to clarify this babble we want to return to a point made in Chapter 1, that employability is a relative concept, not an absolute one. As the labour market fluctuates, so does competition, which means that achievements that might have been good preparation for employability – web design, for one – might lose their appeal because of a collapse in one sector of the economy. Hillage and Pollard capture something of this in their four elements description of employability as:

- What people have to offer employers – i.e. their **'assets'** in terms of knowledge, skills and attitudes
- The extent to which they are aware of what they have got and how they choose to use it – **'deployment'**
- How they **present** themselves to employers, and
- The **context** in which they seek employment.

(Hillage and Pollard, 1998: 12)

The account of employability that we shall develop in the next chapter concentrates mainly on their first point, although it recognizes the importance of awareness of one's achievements and previews the idea of claimsmaking, which is introduced in Chapter 8 and has affinities with Hillage and Pollard's presentation element. Both deployment and presentation are elaborated in later chapters. Of the context element we shall say little more, since neither higher education nor students can do much about the demand for graduate labour.

## Higher education and employers' wish-lists

Suppose that a group of teachers in higher education were given the following list and told that it was a research-based list of outcomes of the undergraduate years that teachers in higher education value:

> initiative; working independently; working under pressure; oral communication skills; accuracy, attention to detail; time management; adaptability; working in a team; taking responsibility and decisions; planning, coordinating and organizing.
>
> (Brennan *et al.*, 2001: 25)

Would they say that these outcomes[4] are at odds with the outcomes they would like their students to achieve? There might be some reservations but, by and large, the things that graduates say they need in their workplace and that employers want are things that teachers – certainly those participating in the Skills *plus* project – value. Academics recognize that good learning depends upon some of these valued achievements and that many of them are likely outcomes of the full engagements we intend our students to have with complex and worthwhile subject matter. In later chapters we shall consolidate this claim that there is a great deal of common ground between the accounts of employability that we favour and the outcomes we wish our students to display on graduation by arguing that the pedagogies for employability are congruent with those for good learning in most, probably all, subject areas.

We accept that vocational, occupational and professional programmes will be sensitive to employers' and professional bodies' views on what students should learn. We reject claims that there is a basic tension between the achievements that employers want and those valued by teachers in higher education. Academics' fears, as summarized in Table 1.1, may be legitimate where employability is understood as the intrusion of 'skills' into the curriculum. In Chapter 3 we elaborate the brief description of employability with which we began in Chapter 1 and, in so doing, identify similarities between academic values and a concern for employability, while trying to offer an account that clarifies the proliferation of lists that has characterized this chapter.

# Notes

1   He says elsewhere that 'in transport and communications, the proportion of graduates classified to occupations below professional level in 1998 was one in three, up from 26 per cent ten years earlier' (2002: 453).

2   Bloom's taxonomy (1956) is the usual point of reference when thinking about educational hierarchies but it is open to severe, arguably fatal, philosophical and psychological challenge (Anderson and Sosniak, 1994). 'Bloom's framework only approaches a taxonomy' (Marzano, 1998: 64). A revised version (Anderson and Krathwohl, 2001) provides a useful set of loose generalizations about the levels of demand that *tend* to be associated with different tasks and processes. If reservations are valid when applied to internationally-respected work, care should be taken before accepting lesser claims to have mapped levels, sequences and hierarchies. The common sense which infuses the UK Quality Assurance Agency's subject benchmarks may be mistaken for expertise, to use a distinction drawn by Bereiter and Scardamalia (1993).

3   This list was developed from a questionnaire prepared by Dr Ray Wolfenden of the University of Manchester.

4   These are the ten competencies that graduates said were needed in their current work in ten European countries.

# Chapter 3

# A new view of employability

## Beyond skills

Until now we have treated employability as a set of achievements, understanding and personal attributes that make individuals more likely to gain employment and be successful in their chosen occupations. But what are these achievements?

Consider an influential North American view. Reich (2002) argued that advanced economies need two sorts of high-level expertise: one emphasizing discovery and the other focusing on exploiting the discoveries of others through market-related intelligence and the application of interpersonal skills. In an earlier book (Reich, 1991) he argued that such professionals, whom he described as 'symbolic analysts', shared a series of achievements. 'Symbolic analysts', he said, are imaginative and creative, have at their fingertips relevant disciplinary understanding and skills and the 'soft' or generic skills that enable the disciplinary base to be deployed to optimal effect. Higher education's key contribution to national prosperity lies in development of graduates with such achievements at their disposal. This means that undergraduate programmes should be concerned with four areas in particular:

- abstraction (theorizing and/or relating empirical data to theory, and/or using formulae, equations, models and metaphors);
- system thinking (seeing the part in the context of the wider whole);
- experimentation (intuitively or analytically); and
- collaboration (involving communication and team-working skills).

Educational institutions are not always successful in preparing learners for the complexity inherent in the symbolic analyst's role, for learners are often expected to learn what is put in front of them and to work individually and competitively; and subject matter may be compartmentalized. Plainly, the education of symbolic analysts (who are likely to be at the leading edge of economic developments of one kind or another) challenges some higher education pedagogic practices.

Higher education is emphatically not, however, only about the education of symbolic analysts. There are other ways in which it can contribute to economic development: as well as preparing young graduates for employment-related roles, it has an acknowledged role in life-long learning – such as in educating further the middle manager so that they can manage more effectively, in upskilling the teacher or process worker, and in facilitating the development of active citizenship.

Whatever the strengths of Reich's account, it is couched in terms of the cognitive face of employability, although in Chapter 2 we noticed that a number of non-cognitive elements are associated with employability.

Consider instead the USEM description produced in the Skills *plus* project, which used a coarse level of analysis to suggest that employability consisted of making convincing[1] claims in four areas:

- Understanding,
- Skilful practices,[2]
- Efficacy beliefs, and
- Metacognition.[3]

Table 3.1 outlines the logic of this analysis, which we elaborate in Chapter 6. Behind it is an attempt to put thinking about employability on a more scientific basis, partly because of the need to appeal to academic staff on their own terms by referring to research evidence and theory, and partly in response to the view that

> Policy makers are concerned with the skills and competencies required for young people to succeed in school or work and to be active participants in their communities. Linking research findings to such goals will enhance their value to policy makers.
>
> (Donovan *et al.*, 2000: 28)

The USEM account is an attempt to do just that, to base action to enhance employability on research findings.

## Educational research and the face validity of USEM

Although unknown to the Skills *plus* team until 2002, the USEM model aligns well with work reported by Marzano (1998). He performed a meta-analysis that used over 4,000 reported effect sizes (an effect size is a standardized measure of the impact of an intervention, such as a new teaching programme) involving an estimated 1,237,000 subjects, ranging from kindergarten to college students.[4] His analysis

> posits the interaction of four aspects of human thought operating in most, if not all, situations: (1) knowledge (2) the cognitive system (3) the metacognitive system (4) the self-system.
>
> (Marzano, 1998: 8)

Table 3.1 The USEM account of employability

| Element | Explanation | Comments |
| --- | --- | --- |
| **U**<br>Understanding of subject matter | Propositional knowledge in the form of mastery of the subject matter of the degree. | 'Understanding' is preferred to 'knowledge' because knowledge is often confused with retention of information. In some 50 per cent of cases, employers are indifferent to the subject of the degree – they use subject-matter understanding, symbolized by good grades or degree classes, as a proxy for critical thinking, perseverance, information-handling, etc.<br>They tend to use a threshold criterion such as an upper second class degree but, even where they specify a degree subject, they often use the other three elements [SEM] when choosing amongst short-listed applicants. |
| **S**<br>Skilful practices | What are often called 'generic skills' as well as subject-specific skills. These can be characterized as procedural knowledge. | Although 'skills' is a widely used term, it may be invalid. The language encourages at least two fallacies: that one can 'have' skills and that they are transferable.<br>What are often called 'skills' are better seen as practices, situated, not necessarily transferable, improved through repetition and assessed with difficulty. |
| **E**<br>Efficacy beliefs | Belief that one generally can make some impact on situations and events. This dispositional element can be loosely interpreted to refer to other aspects of personality. | Beliefs affect one's willingness to act. Dweck (1999) refers to self-theories, a class of beliefs that affect the ways in which people, even high achievers, respond to new and difficult problems.[5]<br>Associated with these self-theories are other beliefs about what sorts of persons we are and what we can do and can be. |
| **M**<br>Metacognition | Awareness of what one knows and can do, and of how one learns more. | 'Reflection', which is a metacognitive process, is widely associated with superior performances.<br>Metacognition is about being mindful and disposed to keep learning. |

One conclusion of the meta-analysis was that '... the constructs of the self-system, metacognitive system, cognitive system and the knowledge domains appear to be useful organizers for the research on instruction' (1998: 128). The analysis centred on 'the effect of classroom instructional techniques ... defined as alterable behaviours on the part of teachers or students' (1998: 66). Although some differential effects across the grade levels were identified in the meta-analysis, 'none of these differences was significant ($p<0.05$, two-tailed)' (1998: 83). His conclusions are summarized in Table 3.2.

Marzano concludes that there needs to be clarity about the goals of instruction; general instructional routines with high power to stimulate learning should be adopted; and specific instructional techniques should be matched closely to instructional goals. A later publication (Marzano *et al.*, 2000), drawing upon the meta-analysis, advises on eleven broad approaches to classroom instruction, concentrating on fruitful sorts of learning activity.

*Table 3.2* Four aspects of human thought, Marzano (1998)

| System description | Effect of interventions addressing this system |
|---|---|
| 'The self-system consists of an inter-related system of beliefs and processes ... the self-system determines whether an individual will engage in or disengage in a specific task' (p. 57). | 'The five categories of beliefs within the self-system appear to control all other aspects of human thought and action. One's beliefs can affect the functioning of the metacognitive and cognitive systems as well as the knowledge domains' (p. 126). |
| 'The metacognitive system can control any and all aspects of the knowledge domains and the cognitive system... it has been described as responsible for the "executive control" of all processes' (p. 54). | 'The metacognitive system appears to be the primary vehicle for learning. Specifically, instructional techniques that employed the metacognitive system had strong effects whether they intended to enhance the knowledge domains, the mental processes within the cognitive system, the beliefs and processes within the self-system, or the processes within the metacognitive system itself' (p. 127). |
| 'The processes within the cognitive system can be organized into four categories: (1) storage and retrieval (2) information processing (3) input/output and (4) knowledge utilization. These mental processes act on the knowledge in the knowledge domains' (p. 36). | 'The overall effect for techniques that utilize the cognitive system are not as impressive as the overall effect size for techniques that utilize the metacognitive and the self-systems' (p. 106). 'The metacognitive system seems to be the "engine" for enhancement of the mental processes within the cognitive system' (p. 116). |
| 'The element of human thought that has been referred to ... as knowledge, is comprised of [sic] the information, mental processes and psychomotor processes that are specific to a given subject matter (p. 29). | Knowledge domains enhanced mainly by techniques that develop cognitive, metacognitive or self-systems. |

There is a resemblance between the Skills *plus* USEM summary of research into employability and Marzano's scientific analysis of thousands of instructional interventions. Marzano's emphasis on metacognition and self-systems, which maps on to the **E** and **M** of USEM, is particularly significant. Since discussion of employability in the UK has largely been confined to thinking about the content relevance of degrees and, post-Dearing, about 'key skills', the Skills *plus* view that metacognition and self-theories were important was a novel one. Marzano's evidence that they matter greatly in human learning adds face validity to the USEM description of elements of employability.

So too with a long-overdue re-working of Bloom's *Taxonomy*. As Anderson and Sosniak (1994) observed, when used as intended, the *Taxonomy* was a handy heuristic, especially if its claim to be a taxonomy was not taken too seriously. However, it was widely used by those who had never read the original and who were insensitive to the trenchant philosophical critiques of its claims and ramifications. The new edition (Anderson and Krathwohl, 2001) is a very different, more robust creation.[6] Its essence is illustrated in Figure 3.1. Attention is drawn to the significance of metacognitive knowledge (the **M** of USEM), to procedural knowledge (**S**) and to factual and conceptual knowledges (**U**). Again, the work was not designed to describe employability but to be a taxonomy (in rather a relaxed sense) for learning, teaching and assessment. However, the similarities between this account of learning and the Skills *plus* description of employability lend weight to the claim that employability ought to be understood as more than a few key skills and some knowledge.

There are also similarities between USEM and the model of adaptable learning suggested by Boekaerts and Niemivirta (2000: 422). They hold that in any situation (and learning situations vary considerably), 'declarative [**U**] and procedural knowledge [**S**], cognitive strategies that have been successful in that domain, and metacognitive knowledge [**M**] relevant to the learning situation' come into play

| The knowledge dimension | The cognitive dimension | | | | | |
| --- | --- | --- | --- | --- | --- | --- |
| | 1 Remember | 2 Understand | 3 Apply | 4 Analyze | 5 Evaluate | 6 Create |
| Propositional knowledge: 'Knowing that' | | | | | | |
| Procedural knowledge: 'Knowing how' | | | | | | |
| Metacognitive knowledge | | | | | | |

*Figure 3.1* The taxonomy for learning, teaching and assessment (after Anderson and Krathwohl, 2001: 28)

Note:
The factual and conceptual knowledge categories in Anderson and Krathwohl's taxonomy have been collapsed, since they can be subsumed under the broader heading of propositional knowledge, or 'knowing that'.

with 'the students' self-system, including their goal hierarchy ... values, and motivational beliefs'. (The capital letters U, S and M are our addition.) We read Boekaerts and Niemivirta's account of 'motivational beliefs' to resemble 'self-theories' [E]. This is consistent with Locke's account (1997) of motivation to work which emphasizes efficacy beliefs.

It might be objected that these studies have a great deal to say about learning and, by extension, teaching and assessment, but they are not analyses of the concept of employability. One response is that as accounts of learning they describe fundamental workplace processes: employers expect graduates to learn, fast and continuously. It is therefore worth taking note of the US National Research Council's view that metacognition is important, partly because it can improve understanding and transfer to new settings and events (Donovan *et al.*, 2000: 15). Such studies are therefore descriptions of something that is a fundamental aspect of employability, the capacity for learning.

A second response is that learning is a form of work, and when the learning in question is the complex and varied learning envisaged by the USEM account, then the similarities between learning and work are pronounced,[7] although recent graduates do identify differences. Our argument is that similar processes are likely to drive success in higher education and, with some reservations, in the workplace. For example, Lent *et al.* (1994: 112) report 'a direct relation between self-efficacy, and academic/vocational performances indices'.

We finish this section with the notion of practical intelligence, introduced in Chapter 1 as a theory of performance in the workplace and in life generally (Sternberg, 1997; Hedlund and Sternberg, 2000; Sternberg and Grigorenko, 2000a; Sternberg *et al.*, 2000). They see practical intelligence as an effective way of dealing with authentic problems. It is not stable, as academic IQ is supposed to be, but grows with life experience. It has a domain-specific tinge.

> ... practical intelligence ... may be distinct from the kinds of academic intelligence associated with school success [and] expertise developed in one environment (for example, school) may have limited application in other environments.
>
> (Hedlund and Sternberg, 2000: 155)

Transfer is not presumed. A 'skill of transfer' (Bridges, 1993) is needed and there is no presumption that any transfer will be easy, let alone automatic.

The parallels with USEM are:

- Knowledge, especially tacit knowledge, is central to practical intelligence. Although this resembles USEM's understanding element, there is a difference in that USEM simply specifies that evidence of understanding is important to the employability of new graduates whereas practical intelligence (PI) emphasizes the role of appropriate, domain-specific knowledge. In terms of employability, practical intelligence highlights the knowledge that is needed in employment, whereas USEM suggests that evidence of being able to understand complex material is often sufficient for getting a job. Of course, where jobs require specialist expertise, as in the professions, then the difference of emphasis between USEM and PI is reduced.

- Skilful practices. Both USEM and PI value procedural knowledge. Again, PI is more context-specific, stressing that procedural knowledge needs to be appropriate to the tasks in hand.
- Efficacy beliefs. PI has no problem with this area but current work places more emphasis on procedural knowledge, recognizing that working successfully involves appropriate self-theories and beliefs.
- Metacognition. PI attends to knowledge that is largely tacit, acknowledging that versatility and flexibility are associated with good strategies for identifying, transferring and deliberately developing it.

So too there are parallels between USEM and de Corte's summary account of what is involved in developing expertise in a domain:

[It] involves the mastery of four categories of aptitudes, namely:
- A well organized and flexibly accessible domain-specific knowledge base;
- Heuristic strategies for problem analysis and transformation;
- Metacognitive knowledge and self-regulating skills;
- Positive beliefs, attitudes and emotions related to mathematics [or to whatever other domain is in question].

(De Corte, 2000: 253)

Our claim, then, is that USEM has more scientific substantiation than old notions that employability = skills.

## Advantages and disadvantages of USEM

### Advantages

Six advantages are claimed for the USEM account:

1   It is economical, comprising just four headings.
2   Following the principle of subsidiarity, it is permissive, allowing departments and universities to put under those four headings the understandings, skilful practices, etc. that they judge best.
3   It is a plausible representation of employer views that also connects with research into learning and, by extension, into performance as well.
4   It raises the eyes from a skills-and-drill approach to employability.
5   It is consistent with academic values, in the sense that the things to which USEM points approvingly are also things that many teachers in higher education also value.
6   It is general enough to be applicable outside England.

## Nine objections

Nine objections and our responses are summarized in Table 3.3.

## A tenth objection

The USEM description of employability is open to an objection more serious than any contained in Table 3.3, namely that it disturbs the curriculum and established practices.

USEM is broadly neutral in terms of subject understanding if it is understood as an endorsement of the good learning and teaching practices. The emphasis on 'understanding' rather than 'knowledge' might be read, though, as a threat. 'Understanding' implies the capacity to transfer learning to ill-defined problems 'in the wild': it implies transfer and authenticity. The difficulty is that one way of helping students to perform to levels that might generally be beyond them – to get a 2:1 or *magna cum laude* – is to set them tame tasks, providing scaffolding and support. From the outside, performances then look meritorious but there are questions to ask about whether they show understanding or just competence on tame tasks demanding near transfer. USEM could imply more demanding approaches to the high-stakes assessment of achievement, which would have implications for teaching, curriculum and percentage of students getting good GPAs or degree classifications.[8]

The implications for what have been called skills are also rather ambiguous. Where there is evidence that existing provision for the development of subject-specific and generic 'skills' is effective and that the set of 'skills' is sufficient, then there may be little need to do anything more than check that care is taken to help students to recognize what they are learning and to develop ways of transferring the practices learnt in one context to others. However, we cannot call to mind any psychological text that commends one-off skills development units and recall many that say 'skills' are best developed by being applied to a range of worthwhile material. Skilful practices are best developed across a whole programme in order to provide practice, reinforcement and opportunities to apply these practices to different content and through a range of increasingly-authentic tasks. This is a challenge of significance to departments that have dealt with skills through dedicated skill-building modules, typically at level 1 (or in the freshman and sophomore years in the USA).

Efficacy beliefs and self-theories are rarely addressed in higher education or touched upon by counsellors and other pastoral staff. However, Rogers (2002) and Cannon (2002) explain the importance of taking seriously students' self-confidence, sense of self-worth and of promoting malleable thinking over fixed. The implication is that these are aspects of undergraduate learning that are not usually considered – a sample of Portuguese students (Vieira, 2002) reported that teachers have too little care for their self-esteem. Again, any actions would need to be at least programme-wide, although substantial reviews by Pascarella and

Table 3.3 Objections to the USEM account of employability

| Objection | Response |
|---|---|
| 1 It is too vague – it is left to teams and departments to establish the achievements that employers value and which they will incorporate into their work. | Partly true. Of course, departments would often resist more prescriptive formulations. Yet they are likely to welcome guidance and we note that, in the UK, ESECT and the LTSN Generic Centre are working with LTSN subject centres to elaborate USEM for departments and teams. |
| 2 The challenge to skills is not welcome. It has been a struggle to get the language of skills into higher education. To excoriate it now risks bringing the educational development movement into disrepute, especially as the distinction between 'skilful practices' and 'skills' may be too fine for some to perceive. | Insofar as the language of skills has prompted enthusiastic amateurs to make assumptions, quite at odds with extensive psychological evidence, that it is possible to 'have' a skill, that skill levels can be specified in general terms, without reference to context and content, and that skills are transferable, then it has been – to put it mildly – unhelpful to employability. No apology is made for challenging it. |
| 3 It is not based on sustained research, being just one reading of the data. | Partly true. It is open to challenge from other readings. However, it is a reading of the data that has proved useful, which suggests it has some face validity. Some correspondence with theories of learning has been demonstrated. |
| 4 The E (efficacy beliefs) is poorly named. The alternatives, 'self-theories' and 'self-systems' are more helpful. | Possibly true, although work on schoolchildren's learning emphasizes that 'learned helplessness', which is a loss of efficacy beliefs, is fundamentally corrosive (Peterson et al., 1993; Seligman, 1998). |
| 5 'Metacognition' is jargon. | Agreed, but the concept is important and is gaining ground in higher education. |
| 6 It is not certain that higher education can influence self-systems. If it can, then there is a marked lack of knowledge about how to foster appropriate self-theories and metacognitive strength. | There is some evidence that HE can make a difference here (Pascarella and Terenzini, 1991; Astin, 1997; Perry, 1997; Dweck, 1999). And although less is known about how to foster E and M than we might like, there are useful pointers. |

| Objection | Response |
|---|---|
| 7 What is known about the development of **SEM** (skilful practices, efficacy beliefs and metacognition) suggests that there is a need to think in terms of whole programmes, not of individual modules, units or courses. This is a challenge to practices, values and systems, notably in the USA and in highly-modularized universities in the UK. | Agreed. The question is whether the challenge is in the interests of students, then of employers. If it is, it becomes a question of costs – how much will teachers in higher education have to do (for example, in articulating modules) in order to adopt a programme-wide approach to the sorts of achievements they want students to be able to claim on graduation? |
| 8 In England, USEM cuts across the priorities identified by the Quality Assurance Agency's (QAA's) subject benchmarking statements which are, for example, silent on self-systems. It compounds complexity. | Perhaps it supplements, rather than 'cuts across'. For example, the Department of Educational Research at Lancaster University, UK, added a section on beliefs (**E** and **M**) to Part 10 of its programme specification. |
| 9 Much of this, especially **EM**, resists assessment. Since we believe that only that which is assessed gets taken seriously by students, there is the likelihood that **EM**, and probably some skilful practices as well, will not be taken seriously by anyone. USEM is a tokenist's charter. | It resists grading but not assessment. See Chapter 8 on assessing 'fuzzy' outcomes, such as **E** and **M**. |

Terenzini (1991) and Astin (1997) imply that the whole higher education environment may be implicated.

Many programmes, especially professional programmes, promote the virtues of reflection, which is certainly a process that can contribute to the development of metacognitive knowledge. The development of programme portfolios (Cambridge, 2001) and of personal development planning in England (QAA, 2001a) can also sustain reflection and the development of self-knowledge. Notice the programme-wide emphasis. There is certainly promise here if students can be induced to participate, but it is most likely to be realized when programmes are infused by research-informed strategies for helping students to know what and how they know.

The tenth objection is not that USEM might disturb existing practices in higher education modules. It is more serious. The objection is that USEM seems to depend on all courses being brought within the iron grasp of programme specifications, boards and directors. Worse, the message seems to be that unless university teachers put themselves into this thrall, little can be done to enhance student employability.

There is certainly truth in the objection that USEM directs attention to programmes, of which modules are but parts. We stand by the claim that the best chances of enhancing student employability come from orchestrated, programme-wide actions, believing that research points strongly in that direction. However, in Chapter 12 we shall use the concept of 'tuning' the curriculum to argue that it is possible to have programme-wide coherence and, through the application of subsidiarity, to respect diversity. In Chapter 7 we also show that there are many individual initiatives of value and argue that a lively co-curriculum[9] is an important adjunct to a good curriculum – but not a substitute for it.

## The dynamics of employability

Our approach to employability is a dynamic one. Table 3.4 depicts the contribution to employability that can be made by experiences prior to higher education and in the different phases within higher education. It shows transitions and notes some of the work that has to be done to reduce the disruption that tends to accompany them. It also indicates that employability does not rest when the first graduate job is achieved. This is implied by the term 'portfolio careers', which was quite a common way in the 1990s of saying that in the labour market people were as employable as could be discerned from their portfolio of (updated) skills. In the face of invasive professional obsolescence, employability needed to be continually renewed to be sustainable. Actions that may groom students to get a fair job on graduation are not really contributing to *employability* unless they include the development of expertise (Bereiter and Scardamalia, 1993) and the enhancement of practical intelligence (Sternberg *et al.*, 2000). Such strategies might enhance an institution's employment rates but unless they are dovetailed with the systemic good learning that makes for sustainability, then they contribute little to employability.

Table 3.4 A dynamic view of employability

| Moments in the transition to graduate employments | Implications for employability |
|---|---|
| 1 Awareness of the employability process | It is common to find naïve beliefs about the value of a degree in the labour market and lack of awareness about employer expectations. Schools and colleges can challenge this through personal development planning and careers advice that highlights the significance of USEM or some similar broad account of employability. |
| 2 Entry to higher education | Good induction arrangements will last longer than a week or two – a semester or year is better. Students need to learn the 'rules of the game' including the 'employability game'; begin identifying achievement and supporting evidence; experience teaching, learning and assessment. |
| 3 The first year experience | Methods that promote learning that is consistent with USEM or some similar account; succeed as learners. |
| 4 On course | Acquiring 'employability assets' – developing well-grounded claims to the elements described by USEM or a similar description. Representing achievements in convincing forms; learning to present claims of achievement in various ways to different employers with different requirements; identifying appealing career opportunities and learning to deal effectively with applications, interviews and assessment centres. |
| 5 Job getting | |
| 6 Entry to the workplace | In the midst of disorientation, using metacognition and self-theories to cope. |
| 7 Career development with workplace learning | Identifying development needs and collecting evidence of the learning that is occurring informally and non-formally. Career planning and management. |

Having identified employability as an important component of life-long learning, we shall now concentrate upon the undergraduate years, noting that the *Perspectives* series of papers on employability has papers on the pre-HE experience (Ward and Pierce, 2003), the first year (Yorke, 2003a), the later undergraduate years (Yorke and Knight, 2003) and transitions to the workplace (Harvey, 2003).

In Chapters 6–13 we describe some small and larger-scale ways in which the curriculum can be geared to enhance employability. First, though, we consolidate the claims for the USEM description (Chapter 4), complement it with an analysis of how studying an Arts subject (English) can lead to various kinds of employment (Chapter 5) and then in Chapters 6, 7 and 8 consider general implications for the curriculum and assessment.

## Notes

1   How convincing the claims prove to be is related to the state of the labour market in which individual graduates pitch themselves. Claims convincing in one industry or region may not work in others, while claims made by 'blue-eyed' social groups seem to be more likely to convince than similar claims made by less advantaged ones.

2   Early project papers referred to 'skills' because the term had wide currency. For reasons explained in Box 2.2, we have slowly moved our public work over to the phrase 'skilful practices'.

3   In the early days of the project 'strategic thinking' was preferred to 'metacognition', largely for fear that 'metacognition' would be seen as jargon. We now think that 'metacognition' is becoming accepted and appreciate the advantages of a term which has attracted a great deal of psychological research.

4   His analysis omits some forms of research that are not amenable to meta-analysis (Light and Pillemer, 1982).

5   Her thinking centres on a distinction between fixed self-theories (I am intelligent, outgoing, caring) and malleable, or incremental, theories (I can behave intelligently, outgoingly, caringly by thinking well and working at it). The 'dynamic, incremental view of human reality ... allows more room for change ... [and] may reduce the likelihood of helpless responding and promote mastery-oriented coping in the face of aversive events' (Dweck, Chiu and Hong, 1995: 283).

6   In the 2001 'taxonomy' there can be overlap between the six cognitive processes: 'analyze' is not always easier than 'evaluate' and there must be doubts about the assumption that 'conceptual knowledge' always precedes 'procedural knowledge'.

There is a competing view that levels of difficulty reside in tasks: 'tasks have a pull to certain levels' (Fischer, 2002). Turiel (2002: 290) adds that people appear to be inconsistent in their judgements, which poses assessment problems. In fact, 'these might not be inconsistencies but variations in the applications of different judgements to different contexts'. These findings, which fit with other research into 'situated cognition', have significant implications for attempts to design progression into degree programmes and for the certification of competence.

7   Employers and new graduate hires both talk about the need to work to deadlines, under pressure, to a budget and with a keen eye to client satisfaction.

8   Worried by 'grade inflation', Harvard has decided to limit the proportion of A grades it awards, a rare example of a university voluntarily reducing the percentage of good and outstanding degrees it will award. However, grade inflation is multi-causal and not amenable to simplistic remedies (Yorke, 2002a).

9   'Co-curriculum' is a North American term which conveniently refers to all those arrangements made outside the 'regular' curriculum for the educational enrichment of the undergraduate years. While referring to things that are optional, it avoids the unfortunate connotations of the English term 'extra-curricular'. We say more about it in Chapter 7.

# Chapter 4

# A research study of employability

## Views from the workplace

As described in Chapter 3, USEM provides a way of thinking about employability that is at a sufficient level of abstraction to be widely applicable as a heuristic. This chapter looks at what recent recruits into employment and their more experienced colleagues have to say about employability.

As part of the Skills *plus* project, semi-structured interviews were held with 97 recently appointed graduate employees and 117 colleagues from the same organizations who had been in employment for rather longer. Some of the latter were fulfilling a supervisory role in respect of the new recruits, others were simply more experienced co-workers. Unlike much research into 'the views of employers', the interviews avoided, as far as possible, those with roles such as 'human resources manager' for three reasons: first, existing research has been sensitive – perhaps too sensitive – to the views of such people; second, the consequence tends to be a bias towards larger organizations and away from small and medium-sized enterprises (SMEs); and third – and most importantly from our point of view – 'employability' as understood close to where the graduate recruit's work is actually being carried out may be rather different than that as understood at the top of an organization. In this chapter we use the term 'senior' (coded S) as a shorthand to denote those of our 214 interviewees who had been in employment for some time (irrespective of status in the organization) and 'junior' (coded J) to denote those relatively recently recruited into employment.

The interviewers were people with experience of the educational service, some having retired from higher education. The interviews were recorded in the majority of instances, and the recordings were transcribed. Where this was not possible, notes were made of the interviews. All interviewees had been informed of the purpose of their interview and had signed an agreement for the interview data to be used on an anonymized basis.

## The informants

Three-quarters of the junior informants were 26 or younger at the time of interview. There was an even split as regards gender, 46 being male and 49 female.[1] Forty-nine had obtained an arts-related degree, and 34 a science-related degree, with 65 obtaining upper second class honours or better. At the time of the interviews, 76 had been in their post for less than 18 months. Forty of the junior employees were in public sector posts, and 53 in the private sector. Where the size of the organization was identified, 63 of the junior employees were in organizations of more than 100 people, and only 17 in smaller organizations.

Of the more senior employees, 78 had been in full-time employment for ten or more years. There were proportionately fewer men than women in this group (50 as against 66). The senior informants divided evenly between public (56) and private (57) organizations which, where their size was identified, were predominantly large (71, compared with 22 identified as small). The senior employees' relationships with the junior employees varied: 18 were co-workers; 3 mentors; 49 supervisors or line managers; and 25 senior managers.

There was a bias in the interviews towards the practical because informants were graduates in employment and those working alongside them. The research approach reported here is likely to have brought to the fore comments on practical intelligence and may have tended to overshadow an appreciation of academic intelligence in action.

We organize this summary of these interviews around the USEM account, with which informants' views were broadly consistent. We acknowledge that such a complex data set might be analyzed in different ways but choose USEM as our point of reference on account of the advantages reviewed in Chapter 3. There are methodological difficulties in all such analyses (Knight and Saunders, 1999) and we present ours as one careful and plausible reading of a substantial archive.

## The broad picture[2]

### Junior employees

Asked what had helped them to gain employment in their graduate jobs, the junior employees' responses pointed to four general reasons:

- Degree experience
- Personal qualities
- Communication skills
- More pragmatic aspects.

In some instances, the academic nature of the degree programme was important (as would be expected). In addition to subject-specific expertise, mention was made of more general employment-related capabilities enhanced through degree-level study. However, set against this was the suggestion by a few informants that their degree programme had not helped them to develop the pragmatic under-standing and skills[3] that they found themselves needing in employment – here, time-management, prioritizing of work, and working with others were noticeable. Some informants also mentioned an absence of practical, 'real-world' experience;

a lack of attention to communication and general interpersonal skills; and a lack of training in information technology.

Personal qualities were significant in the 97 junior employees' minds. They produced, between them, 108 attributes which could be located in the general area of personal qualities. Allaway, in analyzing the data for the Skills *plus* project, notes tendencies for the type of attribute to vary with the type of organization in which these employees were working. There was a tendency for those in the industrial sector to produce attributes such as 'active', 'cope with pressure', 'extrovert', 'leader', 'proactive', 'reliable', and 'self-driven', whereas those from the health and social services sector were more likely to suggest attributes such as 'approachable', 'concern for people', 'empathetic', 'helpful', 'self-aware', and 'sensitive'. This raises the issue of the psychological 'fit' between the graduate and the organization's value system – an issue that awaits further elucidation.

Ability in various aspects of communication, such as listening, presentation and negotiation, were believed to have been significant in the acquisition of the junior employees' current jobs.

The vast majority (81 of 93 valid responses) of junior employees considered work experience (often relatively low-level and casual) to have contributed considerably to their employability. It demonstrated the desire to work, exposure to – and awareness of – more than just an academic world and, in their terms, the development of relevant skills. In a fair number of instances the work placement had been of direct relevance to their current job (notably for posts in industry and in health or social services). For a few, the work experience had been followed by recruitment to the same organization.

A junior informant from a small organization (138 J) pointed to the importance of being multi-skilled, since it was unable to operate on the basis of fairly rigid role-definitions.

### Senior employees

The 117 senior employees (whose status, it will be recalled, varied within their organization) pointed to five main groups of characteristics when describing what their organization sought in applicants:

- Quality of, and performance in, education
- Knowledge and skills
- Personal characteristics
- Communication skills
- Work experience.

Forty-seven informants made explicit reference to the value of work experience, but this may under-represent the true picture since some of the other characteristics mentioned may have been developed through work experience without being explicitly acknowledged.

Educational experience had two components – the quality of the higher educational experience (where the perceived quality of the institution was, in some instances, taken as a criterion), and the performance achieved by applicants on their programmes of study (though, as is noted later, the occasional informant was less concerned about the degree performance than about the potential of the applicant to fulfil the requirements of the job).

The 'knowledge and skills' group of characteristics subsumed not only specialist and 'generic' knowledge, but also 'soft skills' such as those related to working with others (which spill over into communication skills). The desirability of communication skills aligned quite closely with what the junior employees said, with self-presentation, oral and written communication and other interactive skills prominent. One, implicitly critical of the capacity of graduates to express themselves, stated:

> I expect [higher education] to teach them the difference between good and bad grammar.
>
> (183 S)

though the comment might in part be addressed to the compulsory stage of education.

More than 550 references were made to personal characteristics, hinting at their heavy weighting in the judgement of employability. These could be loosely categorized under headings such as intelligence; thoughtfulness; motivation; responsibility; self-efficacy; and sociability.

When higher education was criticized, these informants used terms that were similar to the criticisms made by the junior employees. Personal qualities and practical, work-related knowledge and skills dominated the criticism, with communication and general interpersonal skills also featuring quite strongly. Against this, it was recognized that some of these characteristics would be developed in the home, in groups outside the educational field, and through leisure activities of various kinds.

One comment from a senior employee relates to the economic implications for graduates of their increasing number:

> I think sometimes the universities give a slightly unrealistic view of what to expect when you go out and get your first job … they will … say to you 'When you've got this qualification you will … get a £20,000-a-year job' and in the real world it doesn't always happen like that, in fact it's quite rare. So the biggest thing … a university could do would be perhaps lower the expectations slightly. We don't have many apprenticeship schemes in this country any more but effectively that is what you're doing …
>
> (162 S)

## Understanding

### *Subject understanding*

There is a fair amount of evidence from the senior employees that, where the degree subject has a direct relevance to the field of employment, the graduate's disciplinary understanding is taken as read (though in some cases there was pressure on the applicant to demonstrate their disciplinary capabilities by asking them how their disciplinary understandings could be turned to useful account). Where the employer was less concerned about the actual subject(s) studied, and was more interested in a general capability, the emphasis in the interviews veered towards more general attributes and performances. In other words, more than 'just a degree' was wanted: for example, one senior employee said:

> ... if all the person had was their degree then they wouldn't have got shortlisted.
>
> (185 S)

However, one senior employee (120 S) was concerned that 'good workers' might get weeded out during the selection process whilst academic high fliers progressed (here we might see 'knowing that' given precedence over 'knowing how'). Yet, for another senior employee, the classification of the degree was not the most important thing:

> I'm looking for a balance between accomplishment at a technical level, in terms of a reasonable degree. I'm not after a first, or even a 2:1 when it comes to that. Basically, someone who's gone through the course and understands what they've done, but also somebody with a personality ... to me the personality side is always 51 per cent ... because unless you can get on with the various departments ... your job can be made ten times harder, or if you can get on with them it's made ten times easier.
>
> (180 S)

Academic knowledge may miss the multiple perspectives that the world of employment desires. One junior employee criticized her programme for focusing on the consumer at the expense of considering the supply side:

> Everything's got to be manufactured to a price, for a reason. Although we did study economics and marketing we were kind of brainwashed too much, throughout the course, on consumerism and the end user, not the implications for the manufacturer.
>
> (179 J)

She was unhappy with the extent to which her programme had prepared her for the complexity of the computer systems that had confronted her when she arrived in the retail industry:

... a lot of the retails have got new specification systems, which are like big computer databases and I'd never seen one before, and I think that's really bad, that you get to your first job and you've never even experienced something typical of the retail industry. A lot of it is theory, and probably lacking a few essential skills for *today's* retailing.

(179 J)

Another (161 J) had taken it into his own hands to develop the skills in information technology that he needed for the career that he had envisaged.

### General understanding

A lot of interviews emphasized the relevance of general understandings – often the kind of tacit knowledge that a person picks up when they are immersed in a situation, without it necessarily having to be spelt out. The acquisition of work-related understandings has, of course, been a longstanding justification for sandwich (or co-operative) education, in which the student spends time in some form of work placement as part of their studies. In recent times (and probably stimulated by the Enterprise in Higher Education initiative of the late 1980s)[4] the justification has been extended in the UK to programmes other than those designated as sandwich programmes. One junior informant pointed to work experience as a way of determining whether a particular kind of employment would suit her:

... it's OK doing the theory but you might not like it when you actually get the job.

(152 J)

Another offered a much more positive testimonial to the value of work experience:

[The work experience] just kind of lifted me off really into what I'm doing now and helped me with new skills.

(161 J)

The value of general work experience to a potential employee was stressed in a number of interviews, one senior employee for example noting that

... we would expect everybody to have had some sort of work experience, even if it's holiday working, part-time working ... just any working environment where they've had to work with people, understand some of the politics that goes on and maybe see if they understand any of the financial aspects as well.

(117 S)

Not unrelatedly, senior employees pointed to some applicants' poor appreciation of how the world of employment worked, one noting that

> There are things that [people coming out of an academic environment] just don't seem to have a clue about.
>
> (182 S)

This was given a more explicit focus by another who referred to graduates' scant awareness of hierarchy and bureaucracy.

> (186 S)

Knowing 'how the world works' requires practical experience as well as academic learning. As one senior employee put it succinctly:

> Common sense real life isn't as in the textbooks.
>
> (196 S)

Another (210 S), commenting on a junior employee, noted that she had not yet acquired the world-wisdom through life-experiences 'to be able to make … on the hoof judgements'.

However, it was clear that some junior employees had appreciated the value of prior engagement in the world of work:

> [part-time work] makes you more, I would say, streetwise, more reliant on yourself. [He worked in a bar and as a Student Union door steward.] [You] need to be very confident in that sort of situation because you do get situations that can arise that are rather nasty … you need to be level-headed as well, 'cos if something does occur and you're responsible for that you have to react very quickly, or there'll be first aid …
>
> (171 J)

The year out was one of the biggest aspects of why I can hit the ground running with this company. People who have not done a year out … are not used to all the day-to-day issues that I had to deal with in surveying.

> (181 J)

> … the actual placement that I undertook gave me a chance to have an insight into statutory work, so that filled in a massive void that I felt was missing on the course … they just talk of law in general, they do a lot on the Children's Act, but it's much different to the things written in practice and actually applying the stuff.
>
> (122 J)

The differences between academic and practical understandings were caught in a number of interviews. A former mature student pointed to the advantages that she had regarding her understanding of how things 'worked' in employment:

> ... when [younger students] come out of university it's a different kettle of fish altogether. I was prepared [as a mature student] for what it's like to work in the proper workforce whilst students aren't.... I just think that where the university let us down was ... the placements should have been longer [than 3 weeks].

> (128 J)

Another junior employee had come to wonder whether the balance of her academic programme in nursing had been optimal:

> ... maybe there was too much ... theory behind the management and different philosophies of management, rather than practical advice about how to manage certain situations and how to manage a ward, and what you would do if this happens, or that happens.

> (213 J)

Of course, what she may have missed is the deferred impact of theoretical understandings when she is faced with other kinds of management challenge as her role in the organization evolves.

The need to bring formal academic understandings into play with practical understandings is a theme of Bereiter and Scardamalia's analysis (1993) of the development of expertise. There are examples in the interview transcripts:

> ... you can read things and you can be taught things but it's very different to actually being in a room where you've got a family who are in the middle of a heated conflict and trying to work out how you actually manage that situation and deflate some of the anger there. So you can read but you actually have to get involved and practise those different scenarios [sometimes by observing, sometimes by viewing a video and commenting on it]. Shadowing can be difficult because of the confidentiality, etc.

> (135 S)

> ... you might read all the theories, say about attachment theory, you might be very clear what attachment theory is and how it should work, but it's very different when you're translating it into this family or family A, or family B or family C. They might respond in a totally different way and it's crucial that you don't over-interpret that response from a purely theoretical perspective, that you've got to put it in context as a whole this family's functioning 'cos they don't just function, you know you can't just pigeon-hole families, you can't just look and say 'this is what's happened to this child so this is how this child is going to respond' because A and B doesn't equal C, there are a whole host of

other issues so you need to be very open-minded, flexible and interpret as a whole, really, and not just individual aspects of the same situation.

(123 S)

Local knowledge is similarly important:

... what they need to do is [to interpret] the things you've learnt at university into local practice, about what we do here in [Town A] 'cos how we do it here ... is different to how we do it in [City B] which is different to how they do it in [City C and Town D and Town E] and everywhere else, so people need to learn local policies and procedures and about how we then interpret what we do.

(123 S)

... even though [the authority's procedures stand up very well nationally] the inadequacy of the systems is just unbelievable – nothing is logical, nothing logically follows, nothing triggers off another system automatically, you have to know about all the systems and that is very hard.

(120 S)

## Organizational understanding

The need to contextualize one's employment within an understanding of the organization was mentioned by a senior and a junior employee from very different work environments. In a factory, for example,

it's as important to know what's happening out there as it is doing your job.

( 178 S)

and in the field of law enforcement

The ability to understand the workings of a police force is always important even if you've got a clerical job in finance or something like that 'cos it is very unique – it is one of the emergency services and ultimately the work that support staff do could influence whether somebody dies or lives after a police officer responds to an incident.

(161 J)

However, the breadth of desirable understandings extends beyond the boundary of the organization to include

wider issues, sociology issues, whatever the latest White Paper is ...

(214 S)

## Enterprise

Some senior employees in private organizations thought that new recruits ought to possess more commercial acumen than they appeared to have. This reinforces the argument for work experience and ties in with the broader point, made earlier, that graduates needed to have developed their understanding of the world of employment – provided that the work experience is sufficiently focused to enable students to gain this kind of understanding.

The issue of enterprise was picked up, albeit negatively, by one senior employee who stated that graduates analyzed but tended not to come forward with ideas. Although they may have researched a topic whilst studying,

> they didn't then come forward and say 'As a result of my research I think it'd be absolutely terrific if you make green sponge puddings', for example.
>
> (200 S)

There is more than a hint of creative problem-solving in the preceding example. Creativity was more explicitly valued by a junior employee who saw the value of being able

> to think outside the boundaries of normal [job] activity and be able to come up with solutions ...
>
> (161 J)

There was, particularly amongst senior employees from SMEs, an expectation that graduates should exercise their initiative, and not wait to be told what to do. The strongest expression of this came from one senior employee who was also at pains to point out that trying to achieve success at the expense of others ('over bodies') would not be acceptable and would be counter-productive:

> If there's something that needs attacking, that needs doing, you grab it. You're never given a job, you know: it's up to you, you make your own, but not through [playing] politics. That won't work here.
>
> (196 S)

The junior employee in this SME appears to have 'got the message':

> ... when I was ... offered the chance to maybe do a little work somewhere else [in the SME], I made the most of it and did as well as I could, and I showed an interest. I mean I *am* interested and I grabbed ...
>
> (195 J)

A senior employee of an SME was very definite that the business needed people who were proactive and not reactive. The demands of the business were such that there was no room for taking things easy, or spinning tasks out unnecessarily. The informant put it bluntly:

> I want somebody who compacts their work to make more time available.
>
> (200 S)

## Skills

We remarked earlier in this chapter that the languages of skills were commonly used. Our problem is that they were used too readily, with the result that it is not possible to say much that is useful about 'skills'. However, most of the comments relating to skills were references to generic achievements, not to site- and sector-specific ones. One aspect of 'skills' which did attract comment that resonates with perceptions from elsewhere was the graduate's ability to organize what they had to do within the time available to them. There was also a distinct group of comments about the significance of interpersonal skills.

### *Organizing*

Organizing and prioritizing one's work was widely noted as being important – something that one might infer from the transcripts that had perhaps not been sufficiently recognized by the junior employees when they were students. Yet the changing nature of higher education in the UK and Australia (and wherever students are having to combine study with part-time work and – in some cases – caring for dependants) makes prioritization a necessity. Prioritization could be seen in terms of self-organization or time-management, which a preliminary survey of undergraduates has indicated is an aspect of weakness (Leon, 2002).

The organization of paperwork is critical to success in a number of work environments, especially where others have to be able to find and use the relevant information:

> ... if you look at our team we all operate so differently and some of us are organized and some of us aren't, but ... organizing your time, organizing your files, is very – actually to be honest that's very underrated, because the times when I've gone to people's files to try to find information and they're just in no order, it's infuriating.
>
> (121 S)

### *Interpersonal skills*

The ability to work with a range of people was widely mentioned in the interviews. Not only was being a 'team player' seen as important, but so too were being culturally aware and able to relate fairly easily to those with whom one came into contact. One recently employed graduate acknowledged the value that he had extracted from working with refuse collectors. He had also travelled to other countries and had learned their languages, and therefore had an appreciation of other cultures that appeared to be unrivalled amongst the sample of junior employee informants.

Treating people with respect, and 'speaking their language' were important, as was not pretending to expertise that one did not possess:

> ... being able to handle people is a skill, being able to talk to the public in a language they understand, you're dealing with a typical northern town where people can smell a rat and they know when [you're bullshitting].
>
> (131 S)

Some were faced with the need to deploy the skills of advocacy and persuasion (177 J). Empathy, too, was important, and some of this could only come as a consequence of experience in the job:

> ... the ability to leave your office and go and face people in the community, not knowing how those people will be in terms of their social situation, their mental health and also how they're going to perceive you and deal with that social-work jargon ... that requires a degree of skill that I don't think a graduate would necessarily come with ... [it] only comes with practical experience ... you don't need a social-work qualification ... to be able to think about how people function under stress, under difficult situations.
>
> (136 S)

However, as a junior employee (137 J) in the same area pointed out, one had to be aware of the limits to which one could go in empathizing with clients.

Some new recruits had appreciated the need for the kind of sensitivity that Goleman (1996) terms 'emotional intelligence' when dealing with people. There is, in some jobs, a particular requirement for tact and diplomacy:

> you had to be sensitive sometimes if you had a larger lady [in the gym] and she wanted to lose weight ... saying what she wanted to hear but you'd tell it to different people in different ways, you'd know one person would want motivating in one way and another person would want motivating in another way ...
>
> (148 J)

Diplomacy was not always apparent, even between professionals. One junior employee, exposed to a situation in which divergences in professional judgement had emerged, had been concerned about the manner in which the disagreement had been conducted and she seemed to have had a sensitivity perhaps lacking in her colleagues:

I just felt that it was very inappropriate to slag off another professional in front of clients.

(137 J)

## Efficacy

In this section the concept of self-efficacy is treated broadly, encompassing various aspects of a personal commitment to success and a belief that, even if the person does not succeed every time, they can make a difference to many situations in which they find themselves.

### Motivation

A number of recent employees said that they had strong self-motivation. For one, it was explicitly acknowledged in finding, as an undergraduate, a work placement. For another, self-motivation was maintained by inventing short-term targets, exemplified in part-time work in a bar:

I've probably set myself little challenges in my head to … serve three people before the next person's served one, and just little things like that … keeping myself interested.

(175 J)

### Determination and commitment

Determination (or will) was often mentioned as a desirable attribute, which carries strong connotations of commitment. This was caught by two recent recruits and one more senior colleague:

I'll get my teeth into things and won't let go until I'm satisfied that I've exhausted it or [found] whatever I'm looking for.

(140 J)

… if a job's worth doing it's worth doing well, and I take pride in what I do, and I see it through to the end, quite determined, instead of saying 'oh I haven't got the time', pass it on to someone else, you know. I stay late if something needs doing, although I'm not a workaholic or anything… [laughs].

(179 J)

However, only the third of these informants referred to the possibility that determination might be 'developable':

I guess that's all to do with the personality, the strong will, the confidence, which I think may not be there in the university training. Whether it should be or not, I don't know. I think that strong will or maturity is something that has to be taught. I mean some people are strong willed anyway, but I think you can improve people who aren't strong willed, and that's what's happened with [new appointee].

(178 S)

## Confidence

Self-confidence is obviously a desirable attribute. A person who believes that they can achieve something is more likely to be successful than someone who lacks self-belief. One senior employee referred to a 'can do' spirit. Another referred to an optimistic approach. One recent recruit said:

I'm one of the best and that was the motivation. I can make it, as long as I put the work in.

(140 J)

Confidence is close to self-belief, and was often identified as a desirable characteristic. Important as it was, it needed to be tempered by a realization that some decisions had to be made on the basis of incomplete information:

somebody who has confidence, who has a personality, who can stand up and not necessarily be the expert – you're far from being the expert in terms of knowledge – but have the confidence to stand up there and make a decision …

(173 S)

Dealing with people could be potentially tricky, particularly if one were the bearer of unwelcome news. As one senior employee of a statutory agency remarked, for the agency's employees, confidence was

one of the key things because they do have to be going out and speaking to people who in most cases are not going to be best pleased with some of the information they're receiving.

(185 S)

## Assertiveness

One junior employee had been very assertive, as a student, in seeking help with the preparation of her *curriculum vitae* and had had to push the institution's careers service hard to get what she wanted:

Interviewer:   Did *you* have to go to them and was it optional?
Graduate:      Yes I had to go to them; yes, they didn't come to me.

Interviewer:    So you were motivated, then?
Graduate:       Yes, I pestered them.

(112 J)

Assertiveness was applauded by one senior employee:

> ... they very quickly seize on [new ideas] and they want to be part of any working parties or initiatives, and they very quickly sort of, suss out exactly what is expected of them, and they're very organized in their approach and being able to, then, implement something. Er – not to be fazed, say, in a large working party or something ... able to argue your point and not be intimidated at all by other people ...

(212 S)

## Autonomy

A few junior employee informants made reference to their development of autonomy.[5] One referred to moral courage and the need to lead by example:

> moral courage ... lead by example. Very easy to go with the pack; never easy to stand up and say 'No that's wrong, we shouldn't do that' [to subordinates and superiors].

(174 J)

Another pointed to the need to stand one's ground:

> the ability not to be swayed by other professionals – I don't mean to be arrogant by that.

(137 J)

As an undergraduate, this informant had demonstrated her autonomy, arguing successfully for the right to undertake a particular project despite the initial objections of the academic staff involved.

Other informants (214 S; 122 J; 160 J) noted the importance of being aware of, and acting within, ethical standards of behaviour in respect of their work.

## Coping with stress

Employment, as life in general, throws up stressful situations. Being able to cope with stress of various kinds was noted as important by both senior and junior employees. A new employee might, for example, have to come to terms with the recognition that what they had learned in higher education might not align perfectly with what was needed in the employment situation – research into transitions, summarized in Chapter 1, predicts that there will often be a period of apparent 'de-skilling' as academic understandings are challenged by practical exigencies. For example, report-writing in the workplace often has to be brief and to the point, in contrast to the expectations of higher education for as complete an analysis as possible within a comparatively generous word-limit.

New recruits, especially in SMEs, were expected to come to terms quickly with the demands made of them. One senior employee acknowledged the shock that this had engendered in a new appointee:

> I think you expect almost to come in and, all right, we'll mollycoddle you for one year or two years [laughs] but that doesn't happen here. … And I think that, really for [new appointee] especially … it really was a bit of a shock for her.
>
> (178 S)

Calmness under pressure was valued, as was not being fazed by not knowing the answer when asked a question. Some involved in 'people organizations', ranging from social work to the armed services, had to be able to cope with the emotional impact of their work.

## Metacognition

Some senior employees observed that there was a need for a reflective approach to be adopted regarding work. They expected it to have been developed in the degree programme:

> If someone … said they'd got a degree … I would expect them to have … been doing certain things that would make them aware of … the way they think …
>
> (214 S)

The expectation was that new recruits would be sufficiently self-aware and self-confident to know when they needed to seek advice from colleagues and when they would be expected to handle things themselves. One senior employee said:

> … we are looking about them having some insight as to when you might need to talk to your manager, when you might need to talk to your colleagues or when you can be expected to resolve those issues yourself …
>
> (119 S)

Some junior employees had acknowledged that what they had already done was of value in this respect, and they had been proactive in their self-development.

One, for instance, had undertaken an intermediate-level course on counselling which helped in communicating with and 'getting alongside' people.

Another had been motivated to undertake a personal SWOT (strengths, weaknesses, opportunities, threats) analysis, and had appreciated its value in her chosen caring profession.:

> It is an exercise that I have done for myself, at home, analyzing my strengths and weaknesses and opportunities, just because I felt I needed to do it, not because it was part of my training.
>
> (179 J)

### Learning to learn

There was a general, and unsurprising, acceptance that employees would need to continue their learning, whether through formalized continuing professional development or otherwise. As one senior employee noted, there was a need for people to be prepared to develop their talent and skills; another said that there was no place for 'know-alls'. The requirement for the ability to 'learn how to learn' was captured by one who said:

> ... the skills and knowledge base is so wide that if you haven't got the skills or the knowledge you need to know how to find them and you need to be fairly independent ...
>
> (120 S)

Some new employees appreciated the importance of keeping up to date:

> you've got to keep on top of the game, you've got to know exactly what's going on especially in the fashion world ... you have to be up to date with everything, all the new technology as well ...
>
> (146 J)

> I thought if I wanted to stay in this then I have to force myself to learn fast and I did that and it's worked.
>
> (140 J)

The assertiveness implicit in learning to learn was recognized by one junior employee:

> I'm not frightened of asking questions, me. I'm not a [person] who'll sit there and think 'God, I can't do this' and stick my head down and just ignore it. I'll ask questions and that's the way I learn and find out things ...
>
> (128 J)

## Problems

Researchers, including ourselves, have explored the meanings of employability as a construct. Given that the development of employability has become a direct policy priority in England and is an implied priority in many other countries, such research brings with it a tacit syllabus for the promotion of 'employability' and directs the attention of higher education towards a new set of concerns, such as students learning to present themselves in an appropriate way. This is double-edged. On the desirable side is the educational virtue of helping students to appreciate just what they have to offer to employers – something that some (and perhaps particularly those in non-vocational disciplines) lack. One senior employee expressed some frustration with the inability of some graduates to recognize that they had, in fact, already developed considerable skill in time-management:

> Mature students juggling home life and further study ... I think 'Come on, you can see that they've got good organizational skills, they must do!' I mean they've certainly got a bit more about them ...
>
> (214 S)

Pilot work with ten unemployed graduates (Knight and Knight, 2002), undertaken as part of the Skills *plus* project, hinted that at least some had not made as strong a case for employment as their achievements might have led one to expect, with the implication that the possession of a degree was being perceived as sufficient by itself, in contrast to the views expressed earlier in this chapter. The remedy might include some form of training in presentation, one senior employee observing that

> ... coaching in interview skills is an absolute necessity these days ...
>
> (134 S)

Some students had developed imaginative approaches to self-presentation in order to 'get themselves noticed' amongst the piles of applications likely to land on an employer's desk. One, for instance, had written a *curriculum vitae* in terms of a press-release in preference to adopting the typical presentational format.

The less desirable side of self-presentation is the risk that universities, colleges and undergraduates will concentrate on the development of a performative veneer which might mask things that would render an appointment problematic. One senior employee in the caring professions put it thus:

> I think that some people who come through the mill have learnt political correctness and the words are quite hollow but they get lots of ticks when they come to interviews because they can say the right things but in reality it's sometimes – in my experience – it's not very honest.
>
> (120 S)

There is a hope that the preparation of a portfolio of achievements, supported by evidence, could be of use to both parties to an appointment process. The student could have at their fingertips the evidence to support a claim for consideration, and the employer could ask the applicant to draw on that evidence to elaborate points made before – or even during – an interview. There is, however, the danger that this too will become an exercise in veneering.

## Retrospect and prospect

We have criticized many of the common ways of talking about employability and proposed an alternative, the USEM account. This chapter has suggested that it is consistent with research evidence collected in the Skills *plus* project. Chapter 3 argued that USEM is consistent with other research evidence as well.

The next chapter explores the themes we have been addressing in Part I by examining what employability can mean in the context of degree programmes in English.

## Notes

1   There were, for each item of data, a relatively small, but variable, number of non-responses, so totals seldom add up to 97. Responses coded as 'other' have been omitted here.
2   This section relies heavily on analyses conducted by David Allaway of Lancaster University.
3   Our reservations about 'skills' notwithstanding, informants talked skills languages, often using 'skills' to cover anything that is desirable in the workplace.
4   This initiative began under the auspices of what became the Employment Department of the UK Government.
5   Perry (1970/1998) offers a view of student development that moves, in broad terms, from acquiescence to authority to functioning on an autonomous basis. Autonomy, for Perry, implies the preparedness to act according to self-held principles, even in hostile circumstances.

# Chapter 5

# The study of English and the careers of its graduates

*Philip Martin and Jane Gawthrope*

## Overview

This chapter illustrates concerns that have been addressed in Chapters 1–4. It describes the key issues and features of the English degree's relation to the world of employment. It does this by examining the nature and value of the discipline itself in relation to the employability debate, by considering the evidence gathered from research and statistical surveys, by presenting the personalized accounts of selected graduates, and by a discussion of the English curriculum and its pedagogy in relation to skills profiling.

## English and 'employability'

### The statistical dimensions of the study of English in UK higher education

The Quality Assurance Agency's Benchmarking Statement for English[1] defines the subject as:

> a versatile academic discipline characterised by the rigorous and critical study of literature and language. It is concerned with the production, reception and interpretation of written texts, both literary and non-literary; and with the nature, history and potential of the English language.

Over 130 institutions out of a total of 171 offer degree-level programmes in English, so the subject is very widely taught. In January 2003 the website of the Universities and Colleges Admissions Service (UCAS)[2] listed 3,364 undergraduate English courses. To put this into perspective, there were 3,550 engineering and 4,079 history courses. According to figures from the Higher Education Statistics Agency 10,555 students were recruited to undergraduate and postgraduate English programmes in the year 2000.

The subject is therefore broadly comparable with others in terms of student recruitment in the same year:

- Maths, statistics and operational research: 10,611 students.
- Geography, earth and environmental sciences: 11,095 students.
- Hospitality, leisure and tourism: 9,716 students.

## A brief history of the discipline

As a discipline, English is historically conditioned by controversy and interrogation, yet the current debate about its relation to the world of employment is different. Where previous questions have been concerned to locate the purpose, value and practice of the degree, its relevance – in these categories – has been circled by intellectual boundaries. Now English is being asked to demonstrate its value in relation to pragmatic measurements. How useful is an English degree in the world of employment? What practical benefits does it bring? And most brutally, perhaps, how do the salaries of English graduates compare with graduates from other disciplines? What is a degree in English worth in financial terms?[3]

## Issues

One response to these questions would be to admit that English, in comparison to the vocational subjects, is not well-prepared to answer them.[4] The degree is not on its own in this respect, in terms of either its knowledge or its skills. How, for example, would a pure scientist explain the relevance of a recondite area of knowledge such as string theory to an employer looking for a skill-set relevant to the selling of advertising space? No better, I suspect, than we would in an explanation of how Wordsworth's relationship to picturesque aesthetics might fare in the same context. Another response – and a better one entirely – would be to reverse the poles in a re-organization of the question's implicit hierarchies. How can an employer make the most of an English graduate's knowledge and abilities?[5] And how can English graduates be best prepared for making the most of their attributes in these respects? A further re-organization might re-centre the question again: how does an English degree help a student in the series of choices they will make about – and within – the world of employment?

It is important, we believe, to get these questions the right way round from the outset. The purpose of a non-vocational degree (and possibly others too) is not purely nor primarily to equip its graduates for employment. If that were the case, then we may as well abandon academic disciplines by and large, and construct degrees out of skills courses evacuated of content, which would be cheaper and quicker than using academic subjects as awkward vehicles for the imparting of training needs. Equally, academic subjects cannot ignore the demands of the economy, nor can they deny their students' need to establish themselves as good employment prospects. A non-vocational degree such as English is primarily focused on developing knowledge about particular cultural forms and histories: its purpose is to involve the student in the revision of existing knowledge through the value it attributes to informed and educated *individual* opinion. In this regard its primary purpose is not direct training for employment, but the development of a rich fund of cultural and human knowledge, which in turn is subject to critical enquiry of many different kinds. However the degree is structured or conceived (and there is a deal of difference between many English degrees), the high value given to the individual view is generally endorsed. And at the heart of the degree, in almost all cases, will be the refinement and sophistication of argument, creativity, deduction and debate, exemplified in the overwhelming prevalence in the degree of the discursive essay, and the seminar – or small group – discussion. However, it is important to be clear about the nature of this emphasis. English values individualism but it does not blithely credit opinion for its own sake. The individual view has to be backed up by knowledge, by sophisticated creativity which – for example – is capable of re-organizing existing knowledge in new and unexpected combinations, of seeing the relative merits of opposing or contesting arguments, or by an understanding of the deep complexity of language itself in many different forms, historical or contemporary. To this end, the degree is taught and assessed in such a way as to give high priority and visibility to the individual understanding.

Profiling the attributes and abilities that English departments intend to foster is demanding, and difficult for a host of reasons, but not impossible. Undoubtedly, this notion of individualism should be given some priority: English graduates are good at employing independent analysis but, at the same time, they are taught through processes which give the highest regard to dialogue – with peers, with tutors, with established bodies of thought. They are therefore accomplished in considering the views and opinions of others, and of different schools of thought, and in positioning themselves in relation to all of these. Their reading experiences, dependent for their success on imaginative and creative engagement, as well as analysis, make them imaginative, creative and analytical. And because both literary forms and linguistic analysis make them highly conscious of the complexities of language, they are used to dealing with demanding material, suspicious of over-simplification, and appreciative of eloquence. They have great reading stamina, and because of their historical and cross-cultural reading, they have a developed sense of history, and of other cultures. Their ability to communicate effectively on paper and in speech is likely to be well developed. They will often have been set research tasks, and so will be good at finding things out and, more importantly, will know the kinds of questions to ask. They will, in all likelihood, have a continuing appetite for learning and reading, and they will be curious of the social world around them, since so much of their study in literature and language will have focused on acts of social communication. This would be a starting point for profiling the English graduate's abilities.

Yet there are also a whole range of factors to take stock of here. First, it is important to acknowledge the limitations of terms like 'the world of employment' and, indeed, the skill-sets that are usually drawn down to summarize employers' needs. Employment opportunities are far more differentiated than such lists imply;

graduates' implementation of these attributes are likely to be differentiated to an equivalent, or greater, degree; finally, graduates do not glean all their attributes from the programme of study, and indeed there is evidence that their employability prospects are more strongly linked to other influences (Brown and Scase, 1994). At the same time, there is a certain strength in the generic vagueness of both terminologies (employment and skills), for the ground is so differentiated that it is impossible to map in such detail. It could be argued that the strength of the skills identified for graduates is that their very generalism implicitly acknowledges further differentiation (for it is extremely likely that most disciplines will draw down the same lists in the identification of their graduates' strengths).[6] These caveats might appear to be a set of impossible denials (there is no such thing as the world of employment, no such thing as graduate attributes, let alone an English graduates' attributes) but what we mean by them is that none of these categories or quantities are archetypally definitive; rather, they are generally indicative. It is important to recognize this to avoid the instrumentalist trap of regarding skill-sets religiously, or indeed, as non-negotiable outcomes; an approach which is also liable to deceive students through false expectations. Neither students, nor the co-ordinates of employment, nor the economy itself, are so amenable: these are complex, rich, and volatile quantities, and we need to be aware of them as such.[7]

The dilemma therefore divides like this: do we stick with our generic notion of graduateness, aware of its provisionality and the space it therefore acknowledges for further differentiation, or do we begin work on a more refined, more accurate, and more individually responsive means of accounting for graduates' abilities, such as that initiated above? Do we stick with the certainty of a general law, or go in pursuit – possibly in vain – of precision? Bearing all this in mind, and noting that we are now in the relatively early stages of either process, our response to this has been to gather further evidence, to find out more about the current situation of English graduates in employment.

## Generalized subject choice and career patterns

In the autumn of 2001 the English Subject Centre noted an increasing level of interest in employability issues amongst its community in UK HE. This was against a background of the government's desire to achieve a 50 per cent participation rate for young people in HE, a growing public awareness of the level of debt incurred whilst studying for a degree, and the subject's perceived competition with more vocationally oriented subjects. Departments were feeling under pressure, perhaps for the first time, to indicate the strengths and aptitudes developed in the study of English literature, and to demonstrate to potential recruits how these might lead to 'successful' careers after graduation. There was, however, little evidence to inform the subject community's view of how its graduates related to the world of employment, and so the English Subject Centre commissioned the Centre for Higher Education Research and Information at the Open University

(CHERI), a unit with established expertise in the field of graduate employment, to survey the field of the English degree and graduate careers. Most of the information on generalized career patterns given here draws on this work by Brennan and Williams (2003). The Subject Centre was anxious to avoid relying solely on first destination statistics collected only six months after graduation. CHERI had access to a data set taking a longer profile extending to three or four years after graduation and therefore giving a fuller picture of career patterns.

## Motivations to study English

Why is it that over 10,000 students per year choose to study English, and what influence do career considerations have on this decision? Data collected by Brennan and Williams (2003) from sixth formers and their teachers show a mix of attitudes towards English and graduate careers. It scores low on direct career relevance, with decisions to continue studying the subject for pure enjoyment often being hedged with take-up of another, more applied subject, in a combined programme. On the other hand, others regard the acquisition of a good class of degree regardless of the subject as of primary importance; some see English as a 'blue-chip' subject that conveys evidence of potential to employers, much as classics used to do. When teachers were asked how English might be made more attractive at degree level there was no support for trying to make it more job-related. Rather there was a considerable body of opinion suggesting that English could market itself better, emphasizing its value in employment terms and expounding the range of occupations for which it might serve. It is therefore an oversimplification to say that even amongst sixth formers, English is labelled as a non-vocational subject: the Brennan and Williams study found some recognition of the deeper competencies bestowed by academic study.

This is an important lesson for English departments under pressure to demonstrate in crude ways the employment relevance of their courses. Generally speaking students are not motivated to study English because of any direct career relevance, but because they enjoy the subject and see it as a 'high status' one. The career relevance comes not from the subject studied *per se*, but from the way in which it is seen to prove the students' wider intellectual abilities, which might broadly equate to the 'Understanding' and 'Metacognition' of the USEM model.

## Generalized career patterns

In this section, we look at the information that can be gleaned from statistical data about the career profiles of English graduates, and how this compares to other subject groups. The data examined are those generated by the national First Destination Statistics (FDS)[8] which are collected six months after graduation, and data collected in a survey conducted by CHERI three to four years after graduation (Brennan *et al.*, 2001).

When making career choices, the number of possibilities open to English graduates, like other non-vocational graduates, is immense. Most 'top' employers in the UK make most of their jobs open to graduates irrespective of the subject of their degrees. For English graduates then, their subject of study can therefore be regarded as less important than other factors such as intellect, attitudes, social fit and prestige of their university.

## Level of employment

The FDS data are, of course, limited in that former students are surveyed only six months after graduation, when the transition to stable employment typically takes two to three years. The 2000/1 data indicate that 58 per cent of English graduates were in employment six months after completing their degrees, a figure which is similar to that of other non-vocational graduates. Twenty-eight per cent were still studying and only just over 7 per cent were actually without work and were seeking it. Of those employed, 75 per cent were working in a full-time paid position and 41 per cent were in a graduate level occupation. In broad brush terms, this paints a picture of graduates not yet embarked on a settled career path, taking further qualifications in order to equip themselves for one or working at what they might regard as temporary jobs. A mere six months after graduation this is as one might expect (Purcell and Elias, 2002).

What is the picture if we look three to four years after graduation using the CHERI data? Again, unemployment does not appear to be a significant problem, with only 9 per cent experiencing this in the first three and a half years after graduation. This is close to the average for all graduates. Although in the first two years the proportion working is low among English graduates compared to others, this is largely due to the high proportion engaged in further study, and after three and a half years these differences have largely disappeared. By the beginning of the fourth year the labour market activity of English graduates is similar to that of any other group of graduates, with 84 per cent of them in graduate level jobs. This is slightly worse than average for all graduates, but not worse than Humanities and Languages graduates in general. We can therefore conclude that although the English degree does not equip students for a specific career, it is giving them the capabilities to find and keep jobs at an appropriate level.

## Employment sectors

Both the FDS data and the CHERI data show that there is a relatively high proportion of English graduates in the public sector (45 per cent) and non-profit sector (12 per cent). For all graduates the equivalent percentages are 35 per cent and 6 per cent. This concentration in the public and non-profit sectors, where salary levels are lower than the private sector, probably explains the low average salary of English graduates. At the time the CHERI data was collected (1998–9) there was a gap of £1,500 between the average income of an English graduate and that of all Humanities and Language graduates, and a gap of £4,500 compared to all other graduates.

## Job satisfaction

According to the CHERI data, English graduates' satisfaction with their employment situation is the same as the average among other Humanities and Language graduates, with 46 per cent reporting fairly high levels of satisfaction. Compared to all graduates, however, where 58 per cent had a positive view of their situation, the level of job satisfaction is lower.

English graduates have a less positive view of their jobs when asked to take into account their earlier expectations. Asked whether their work situation met the expectation they had on entering higher education, only 19 per cent of English graduates gave a firm 'yes'. This compares with 30 per cent for Humanities and Language graduates, and 37 per cent for all graduates.

This may point to several issues in the area of the interaction of higher education and the world of work. Most obviously it points to a widespread disappointment amongst graduates, with the quality of working life a mismatch between expectations and experience. Those entering HE directly from school or college may indeed have an idealized image of career development, or an assumption that the degree is a ticket to a lifetime of demanding and rewarding work. However, we must also consider that many expectations are not unreasonable, and the mismatch arises from the pressures and restrictions of jobs which give little room for personal fulfilment.

Whatever the explanation, the situation suggests that most Humanities and Language Departments might benefit their students by providing more opportunities to enhance their understanding of the workplace both in terms of the range of careers available and the satisfactions and dissatisfactions of graduate employment. They need to be prepared for a transitional period of several years after leaving higher education and entering stable graduate employment. And finally, they need to be reminded that because there is no automatic employer demand for non-vocational graduates in particular subjects, English graduates need to be adept at demonstrating a whole range of personal and cultural attributes in addition to their possession of a degree. The challenge for those departments recruiting students from non-traditional backgrounds is that, as the CHERI report puts it, 'for students from non-vocational subjects, questions of what you have studied may be less important than questions of where you studied and your social background' (Brennan and Williams, 2003: 7).

## The workplace relevance of English

How does English as an academic discipline present itself to potential recruits in terms of its contribution to career development? We have already noted that the primary motivation to study the subject comes from enjoyment of language and literature rather than as a qualification for a particular career. Nevertheless, the large financial investment made by students and their parents in higher education means that the question of what comes afterwards exerts at least a background influence in subject choice. So how do departmental websites present career opportunities to potential students?

A survey of a random selection of 33 English Department websites in the summer of 2002 (see Brennan and Williams, 2003: 22) showed that all but three offered information on the abilities, competences and skills developed in students and/or gave examples of the types of career graduates enter. 'Journalism', 'Teaching' and 'Media' were the three careers most likely to be mentioned, closely followed by 'Publishing' and 'Postgraduate study' (Brennan and Williams, 2003: 23). But if one looks at the range of occupations which English graduates actually go into, the conclusion would be that departmental websites are failing to reflect this breadth. The First Destination Statistics 2000/1 show that for those in employment six months after graduation, the largest category is 'Business, consultancy and research' (18 per cent), followed by the 'Wholesale and retail trade' (16 per cent) and 'Manufacturing' (11 per cent) (Brennan and Williams, 2003: 36). If not actually misleading, many departmental websites are therefore underselling the education they offer as preparation for a wide range of different careers. The focus on journalism and media on the websites arises, presumably, from an inaccurate stereotype of the English graduate, or from an assumption that these careers are attractive to potential students. The risk, however, is of deterring those students who do not envisage themselves as working in journalism or the media.

In terms of the types of abilities, competencies and skills English departments said on their websites they would develop, the most frequently mentioned were: (a) written/oral communication skills and (b) critical analysis and evaluation. Both of these figure in the English Benchmark Statement, although they are also mentioned by a number of other subject Benchmark Statements. The CHERI data from a survey of graduates three to four years after graduation (Brennan et al., 2001) asked them how they saw their major strengths *compared with* other graduates at the time of their graduation. This therefore gives us some insight into how well the competencies being claimed on the websites and in the Benchmark Statement are being delivered in recent graduates. Compared with other graduates, English graduates rated themselves particularly highly in terms of:

- Written communication skills
- Oral communication skills
- Documenting ideas and information
- Creativity
- Tolerance, appreciating different points of view
- Critical thinking.

One can therefore see a high degree of concordance between the skills claimed in the websites and Benchmark Statement and those mentioned by the English graduates. (English Departments and the Benchmark Statement might re-consider how study of the subject contributes to creativity, since although these sources do not give prominence to it, English graduates express creativity as being a strength.) Indeed written and oral communication skills and critical thinking are the skills which employers believed the English degree was best at developing in graduates.[9] However, there are some areas where English graduates feel they are weak compared to other graduates. Brennan and Williams conclude that:

> If we compare the skills English graduates feel they lack to those the English benchmark statement reports they should possess, there is a mismatch in terms of developing team work, time management/organization and IT skills. Moreover, these same skills were all mentioned to a greater or lesser extent in the search of websites. And indeed, in the study conducted by the Council for Industry and Higher Education (CIHE), employers felt that English degrees were worst at developing time management and building relationships ... Although the evidence ... is limited, it suggests that English departments may not be developing the full range of attributes and capabilities outlined in the benchmark statement.
>
> (Brennan and Williams, 2003: 27)

This returns us, therefore, to the dilemma we outlined above: should we stick with the broadly indicative categories of 'graduateness' or should we be devising more customized profiles for English graduates, which in turn, can be made even more responsive to individual needs? Certainly there is little will, among academics, to do the latter, and while some of this can be put down to a familiar reluctance to convert intellectual value into utilitarian capital, this is not the only root of the lack of enthusiasm to go further. Evidence currently suggests that graduate generic skills are situated in a confused and misleading discourse primed by policy, but not underpinned by clear ideas of learning (Bennett *et al.*, 2000: 175–7). Academics are wary of the skills agenda, but there are also clear signs from students that they come to their degrees with skills-weariness, and an established scepticism about tick-box charts, content-evacuated courses, and bullet-point lists. Further, there is little evidence from employers that they want more elaborate benchmarks or competence charts. They are hardly having difficulties recruiting graduates *per se*, although it is clear that they find some of them short on what they regard as basic skills (literacy, numeracy, IT, team-working). Making more extravagant claims for the intrinsic presence of transferable skills will not help anyone. It is useful, at this point, to turn to our case studies offering retrospective views on the English degree, since they offer highly particular – but nevertheless interesting – ways of analyzing the long-term value of the English degree.

These case studies are not offered here as typical monuments of the English degree; their status is rather that of oral histories, personal accounts that are not engendered by overstated claims, or the opposite. In each case, it is clear that our graduates were less aware of the attributes inculcated or nurtured by the degree at the time of its duration. Retrospectively, they all achieve a more precise sense of how the degree has helped in particular ways. For one (Jane Arthur) the key elements are analysis and creativity: 'the ability to look for new angles, to select from a wide range of possible exempla'. For another (Val Butcher) the most significant is something she believes to be all too often left out: the corollary to confident communication, she notes, is 'the ability to influence others', and here she identifies something not exclusive to English, but a quality which sits right at the centre of those discursive activities which we used to characterize the degree at the start of this chapter. All English students grow to recognize the place of rhetoric (technically, the power of persuasion) in literary and other texts, indeed, that is what so much of their essay writing and seminar discussion adds up to. Our third graduate (Peter Strachan) is in similar territory when he cites his experience of 'making a written case for a grant to Oxfam's senior management' – a particularly vital persuasive skill, perhaps, and alongside this he stresses the importance of the 'development of thinking within a theoretical framework' and 'reading critically'. These, he notes, are attributes that have stood him in good stead. He has received a training in thinking of a kind, by the very stringency which literary theory demands. Each of our graduates also provides a neat coda for their brief life-sketch. Val Butcher celebrates her experience in English, but wishes she had known what it was doing for her at the time; a ringing reminder perhaps that we owe it to our graduates to make them more conscious of their abilities. Jane Arthur writes positively about the challenge and satisfaction of the degree for its own sake – 'studying English … was the most intellectually demanding part of my life'. Peter Strachan acknowledges the space the degree gave him to think, and the extent to which it was the means of considering the wider cultural and political contexts that underlie all literary texts. He also notes it gave him an enduring love of reading, and then, most potently, quotes his teacher's adage that 'there's not much you can do with an English degree but a whole lot that society can do with an English graduate' – a truism that nevertheless takes us back to the importance of raising the consciousness of graduates and employers about the validity of the degree beyond its programme.

However, 'employability' will not be achieved by a sticking-plaster list crudely applied to an academic programme, and neither will academics be keen to promote the cause of 'employability' if it only takes the form of denying intellectual values, or indeed, of de-professionalizing their work. Most English students come to degree level study because they enjoy the subject in its own right, and because they sense that value to which their teachers will readily subscribe – the value of English in developing the intellect, in permitting individuals to extend their creative, critical and imaginative abilities to the full. It is essential to keep faith with this while simultaneously recognizing the importance of enabling graduates to maximize choice and potential in their careers. That means not making spurious or inflated claims for our graduates' abilities just as surely as it means making sure that we do not undervalue what they do well.

## Jane Arthur: a graduate in English

Jane Arthur read English at Leeds University between 1979 and 1982. After taking an MA in Librarianship at Sheffield University, she pursued a career as a university librarian and is currently Assistant Director of Learning and Information Services at the University of Hertfordshire.

> I read English at Leeds, 1979–82, which was a traditional programme, including Old English, Middle English, Shakespeare, the Novel, and nothing beyond the 1920s in the compulsory courses. However, we had some electives, and I took Science Fiction and History of Language.
>
> In those days, over 20 years ago, transferable skills or vocational skills were not part of an English course, so, of my own volition, I taught myself typewriting and took a computer studies 'O' level evening class.
>
> I did not go to university with a career path in mind, but had the experience of a Saturday job whilst at school – working in the local public library. This at least gave me an idea of the sort of work which I felt confident I could do and enjoy. Nevertheless, whilst at Leeds, I went through the rounds of careers fairs and applications for many posts, which convinced me that I was making an informed choice and not just drifting into a job. I obtained a one-year graduate traineeship at Leeds University Library.
>
> I gained an MA in Librarianship at Sheffield University, where I again tried to develop IT skills by choosing a course in Prolog – in the early days of Expert Systems.
>
> My first post was at Cranfield University (Cranfield Institute of Technology as was) – a postgraduate technological university. I arrived as a newly qualified librarian with no experience, a degree in English and lots of enthusiasm. I ended up staying there in various posts for nearly six years. Work there included searching information databases for postgraduate students and staff, in the days when it was called online searching (there were no CD-ROM or web-based databases) and access was charged at so much per minute, so that ineffective searching could run up a hefty bill; and being the editor of an abstracting service (hard copy and online database) called *Robotics Technology Abstracts*, which was sold internationally, until it was no longer competitive and closed down.
>
> Subsequently, I worked at Dundee Institute of Technology (University of Abertay) for three years as the Deputy Librarian. Then I moved to the University of Hertfordshire, where I have been for nearly ten years, the last three of which have been three days a week, balanced with motherhood. At UH, I have managed campus libraries and learning resources centres (converged library, computer centre and media services); I have been the project manager for a new learning resources centre building; and I have managed library system purchases. Along the way, I fitted in a part-time MBA through the OU.

So, how far has my English degree helped or hindered me? Tricky one. An English degree has never been a prerequisite for any job or course which I have done. In my career, I have had a couple of significant 'breaks': one was getting the postgraduate traineeship at Leeds, and the other was getting the job at Cranfield. For early career posts, most candidates have broadly similar qualifications and experience, so I believe the secret was to have some unusual and therefore memorable hobby or experience. An English degree did not really help here. Later on, jobs were based on previous experience, and track record.

However, English taught me analysis, writing and the ability to handle and select from large amounts of data. The texts I studied had largely been written about *ad nauseam* by scholars, so I learnt the technique of selecting some minor episode or image as symbolic of a wider theme. The ability to look for new angles, to select from a wide range of possible exempla and to demonstrate an understanding of both the wood and the trees, are things that have stood me in good stead when dealing with, for example, the huge amount of detail of a building project; the need to communicate complex issues straightforwardly with users/customers; and the need to write for a time-constrained audience. I don't claim that I always achieve these, but I know what I am aiming for.

Studying English for three years was the most intellectually demanding part of my life. Other studies and work have been satisfying in other ways, e.g. a skill mastered, a project completed, a bid won against competition, the joys of parenting. But I would not have missed the intellectual challenge of studying English.

## Val Butcher: a graduate in English

Val Butcher read English at the University of Sussex and then took a Diploma in Vocational Guidance. She has been involved in careers guidance and careers education in schools, colleges and universities since the mid-1960s.

She is now Senior Adviser for Employability with the Generic Centre of the LTSN (Learning and Teaching Support Network), and a consultant on Higher Education in matters relating to employability in the academic curriculum.

She was formerly Director of Enterprise and then Principal Adviser for Higher Education and Employment at the University of Leeds, and Assistant Director in the Leeds University Careers Service. She is also a Fellow of NICEC (the National Institute of Careers Education and Counselling), a Senior Visiting Fellow at the Centre for Employability, University of Central Lancashire, and a member of the Higher Education Funding Council for England's Enhancing Student Employability Co-ordination Team.

She is a member of the Careers Writers Association, producing articles and learning materials for students and has researched and published extensively on the links between education and the world of work.

'Skills? I don't have any skills ... I read English!' I recall informing a graduate recruiter triumphantly. Skills, I felt, were a lower order of learning, suited to those who had taken apprenticeships – whatever they were.

I soon found out. Having told my University Appointments Officer that I wanted to 'work with people and not be stuck behind a desk' I found myself the youngest student on a course of training to be a Youth Employment Officer. I had explored library work, teaching and graduate secretarial work, all of which seemed to 'use' my degree, although I couldn't say how. Then I had the good sense to consult the professionals, and embarked on a career which I have loved for the past forty years.

What did my English degree do for me?

For many years, I would have said 'nothing' because I simply was not able to distinguish between the content and the process of my learning. I was just very sure that I was never going to read Thackeray again.

It was, I think, when I became involved in training other practitioners and had to identify and articulate what a competent practitioner in my field needed to be able to do that I realized that I was drawing on attributes, attitudes and competences which had been framed during my degree studies.

'Planning/execution of essay/project work' identified in the English benchmarking statement as a key feature of the subject is something I have deployed, fairly obviously, in the writing of bids for funding, progress reports and dissemination materials that I have had to write in my years of managing large development projects on careers education and employability in schools, further and higher education.

The ability to 'understand/develop intricate concepts', also mentioned in the benchmarking statement, has undoubtedly been drawn upon in my research work, which has resulted in publications on a range of careers and learning-related topics.

More creatively – and 'creativity' is one of the attributes cited by English graduates themselves as a quality in which they believe they compare well with other Arts and Humanities graduates – I have produced a wide range of information and learning materials for staff, from writing a video script and workbook on 'Effective Use of Careers Material' to 'Making the Most of Work Experience', a Tutor/Careers Adviser Material on preparing students for work experience. For students themselves, I have written more than I can possibly mention, including four editions of *Taking a Year Off*.

One of the English departmental websites referred to by Brennan and Williams (2003) mentions 'Lucid and confident presentation of argument in writing/speech' and I am astonished that the corollary to this, the ability to influence others, is not mentioned, since this has been a key requirement of my work, and, I am sure, that of many other English graduates.

That the study of literature equips a graduate with tolerance and an appreciation of different points of view (another view English graduates hold of themselves) should not, perhaps, be surprising, but I also believe that it can equip the individual with an emotional intelligence; the ability to sense what other people's agendas might be and to communicate and relate appropriately.

Does all this, forty years after my degree, give the whole picture? Not really. I also feel that I am a competent team builder and networker– where did that come from?

The clue, I think, lies in the holistic nature of the higher education experience.

'Interests? No, I have no interests. Hobbies are puerile,' I informed the same bemused graduate recruiter. What did I do in my spare time? I went to parties; organized parties. I loved parties.

After a predictable rejection (not predictable to me at the time), I stopped being so frank in selection interviews, but had I known it, I had identified a personal resource which has equipped me to work effectively as a change agent in education for many years.

I'm glad I read English, but I wish I had known at the time what it was giving me.

## Peter Strachan: a graduate in English

Peter Strachan graduated from University College, Cardiff in 1977 with first class honours in English Literature. After a year off he started a D.Phil. at Jesus College, Oxford, working on it full-time until 1981 and finally completing it in 1987. After leaving Oxford he became a Voluntary Service Overseas volunteer in a teacher training college in Egypt and after two years took over the management of the VSO programme in that country. He subsequently worked for Help the Aged (Overseas) in London and then managed the Oxfam programme in western Sudan from 1987 to 1990. Upon his return to the UK he took an M.A. in Social Policy at Brunel University and worked first as a benefits adviser for Age Concern in Waltham Forest, London and then as a Development Officer with the National Association of Citizens Advice Bureaux (NACAB). In 1998 he joined Coventry City Council as Policy and Planning Manager in the Corporate Policy Team and has since become the City Council's Area Co-ordinator for two of the most deprived wards in the city. In 2001 he completed a Diploma in Management through the Open University Business School and now swears that he will never take another exam for as long as he lives.

The first thing that I'd have to accept is that I've never really *tried* to make use of my English degree in my career. By the time my research money was running out at Oxford, the only thing I was really clear about was that I no longer wanted to be an academic. I did the public sector bit of the 'milk round' and found very mixed attitudes to my academic background. Generally they liked the First – evidence of either a reasonably sharp mind or, at least, a certain degree of sheer doggedness – but I have no recollection of anyone saying that it gave me the ideal knowledge base for managing a coalmine. The doctorate, not even completed, was the cause of much suspicion and I had to work hard to convince a succession of potential employers that I could take a decision without first spending six months in a library.

Clearly I was successful in convincing the NHS of this as they offered me a place on their fast stream management training scheme, but by that time I'd decided instead to accept a rather less lucrative offer from VSO. Again, it wasn't my degree that interested them, but rather the volunteer adult literacy teaching I'd done during my year off in Cardiff and my campaigning activities with the War on Want and World Development Movement groups in Oxford. The bit of my thesis that did interest them was actually the bit that had least to do with English, as such. My topic involved a lot of theory and this in turn had involved getting up close and personal with a lot of theoretical linguistics. The fact that this meant that I knew the difference between a past perfect verb and an embedding transformation was probably taken into account.

So what did I (and society) get out of my six years studying Eng. Lit. – and, of course, spending several thousand pounds of taxpayers' money? I'm profoundly grateful to have taken my first degree at Cardiff. At the time, Cardiff was developing a reputation for pioneering approaches to English Literature that were still regarded as a little outlandish in many universities, where Bradley and Leavis still ruled the roost. Cardiff emphasized skills over knowledge and encouraged its students to develop their thinking within a sound theoretical framework. Depth of reading was prized over breadth, literary history was considered to be of relatively low priority and value judgements were positively discouraged. Instead I was schooled in reading critically, in becoming highly aware of language and its effects, and in developing arguments that were based on evidence rather than assertion. I was also encouraged to think critically about the various theoretical standpoints on offer and to explore the ways in which this theory could be applied to help cast light on practical criticism (I use the term in both its general and technical senses). These are skills that have continued to inform my work over the years.

The habits of using theoretical tools to analyze practical problems and of developing clear and well supported written arguments are ones that have proved essential in many contexts. These range from making a written case for a grant to Oxfam's senior management five thousand miles away from my base in west Sudan to formulating and evaluating policy options for elected Councillors in Coventry. As a manager, I never cease to be depressed at the poor quality of written English displayed by even fairly senior colleagues. If a graduate in English leaves college with nothing more than the ability to write prose that can be published in a newsletter with little amendment, then that is a skill upon which many senior managers would now place a considerable premium.

In terms of personal development, my first degree also gave me the space and a framework for thinking about life, the universe and everything. Again, the Cardiff emphasis on the value of theory was important here – a more traditional university at that time would not have made the links with politics, linguistics, society and ideologies about which students in Cardiff were encouraged to think.

And it did give me three years in which to develop what has remained an enduring personal love. My most recent collection of holiday reading included *Coriolanus* and my Filofax has pages of favourite extracts from poets from George Herbert to Seamus Heaney to which I frequently return to help restore a sense of perspective at the end of a frustrating day.

My old headteacher at Middlesbrough High School, himself an English graduate, used to say that there's not much you can do with an English degree but a whole lot that society can do with an English graduate. I suppose I've been spending the last quarter century confirming the truth of that observation.

## Notes

1   Available at: http://www.qaa.ac.uk/crntwork/benchmark/english.pdf.
2   www.ucas.ac.uk.
3   One of the most recent studies conducted into this (Walker and Zhu, 2003), which was based upon Labour Force Survey data, suggests that Arts graduates earn less on average than those who enter employment with two A levels.
4   Very little is known about the real destinations of English graduates (for available data see Brennan and Williams, 2003). However, there are many indications that the constitution of the graduate population of the subject will have considerable influence on calculations about its earnings. For instance, for many years English has had far more women than men undergraduates (in a ratio of around 70 per cent/30 per cent); mature returners – almost all of whom tend to be women – commonly made up around 30–35 per cent of English students in post-1992 universities and the colleges until very recently. Large numbers of English graduates go into teaching. When reviewing earnings data, it is important to bear such factors in mind. With clear evidence of women still suffering unequal financial rewards in the workplace, large numbers in underpaid professions, and many English students graduating between the ages of 35 and 55, it is unlikely that they will compare well with graduates of (say) Economics.
5   See the comments made in the Peter Strachan case study, p. 84.
6   The HEQC Pilot Graduate Attributes Profile is a model of 'graduateness' which can be applied to any subject. It is reproduced in *The Graduate Standards Programme Final Report*, Annex C: 86 (Higher Education Quality Council, 1997).
7   For an important conceptual discussion of skills in higher education which argues powerfully for this complexity, see Barnett (1994: 55–68). For a good pragmatic discussion of the factors in play, see Bennett *et al.* (2000), particularly pp. 120–43.
8   Available at: http://www.hesa.ac.uk/holisdocs/pubinfo/fds.htm.
9   Employers were asked in a study carried out by the Council for Industry and Higher Education (2002) how they perceived skills development through undergraduate study and how far these perceptions reflected subject benchmark statements.

# Part II

# Towards the enhancement of practice

In Part I we offered a description of employability in general and argued that it can be enhanced by good mainstream curricula and vigorous co-curricula. Given the closeness of our account of what employers value to common thinking about the processes and outcomes of good higher education practices, the argument was that institutions concerned to enhance student employability would also be enhancing student learning and *vice versa*. What, though, might higher education institutions do to secure these twin benefits?

Part II begins by considering what would be needed to develop understanding, skilful practices, efficacy beliefs and metacognition in the first cycle of higher education. A discussion of ways in which employability may be enhanced in various workplace-related ways then follows in Chapter 7. Given that the curriculum that students *really* experience is shaped by the ways in which their learning is assessed, we take time in Chapter 8 to explain how the fuzzy and complex achievements that are central to *higher* education and to employability may be reached by differentiated assessment arrangements. We notice that there is international consternation about the assessment of learning and argue that a concern to promote employability exacerbates matters. Although it might be convenient to exclude assessment issues from the discussion, if employability were kept in the unassessed attics of the curriculum, neither would it be taken very seriously, nor would the processes and outcomes associated both with it and good pedagogic practices get the attention they need to flourish. So, before we describe curriculum developments favourable to employability, we need to consider assessment issues.

In Chapters 9–11 we survey curriculum development work done within the Skills *plus* project in four universities in the north-west of England between 2000 and 2002. The three accounts and the overview in Chapter 12 describe an approach to curriculum enhancement that we have found transportable, robust and effective.

Chapter 13 goes beyond the specifics of programme development and explores the implications for universities and colleges. In asking what they need, as *institutions*, to do in order to help students make the best possible claims to employability, we are also asking, of course, what they need to do to promote good learning.

Even if the term 'employability' is not widely used beyond the shores of the UK, there are – without doubt – questions about what higher education should be doing in order to stimulate the sorts of achievements that employers around the world regularly say they value and to which higher education itself has long staked a claim.

In Part I we argued that a concern for employability is a concern for much more than narrowly-focused skills. In this Part we show that actions to enhance employability, however parochial the uninformed might imagine them to be, are, in fact, actions to stimulate that which makes higher education *higher*: complex learning and the (co-) curricular processes that favour it.

# Chapter 6

# How we can develop employability

## From theory towards practice

We argued in Chapter 3 that the USEM account had considerable face validity because it can be lined up with an amount of empirical research evidence. We also claimed that it provides a way of thinking about employability that is consistent with academic values. Even if the general thrust of the argument is accepted, there is a need to elaborate some of the detail. In the early sections of this chapter we briefly survey some of the theoretical perspectives that underpin the USEM account, emphasizing efficacy beliefs since our experience is that the 'E' of USEM is generally less well understood than the other components. Though we have separated the USEM components for analytical and presentational reasons, we readily acknowledge that these are interrelated – for example, metacognitive ability feeds into skilful practices. In the later sections of this chapter we comment on some aspects of curriculum design where the intention is to promote complex learning and employability.

## Understanding

Some prefer to use the word 'knowledge' generically for what is learned about one or more subject disciplines. Our preference is for 'understanding' because of the more limited connotations of 'knowledge' that have been influential in educational circles following the publication of Bloom's *Taxonomy of Educational Objectives* in 1956. 'Understanding', too, has broader and narrower meanings, and we have adopted the broader meaning, in relation to the subject discipline(s) involved, which we take to encompass all but the metacognitive in Anderson and Krathwohl's (2001) revision of Bloom's original work (summarized in Figure 3.1).

We expect undergraduate students to remember relevant facts, to understand concepts, to apply their understandings to relatively routine problems that do not call for innovative thinking, and to analyze situations and to bring critical evaluative skill to bear on – for example – the literature. We may or may not expect them to exhibit creative behaviour, i.e. to come up with something new, or some new configuration of material that is already known (an analysis by Yorke (2002b) of the first 22 subject benchmarks published by the Quality Assurance Agency suggested that creative behaviour might figure in only about half of the subject areas covered). We also expect students on science-based programmes to develop the 'know how' to operate safely – say – X-ray diffraction or infra-red spectroscopy apparatus in a manner that will produce trustworthy results. Similarly, we expect students on arts-oriented programmes to develop an understanding of how – say – the critical analysis of texts should be pursued.

## Skilful practices

To some extent, the procedural knowledge we expect students to develop comprises 'skilful practices'. These include practices needed for the deployment of disciplinary expertise and those more generic practices that enable disciplinary expertise to be applied effectively in the employment arena – these are often labelled 'soft skills', under which can be found self-management, the capacity to work productively with others, awareness of the internal politics of organizations, the ability to deal with divergent points of view, and the ability to determine what is possible in a given situation (even if it is not what the person would ideally like).

Whether discipline-specific or more generic, skilful practices are context-sensitive. Whilst there is, of course, a virtue in having an academic understanding of how organizations 'work' and of what might be expected of a person occupying a particular role, there is also a need for that understanding to be converted into the 'knowing how' of success in *particular* practice, as some of the informants quoted in Chapter 4 made plain.

Sandwich (or co-operative) programmes have always stressed the value of work placement experience. Hartley and Smith (2000) offer a typical justification, pointing to the value of such programmes in respect of the following:

- Helping students to see the connection (and, we might add, the disconnections) between theory and practice.
- Assisting in the development of specific skills for which the equipment may not be available in the higher education institution.
- Developing the capacity to work effectively in teams (in the work environment teams tend to be more heterogeneous than those in the higher education environment, which potentially adds educational value).
- The development of characteristics such as responsibility, initiative, ethical behaviour and respect for others (not that these are undeveloped by higher education, but that the different context widens the student's repertoire).

## Efficacy beliefs

We use the term 'efficacy beliefs' in a broad sense, and encompass a number of theorists' contributions within it (Table 6.1).

*Table 6.1* Some theoretical contributions to the 'E' of USEM

| Theorist(s) | Contribution |
| --- | --- |
| Dweck (1999) | 'Fixed' and 'malleable' self-theories |
| Dweck (1999) | Learning and performance goals |
| Dweck (1999) followed by Pintrich (2000) | Performance goals subdivided into 'approach' and 'avoidance' versions |
| Sternberg (1997) | Practical intelligence |
| Rotter (1966) | Locus of control |
| Bandura (1997) | Self-efficacy |
| Seligman (1998) | Learned optimism |
| Salovey and Mayer (1990); Goleman (1996) | Emotional intelligence |

Dweck (1999) makes the point that the kind of self-theory held by a person is likely to impact on the way in which they approach the task of learning:

> … we have seen that holding a fixed theory of intelligence appears to turn students towards concern about performing and looking smart. Holding a malleable theory appears to turn students towards concerns about learning new things and getting smarter.
>
> (Dweck, 1999: 23)

A fixed self-theory is a belief that an attribute such as intelligence is immutable – one is bright or one is not – whereas a malleable self-theory admits the possibility that the attribute can be developed. This quotation also draws attention to the distinction that Dweck also makes between performance and learning goals. Performance goals are concerned with 'doing things correctly' and the sustaining of appearances; learning goals are – as the label implies – related to the desirability of learning new things, and carry fewer implications for 'getting the right answer'. Adopters of performance goals, according to Dweck, are quite likely to find their self-esteem threatened by failure, whereas adopters of learning goals are more likely to be spurred further to succeed.

Pintrich (2000) subsequently showed that performance goals could be subdivided into two types, 'approach' and 'avoidance'. 'Approach' performance goals were based on a person's desire to exhibit mastery, whereas 'avoidance' performance goals were based on a desire not to be shown up as inadequate. Pintrich was able to show empirically that there were circumstances under which there was no significant difference between performances of students adopting learning and 'approach' performance goals, whereas the adoption of 'avoidance' performance goals led to inferior performance.

Dweck's and Pintrich's work points towards a connection with the ideas of 'deep' and 'surface' learning. Performance goals tend to be connected with surface approaches whereas learning goals tend to be connected with deep approaches.

There is another connection that may also be sustainable – with theories of student development (Perry, 1970/1998; Kohlberg, 1964; King and Kitchener, 1994) in which there is a general developmental trajectory that runs between acquiescence to authority and personal autonomy (Knight and Yorke, 2003b). We can speculate that the adopter of performance goals is more likely to take an acquiescent stance in employment than the adopter of learning goals.

Sternberg (1997) suggested that, in addition to the kind of intelligence that is captured in intelligence tests, there is also a 'practical intelligence' which enables people to perform effectively when faced with the complex, often 'messy', problems thrown up by life. Sternberg and Grigorenko (2000a), reviewing the evidence regarding the development of practical intelligence, conclude that the typical trajectory continues upwards throughout a person's life (save possibly towards the end, for pathological reasons). In other words, practical intelligence is 'developable' and, educationally, there is a lot to play for – for employability and life in general. We have summarized similar conclusions about the development of expertise. In contrast, IQ typically reaches a peak in early adulthood, and declines slowly thereafter.

Goleman, in 1996, popularized the notion of emotional intelligence whose origins lie in work done at the beginning of that decade (Salovey and Mayer, 1990). Goleman, drawing on this work, suggests that emotional intelligence subsumes: knowing one's emotions; managing emotions; motivating oneself; recognizing emotions in others; and handling relationships (p. 43). Mayer *et al.* (2000) are concerned at the plurality of meanings that the construct has come to embrace, and indicate their preference for emotional intelligence as a mental (indeed, metacognitive) ability which has four branches: emotional perception; emotional integration; emotional understanding; and emotional management. If success in social situations is – in part – predicated on emotional intelligence, then emotional intelligence is a tributary of Sternberg's practical intelligence.

Rotter (1966) developed the notion of locus of control, and devised a test to measure the extent to which people saw themselves as being able to control events (i.e. they had an internal locus of control), or as being controlled by others (external locus). Although Rotter's approach has been criticized on various grounds, the idea of locus of control has had sufficient face validity to retain some currency. We note here that there is a possible link with the acquiescence–autonomy dimension of student development that we mentioned earlier. We would expect 'externals' to be more acquiescent than 'internals'.

There is also a link with Bandura's (1997) concept of self-efficacy – broadly, a person's belief that they can make a difference to situations. Bandura uses self-efficacy in both context-dependent and context-independent ways; however, the distinction – though important – can be left to one side for present purposes. The point we want to make here is that there is no guarantee that the self-efficacious person *will* make a difference to a particular situation. The construct is probabilistic: other things being equal, a high level of self-efficacy is more likely than a low level to have an impact on a situation. Seligman's (1998) concept of 'learned optimism' implicitly points to the potential for education to make a difference to the way a person faces up to the challenges of employment, and of life in general.[1] Seligman's researches have led him to conclude that an optimistic cast of mind can be developed, and his book suggests some ways in which this might be done.

## The 'developability' of efficacy beliefs

The various theorists' work discussed briefly above suggests, with varying amounts of explicitness, that the 'efficacy beliefs' – the 'E' – aspect of USEM is susceptible of development. However, that development depends critically upon the teacher's awareness of the conceptions, their commitment to facilitating student development, and their pedagogical expertise.

As part of the Skills *plus* project we asked some 2,200 first and final year students across a variety of subjects to agree or disagree with the item: *An individual can't change their intelligence by much.* Roughly two in seven were inclined to agree, suggesting the possibility of a fixed self-theory as far as intelligence was concerned. The opportunity was also taken to use the item with 72 academic staff attending workshops, with an almost identical result (though a couple, quite reasonably, remarked that 'it all depends what you mean by "intelligence"'). If these proportions were sustained across higher education, they would imply that around five of every ten teacher/student pairings were those in which both parties had a malleable view of intelligence, and that in one pairing in ten both parties would hold a fixed view. The other two possibilities (teacher fixed, student malleable; and teacher malleable, student fixed) would each appear on two occasions in ten.

From a pedagogic point of view, the malleable/malleable pairing is the most propitious since both parties believe in the development of intelligence (we do not know what kind of intelligence was meant by the respondents, but speculate that this might be 'practical'). The least propitious is where both parties have a fixed belief, since this could lead to fairly barren learning encounters in which both parties act according to their presumptions. The learning achievements of the student from the two 'crossover' pairings of malleable/fixed will probably depend on the 'malleable' person. If the teacher has a malleable disposition then they may, through the exercise of pedagogic skill, be able to help the 'fixed' student to become more malleable. If it is the student who is the malleable one, then they may need to call on a considerable amount of self-belief if the teacher offers no expectation regarding their practical capacity to develop.

It is important for teachers to become aware, if they are not so already, of the educational significance of the fixed/malleable distinction and of the 'developability' of practical intelligence. This has a particular force when a student cohort might be felt to be lacking in academic ability because of modest entry qualifications even when these might have been gained in difficult educational and/or social circumstances. If students' sense of self-efficacy is not strong, and they perceive the cognitive and cultural leaps expected by their higher education programmes are wide, then they are at particular risk of not bridging the gaps, of becoming demoralized, and of discontinuing their studies.[2] For those students entering higher education from disadvantaged backgrounds, the risk-level is higher. Bandura (1997) implies the need for tasks to be pitched at an appropriate level and graded in difficulty, and he is explicit regarding the need for feedback:

> The less individuals believe in themselves, the more they need explicit, proximal, and frequent feedback of progress that provides repeated affirmations of their growing capabilities.
>
> (Bandura 1997: 217)

Where students have come to overrate their capabilities, they are also at risk of performing badly in higher education and becoming demoralized (and especially so if they are oriented towards performance goals). Naylor and Smith (2002) analyzed performances of students graduating from UK universities in 1993 and found that, compared with pupils with equivalent qualifications from state schools, pupils from fee-paying schools obtained on average a *lower* class of degree. This finding (which might surprise some) could stem from the teachers in independent schools making strenuous efforts to get their pupils to do well in the A-level examinations (after all, their schools' reputation stems in part from pupils' entry to higher education) but not necessarily preparing them as well for the very different learning experience in higher education. Boud (1995) might refer to a comparatively lower 'consequential validity' of the fee-paying pupils' learning.

### Assessment and efficacy beliefs

There have been recent moves in the UK to replace traditional assessments at the end of the first semester by feedback intended to improve learning; many students need longer than a semester to come to terms with what is expected of them academically and early failure is discouraging, particularly if the student's self-theory favours performance goals. Quite apart from the general conditions under which feedback is likely to improve learning, summarized in Chapter 8, there are two points to be made about feedback and efficacy beliefs.

1   The focus of the feedback should be on the strengths and weaknesses of the presented work (and not on the student).
2   The feedback should indicate how the student could develop their work for future tasks (and not – unless the student has to retake the assessment – on how best to re-do the task that is past).

Thought needs to be given to the *manner* in which feedback is given, as well as the content and timing of feedback. Poor grades, unless accompanied by supportive and constructive comment, can lead insecure students to believe they lack sufficient ability to succeed – perhaps because they have adopted performance, rather than learning, goals.

## Metacognition

Flavell's (1979) concept of metacognition can be seen from three different yet interrelated perspectives: strategic thinking; applicability to the task in hand; and personal self-awareness. The first deals with learning, thinking and problem-solving, and can be seen as having a general, cross-disciplinary relevance. The second deals not only with the pragmatic know-how relevant to the task, but also the capacity to stand back and reflect prior to, during, and after the implementation of a course of action. The third refers to the knowledge that a person has about their own strengths and weaknesses. All of these have a clear relevance for employability.

Whilst some metacognition develops without special attention as a consequence of study in one or more subject disciplines (and more quickly if metacognitive capability is fairly well developed already), there is a case to be made for making the development of metacognition an explicit part of the curriculum. The evidence we presented in Chapter 4 indicates how important for employability is the ability to work well with others, and an understanding of how one can, as an individual, use self-awareness to maximal effect.[3] A knowledge of one's strengths and weaknesses can be turned to advantage when one is working with others. Sternberg and Grigorenko (2000b) see the practical application of self-awareness as exemplifying successful intelligence in action, and Belbin's (1981) exploration of team roles points quite firmly towards the value of complementarity in group problem-solving. There ought to be scope in a curriculum for incorporating reflective analysis into group activities, and for encouraging reflection by individual students on their achievements. Work placements provide particular opportunities for personal reflection (Lazarus, 1992). Whilst a lot might happen in the normal course of events, an explicit requirement laid on students to be reflective about their learning from such activity is likely to give evolution a measure of assistance – provided that the staff support for this is available.

Students in higher education are expected to have developed the metacognitive capacity for self-regulation by the end of their programmes. Self-regulation depends on the capacity to recognize and respond appropriately to the demands of the situations confronting them. If students merely respond to statements of standards and criteria without 'making them their own', then the development of a self-regulatory capability may be hindered. Boud puts it succinctly:

> Too often staff-driven assessment encourages students to be dependent on the teacher or the examiners to make decisions about what they know and they do not effectively learn to be able to do this for themselves.
>
> (Boud, 1995: 39)

The corollary is of an implicit pressure to 'come up with the right answer' (i.e. to achieve a performance goal) and not to stretch out – perhaps riskily – in the interests of learning. Put another way, this is tantamount to encouraging 'learned dependence' (Peterson *et al.*, 1993) – which is surely not what higher education intends.

Wolf (1995) showed in respect of academic staff's understanding of criteria that it is necessary to refine understanding of assessment precepts by considering actual examples. On the same principle, it makes sense to engage students with the assessment process, since this can encourage both cognition and metacognition. Dochy *et al.* (1999: 345) concluded, following a review of the literature, that the positive effects of engaging students in the assessment process included, *inter alia*:

• Increased student confidence in the ability to perform.
• Increased awareness of the quality of the student's own work.
• Greater independence in learning.
• Improvement in the products of learning.
• Increased reflection on the student's own behaviour and/or performance.

Gibbs (1999: 43ff) provides an example from Engineering that is consistent with the conclusions of Dochy *et al.* We note that these conclusions indicate that peer assessment can assist the development of self-regulatory behaviour and also indicate its contribution to the broader 'E' and 'M' components of USEM.

The work of Dochy *et al.* points to the broader importance of formative assessment in student development. We note that a desire to strengthen formative assessment has considerable implications for curricula since, in any context where resources are constrained, it implies some redistribution of staff effort. On the whole, traditional approaches to curricula do not accord formative assessment the weight it deserves and, as a consequence, do not optimally serve student learning. In some subjects and universities, staff may invest heavily in high-stakes summative assessment to try to achieve what might be better done through low-stakes formative approaches (see Chapter 8, and the extended argument in Knight and Yorke, 2003b).

Like peer and self assessment, personal development planning (PDP) has the potential to stimulate reflection to an extent probably not hitherto reached in most curricula. The construction of a portfolio of achievements and associated reflection could also serve students well as they put together applications for jobs. However, there are difficulties in devising robust and workable PDP systems and a real problem of getting 'buy-in'. Academic staff tend to be uneasy about 'backstage' innovations, things that distract their attention from teaching students and doing research. Students are also pressed for time and likely to avoid innovations that have no obvious pay-offs. The fear is that PDP may seem too remote from the daily business of lectures, seminars, laboratories, studios and assessment. We believe that the likelihood that PDP would gain acceptance would be at its highest (but it would still be no certainty) if it were presented as a contribution to the building of students' *curricula vitae*.

## Teaching for successful intelligence

Teaching for 'successful intelligence', as Sternberg and Grigorenko (2000b) describe it, aligns quite closely with what we see as the operationalization of the USEM account of employability. Sternberg and Grigorenko are interested in encouraging people to exhibit what Stephenson (1998) terms 'capability':

> Capable people have confidence in their ability to
> 1   take effective and appropriate action,
> 2   explain what they are seeking to achieve,
> 3   live and work effectively with others, and
> 4   continue to learn from their experiences, both as individuals and in association with others, in a diverse and changing society.
> ...
> Capability is a necessary part of specialist expertise, not separate from it. Capable people not only know about their specialisms, they also have the confidence to apply their knowledge and skills within varied and changing situations and to continue to develop their specialist knowledge and skills ...
>                    (Stephenson, 1998: 2, minor presentational changes made)

Strongly implicit in the notions of 'successful intelligence' and 'capability' is that they are holistic rather than atomistic. In USEM terms, understanding, skilful practices, efficacy beliefs and metacognition come together in employability. Hence although there is value in focusing pedagogically on one USEM component at a time for some learning activities, the full power of the account will only be seen in learning activities in which the student is expected to draw simultaneously on most, if not all, components. Work placements and project work are two kinds of activity in which richly complex learning may (though will not necessarily) occur.

Sternberg and Grigorenko (2000b) have prepared a handbook for the teaching of 'successful intelligence', which offers broad ideas for activities intended to develop aspects of complex learning: these need to be fleshed out with appropriate disciplinary content.[4] There are sections on teaching for analytical, creative, and practical thinking whose main virtue is likely to be the prompting of ideas for pedagogy in the higher education arena. Other relatively accessible (and enjoyable) stimuli to thinking about student development can be found in the popularized (and not pedagogically-oriented) accounts of Goleman (1996) and Seligman (1998).

Many of the ideas put forward by Sternberg and Grigorenko (2000b) will already be well known to teachers, though they may not always have been connected to employability. The following list picks up some of Sternberg and Grigorenko's suggestions, students could be encouraged, for example:

- To question their assumptions (after all, any researcher worth their salt does this).
- To explore possibilities for redefining the problem facing them (this could mean 'turning the problem on its head').

- To be aware of the relationship between creativity and intrinsic motivation.
- To organize information.
- To think and plan before acting.
- To check periodically that they have not drifted off course (perhaps because of going down an attractive by-way and losing focus on the main task).
- To engage in constructive critique of their own work, and that of others.
- To be prepared to take risks (after all, as Rogers, 2002: 113, observes, learning 'is an essentially risky business').
- To see setbacks as learning opportunities (following the maxim that 'the person who never made a mistake never made anything').
- To tolerate the ambiguity and indeterminacy that inhere in many problem-situations in employment and life generally, and to recognize that, in many practical circumstances, a perfect answer is unattainable.

However, we have to observe that tightly-defined learning outcomes and curricular structures may militate against learning from situations that reflect the fluidity and 'unboundedness' that are inherent in some of the challenges that can be found in workplaces.

## Designing curriculum for complex learning

The implications of USEM for curriculum design are dramatic but not, as we shall shortly show, unfeasible. They are dramatic because the USEM description of employability brings to the fore something that has often been recognized by those organizing co-curricular activities, namely that opportunities and engagements do not reliably translate into learning achievements. If learning in general can be unpredictable, as is said by critics of attempts to pre-specify it in terms of behavioural objectives and the like (e.g. Stenhouse, 1975), then this is all the more so for *complex* learning.

Complex and complicated learning are not the same. It can be complicated to memorize procedures, formulae, sequences and plots, especially if we have to use several sources in the process. To do this is not necessarily complex because we can define the outcome in fairly convergent, fixed or determinate ways. Nor is formal operational thinking, the highest epistemological level identified by Piaget, complex, because, at least in most of his examples, it is about the application of mathematical and scientific reasoning to solve determinate, convergent problems. It may be tough – for most of us it *is* tough – but there are answers which are generally recognized to be the right answers and there are known procedures for getting them. The learning we want to come from higher education is, in the main, not determinate and therefore beyond the reach of precise, reliable and valid measurement. Complex learning is 'fuzzy' learning and, as we have remarked earlier, a slow business (Claxton, 1998).

We need to think about how many elements of employability are to be promoted by *programme* arrangements that provide a sequence of learning environments to stimulate students to develop well-founded, evidence-based claims to employability. Good learning environments can improve the odds of groups of students becoming more employable but they do not guarantee that any individual will become articulate, emotionally intelligent or self-motivating. There needs to be a certain realism about what higher education can do to affect what has been engrooved, embrained and embodied in the years before people become undergraduates. Consequently, it is important to stress that any claims that higher education can increase the employability of graduates need to be made in probabilistic terms – in other words, about the *likelihood* of making a difference at the *group* level.

The inappropriateness of the apparent certainties of some outcomes-led approaches to education challenges traditional instructional design processes and calls for a different approach to the design of learning environments that is conducive to the sorts of complex learning that concern us here (Ganesan *et al.*, 2002). Rather than imagining that it is possible to pre-specify complex learning outcomes and then line up the correct teaching and learning and assessment experiences to advance them, it is more a case of trying to put in place a series of opportunities or affordances conducive to their emergence, in some forms amongst a worthwhile number of cohorts of students. This begs questions about the sorts of circumstances under which such complex learning is favoured, to which we now turn.

### Learning

Learning does not come from instruction alone. Take, for the sake of argument, Bereiter and Scardamalia's account (1993) of four types of knowledge that experts have: formal, informal, impressionistic and self-regulatory knowledge. They also point out that much of these knowledges is tacit and acquired by informal means, such as the daily practices of work, study, leisure and other social exchanges. Other researchers have come to similar conclusions. Becher (1999) reports that professionals may learn six times as much non-formally as they do formally. Coleman and Keep (2001: 16) argue that much learning is 'embedded in the day-to-day', which is to say that we learn through doing tasks in activity systems and with others in our workgroups or communities of practice (Wenger, 1998).

Some tasks, ways of working and social groupings encourage new thinking and doing; they are rich in opportunities for different forms of learning. This is most likely when people are disposed to tackle problems to increase their expertise, when their goals are learning goals rather than task performance goals (Bereiter and Scardamalia, 1993; Dweck, 1999). On this analysis, direct instruction can be one of many stimuli for learning, but learning can also be encouraged by giving people new tools with which to work, creating new expectations or 'rules', and making it easier for them to share problems, brainstorm answers and talk, face-to-face or electronically. In this view the physical architecture of the place in which work takes place, the electronic architecture, the learning tasks and messages about the 'name of the game' may all affect what they learn. Some of that learning is intentional and the product of instruction but where it is formal, or 'negotiable knowledge' as Bereiter and Scardamalia call it (1993: 61), it risks being crystallized, inert or disconnected. Of course, formal knowledge does not have to be like that, and it may emerge from the construction of meanings in the flux of using good tools, rules and the contributions of other people when tackling tasks.

There is a lot of research evidence about good learning. For instance, de Corte (2000) concludes that

> Research has led to the identification of a series of characteristics of effective learning processes ... learning is a constructive, cumulative, self-regulated, goal-oriented, situated, collaborative and individually different process of knowledge building and meaning construction.
>
> (de Corte, 2000: 254)

The elements contributing to this learning are less obvious. In our paper 'Employability and good learning in higher education' (Knight and Yorke, 2003a) we described learning in higher education as an outcome of the interplay between four elements. These are:

1   *Student approaches to learning in general*, including the beliefs that lie behind them. We know that students who think they are trying to reproduce faithfully information as a part of a 'right-or-wrong' game have less time for sense-making than those who want to transform information by making a sense of it that is fit for a time and purpose (Prosser and Trigwell, 1999, provide a good summary of this research). Good learning, whether directed at employability or not, depends on the quality of students' general approaches and beliefs. There is a lot of evidence that approaches can be changed for the better by well-designed learning environments, programmes and practices.

2   *Student approaches to studying in a domain* – to studying something. They are more specific than students' general learning dispositions. Students may take:
    - 'deep' or sense-making approaches;
    - apathetic, 'just-getting-by' approaches;
    - surface approaches, where the aim is compliance rather than understanding;
    - strategic approaches (which involve using whichever of the other three approaches makes best sense in the circumstances).

    The approaches to study that students use tend to reflect general approaches to learning and the sorts of tasks, lectures or tests we design. There is therefore a case for programme-wide audits of the tasks students do, not least to see that there is some sense in which the tasks are fit for the purpose of promoting valued learning outcomes that have a fit with employability. Examples of such audits are found in Chapters 9–11.

However, we need to know more about good task design and the design of good teaching→learning→assessment sequences – there is no HE equivalent of the seminal work on school classroom tasks done by Doyle (1983), Bennett and colleagues (1984) and Stigler and Hiebert (1999).

3   *A good general learning environment.* This should contain plenty of opportunities for students to mix, work together on problems, network electronically and construct meanings from a good range of resources. In poorer environments there may be, for example, a mismatch between physical resources and valued learning outcomes, or academic staff may sponsor cultures that are at variance with those needed to foster complex learning and employability. Even in such unfavourable circumstances, connections can be made between, say, libraries full of heavy textbooks and what students will tend to learn. As befits what is surely a professional and creative activity, learning design will need to be understood as a probabilistic and fuzzy activity and not the sharper and surer practice of rational curriculum planning (Ganesan *et al.*, 2002).

4   *Instruction, task sequences and assessment processes.* They should be aligned so that the curriculum-in-use is recognizably akin to the espoused curriculum. When they are not, the operational curriculum fits the 'garbage can' model, being just an accumulation of conflicting beliefs, practices and priorities. And if students find it hard to discern a programme learning culture, curriculum coherence or plenty of opportunities for developing valued social practices, it is not surprising if they default to the coping strategies that have worked elsewhere. These strategies will often emphasize the collection and reproduction of information and algorithms, and not sense-making. Individual teachers and their modules may sparkle in 'garbage can' or 'free-for-all' curricula but ultimately contribute relatively little to the complex learning that employability and good learning both need. In the UK the Quality Assurance Agency has pushed institutions to write specifications for their programmes, which has generally prompted departments to think about the match between pedagogic practices and programme aims. In Skills *plus* work with departments we have found that curriculum auditing is a good way to get discussion about this coherence. The process, elaborated in the next four chapters, is simple. Each course tutor records the teaching, learning and assessment methods in use. They are tallied on programme grids, which quickly show imbalances. This pattern stimulates discussion about whether programme-wide pedagogic practices are fit for the purpose of promoting programme goals, which have been framed in response to the employability policy.

This fourfold analysis is a useful prompt to designers, not a template. For example, there is not a *direct* chain of connections between learning environments and student activities (Goodyear, 2002). One explanation of this points to the operation of individual psychologies, which mediate 'objective' environments and, in so doing, give each a distinctive tinge for each individual. We refer here to psychological variations in, at least, self-theories, perceptions and motivations.

## Design

In designing employability-oriented curricula (and, we would add, any curricula) it is important to ensure that the students' learning experiences are coherent and progressive – a matter that has, until recently, been in the background while institutions in the UK have implemented modular schemes. The requirement of the UK's Quality Assurance Agency for institutions to provide programme specifications has re-emphasized the traditional curricular virtues of coherence and progression. It also implicitly focuses attention on the way in which the student experience is developed. Early learning encounters generally need more 'scaffolding' (Wood *et al.*, 1976; Bruner, 1985), which is progressively removed as the students' capabilities develop. As we noted when discussing efficacy beliefs (above), the less attuned the entrant is to the expectations of higher education, the more important it is to have good scaffolding in place, and for progression to be taken seriously in curriculum and task design.

We take from de Corte's work (2000), which was admittedly focused on school mathematics learning, a series of guiding principles for the design of good learning environments:

- Learning environments should induce and support constructive, cumulative and goal-oriented acquisition processes ... through a good balance between discovery learning and personal exploration on the one hand, and systematic instruction and guidance on the other.
- ... As students' competency in a domain increases, external regulation of knowledge and skill acquisition should be gradually removed so that they become more and more agents of their own learning.
- Learning environments should embed acquisition processes as much as possible in authentic contexts that have personal meaning for students, are rich in resources and learning materials, and offer ample opportunities for collaboration.
- ... taking into account individual differences among learners in cognitive aptitudes as well as in affective and motivational characteristics.
- Because domain-specific and domain-general knowledge play a complementary role in competent learning and thinking, learning environments should integrate the acquisition of general (meta-)cognitive skills within the subject matter domains.

(de Corte, 2000: 254)

Yet, that said, there is a real shortage of research into the design of such environments, especially should we think in terms of programme-level designs to afford the best chances that individuals would respond most creatively to the four elements. We offer three general pointers:

- Rational curriculum planning and overly mechanistic approaches will not be able to handle this complexity. Although it may not be congenial to command-

and-control managerialists, curriculum design becomes a matter of bringing together as many sources of potentially productive messages, opportunities and requirements as possible in the belief that they will have some impact at the group level.

- It is vital that students appreciate the opportunities or affordances designed for them and that we foster learning cultures that help them to know what they are learning and why, and that help them to know how to develop the claims to achievement that make them more employable. The Alverno College experiment (Mentkowski *et al.*, 2000) is a remarkable demonstration of what is possible when students understand what a programme, its components and affordances are intended to promote.

- Official thinking notwithstanding, we should not become fixed on the development of individual teachers' instructional skills, important though this is: instead, we should worry a lot more about the development of 'learning departments' that create student learning environments and programmes favourable to the development of employability.

The next chapter describes steps that have been taken in one country, England, to develop employability. Chapter 8 argues that further progress will depend on a working solution being found to the problems of assessment.

## Notes

1 The self-efficacious approach is captured in various popular formats, including Piper's (1946) children's book *The Little Engine That Could* in which the engine puffs 'I think I can, I think I can …' as it attempts for the first time to go over a hill. All ends happily, of course, with the engine seeming to say 'I thought I could, I thought I could …' as it descends the other side. Not every attempt by the self-efficacious is blessed with success, of course.

2 We observe, in passing, that around two-thirds of withdrawals from programmes of study in the UK take place during or at the end of the first year, which is the critical period for adjustment to the demands of higher education.

3 Note that this is another way of referring to emotional intelligence, whose meta-cognitive aspect was noted earlier in this chapter.

4 The materials are intended to be applicable to a range of educational levels and the authors indicate the level(s) for which each suggested activity is suitable.

# Chapter 7

# Engaging students with the worlds of work

---

## Addressing employability

> Companies still complain about the employability of graduates ... despite the cash, government pressure and numerous initiatives, many believe that universities are neglecting the employability factor.
>
> (Utley, 2002: 10)

This chapter shows some of the ways in which higher education institutions have shown that they take 'the employability factor' seriously. For example, St John Fisher College in Rochester, New York, will pay graduates who do not find a professional job up to $5,000 until they do.[1] Similarly, engineering students at the University of Miami can get up to $17,000 of graduate school tuition. Although the emphasis in these schemes is on employability through relevant content, liberal arts colleges are also taking an interest. A leader article in *USA Today* (26/9/97) said that,

> The money-back guarantees are most common at technical colleges that can't turn out graduates fast enough to satisfy high-tech employers. But the popularity of the programs is encouraging liberal arts schools to rethink how best to prepare students for after-college life.

We agree and suggest that a university or college has not really addressed employability until it has a convincing account of the ways in which it enhances not only the employability of those taking programmes with a direct vocational relevance but also that of philosophers, historians and artists.

## Scope and purpose

The account that follows is localized and generalizable. It is localized in that the examples are drawn from England.[2] It is generalizable in that similar initiatives are to be found throughout the English-speaking world[3] (see Gaff and Ratcliff, 1996; Boud and Solomon, 2001).

Many of the initiatives we describe are at the course level or centre upon the co-curriculum, which we define as activities that are complementary to but not an integral part of an academic programme. This is indicative of the problems that systemic, programme-wide approaches cause for those working in high-choice modular systems in which the notion of programme coherence is somewhat hazy and the *module* or *course* is the primary unit of analysis. We return to this theme in Chapters 12 and 13.

We end this chapter with some uncomfortable questions about graduates likely to face disadvantage in the labour market. Are initiatives such as these sufficient, or would it be fairer to aim to enhance employability through mainstream curricula, or is neither approach good enough?

## Work-based and work-related learning

The idea that student employability is enhanced by work-related and work-based learning has considerable face validity. 'Work-related learning'[4] is a loose term covering activities that are intended to contribute to a student's fitness for employment.[5] It includes classroom activities that are designed directly to

- teach propositional or formal knowledge that is of value in an occupation;
- develop something of importance in a particular occupation (triage or classroom management);
- foster generic practices, such as team-working and interpersonal fluency.

A number of higher education institutions provide opportunities for students to get credit for work-related learning – as in the Leeds University Philosophy Department, where credit can be had for the mentoring of more junior students. The School of Independent Studies at Lancaster University has long allowed students to propose ways of securing course credit through work-related activities and through some academically-appropriate activity based upon their work-based activities.

Many things that can be learned on-campus can also be developed in a workplace. Other valued achievements, such as triage or classroom management, demand workplace practice and are likely to be assessed in the workplace. *Work-based* learning is therefore treated as a special kind of work-related learning. A lot of institutions formally accredit work-based learning as an integral part of their (non-sandwich) curricula – offering a module's worth of credit, for example.[6]

So, *work-based* learning is taken as a subset of *work-related* learning: 'work-related' distinguishes an activity from 'pure' academic work, and 'work-based' signifies that learning should be happening in a workplace. Following our summaries of the development of expertise (Chapter 1), practical intelligence (Chapter 1) and generic skills (Chapter 2), we remark that practitioner development will usually come from on-campus and work-based experiences, combine formal and non-formal learning and be promoted through the mainstream curriculum or through the co-curriculum.

In 2000 the English funding council, HEFCE, invited institutions to bid for funding to develop foundation degrees in part-time, full-time and distance learning modes. These degrees were to be work-related, developed in partnership with employers and including substantial amounts of work-based learning. *The Future of Higher Education* (DfES, 2003) stressed the importance of the foundation degrees in government plans for expanding the participation of young people in HE and showed enthusiasm for the continued development of higher education programmes delivered in further education colleges. Although these new pro-grammes could be used to illustrate ways in which work-related and work-based learning can be blended, we will not pay them particular attention but treat them as special cases of initiatives to enhance employability.

## Employability-enhancing practices

### Work-based learning

This can take the form of placements, which are part of the programme of study, or of work done outside the programme but 'cashed in' through personal development planning or enrichment activities, such as *Insight plus*. Harvey says of placements that they are of two types.

> *Embedded* placements may be:
> Optional or compulsory;
> Single block placements (thick sandwich) or multiple block placements (thin sandwich);
> Year long, semester long or for shorter periods.
>
> *External* placements often take place during term-time and may be of variable lengths but are usually single block placements. They are arranged privately by individual students, or arranged through agencies or are part of the recruitment procedures of some organisations.
>
> (Harvey, 1999: 2, 3)

He is wary of the assumption that placements necessarily lead to learning, arguing that

> Unless these external placements are heavily promoted and facilitated within an institution with an expectation, at programme level, that students become involved, institutions should not claim any employability development as a result ...
>
> (Harvey, 1999: 3)

Blackwell and colleagues (2001) described four substantial studies of work-based learning and observed that the experience was not invariably a high quality one, nor did students necessarily consider that they had learnt a lot from it. They did suggest that graduates, looking back, were more appreciative and wondered whether this might be because they, the graduates, had had the time to reflect – they saw reflection as an essential concomitant of work-based learning. They also observed that there are difficulties in assessing work-based learning (see Chapter 8) and argued that good quality work-based learning has six characteristics:

- Stakeholders – students, employers, academic staff and employees – all appreciate the underlying intentions.
- The quality of work experience is greatly enhanced by prior induction and briefing for all concerned; facilitation of ongoing reflection; debriefing, reflection and identification of outcomes.
- Work experience is accredited so that it is taken seriously.
- Low-stakes or formative assessment is used to support the process of learning from work experience.
- Students build up a work-experience portfolio.
- Students can say what they have learned, provide illustrations and, if need be, commentary.

Harvey illustrates several of these points in the following example:

> The University of Bournemouth provides an example of the monitoring and reflection process. Students are required to keep a logbook or diary of their placement (weekly entries) detailing activities, targets, skills used, difficulties encountered and how they overcame them, as well as what they learned. This has to be signed by their supervisor on a regular basis. Towards the end of the placement students also complete a specific assignment of 2,500 words that brings together their findings. Placement development advisors visit students *in situ* on two occasions during the 40-week placement. The advisor speaks both to the student and to the workplace supervisor and produces a report identifying progress made from visit to visit, including learning and skills development. Finally the company is asked to complete a one-page appraisal form (matrix of skills). The pieces of work, the logbook, the personal development advisor reports provide an overall picture of the placement.
>
> (Harvey, 2003: 38)

Noble and Paulucy (2002) offer complementary advice. They also make an important economic distinction between types of work-based learning. They distinguish between that which 'involves the translation of discipline-based university programmes into forms which can be delivered through the workplace' as in the case of an MBA in management practice, and that 'where the focus and context of the curriculum is primarily designed by the learner' (p. 26). This distinction between 'batch processing' and customized provision is important for several reasons, two of which are:

- Customized provision 'requires staff to develop what may be a new set of skills, behaviours and competencies in relation to learner support. Facilitation, networking, brokerage and negotiation are all essential parts of the skill repertoire' (p. 27).
- Customized provision is expensive and probably cannot be scaled-up so that this form of work-based learning becomes part of all students' curricula.

The conclusion that dedicated higher education staff are needed to facilitate and support the development of work-based learning is predictable, as is the corollary that this need is greatest with customized, individualized placements. There are costs too for employers, as is evident from the Association of Graduate Recruiters' briefing paper (2002) for employers on providing good quality work experience. Although the AGR is clear about the direct and indirect benefits to employers, what stands out is that work experience cannot be satisfactory unless it is purposeful and well organized.

There are questions, then, about the feasibility of widespread work-based learning in a mass higher education curriculum and about its affordability, especially in its bespoke forms. Problems with answering these questions have led some programme teams to look instead at strategies reviewed earlier – relevant content, projects, skill-building and entrepreneurship modules.

A number of local and national organizations and networks offer external placements. The Shell Technology Enterprise Programme[7] (STEP) is a long-standing organization that provides some 1,200 placements a year in SMEs. Evaluation evidence shows that STEP placements are appreciated by employers, with 82 per cent of those involved in 1999–2000 saying that the placement would have a long-term impact on the business and 55 per cent saying that they had made a profit of £2,000+ on it (Work Experience Group, 2002: 12). STEP keeps a high profile through such events as its '*UK's Most Enterprising Student*' award. There are also regional and institution-specific initiatives. One is the KITTS project,[8] a development in the greater West Midlands area supported by nine higher education institutions, which helps about 60 SMEs a year to take on graduates to tackle a specific project for up to 13 weeks.

There is, though, general agreement that preparation is needed if a placement is truly to be a learning experience:

> Specific forms of student preparation advocated included practice in identi-fication of learning outcomes and their articulation; practice in articulating cognitive language and concepts to other people (to gain familiarity); and practice in relating cognitive concepts to everyday and work settings to provide relevant anchoring ideas.
>
> (Little 2000: 126)

Despite this agreement, Little found that there was a lot of emphasis on helping students to get placements and

... only a very few of my case studies made reference to discussions about processes of learning, the learning cycle, processes of reflection on actions and experiences, and the language used for articulating the development of higher order cognitive skills and personal transferable skills.

*(Op. cit.:* 126)

When it comes to thinking about work-based learning for part-time students, such as those in the National Health Service University or in the Open University, this emphasis on learning, not on placement, becomes compelling because students will usually already be in paid or voluntary work. The problems are not getting placements but in seeing how learning can be supported through the experience of work in a variety of settings. This is a challenge being faced by Foundation Degree programmes in England, and raises issues concerning the relationship between learning that takes place in the workplace and academic standards.

Watchwords are:

- Learning – what programme outcomes should students be addressing?
- Quality – how is the university to be assured that students receive good quality support and guidance, especially when the student is the only person formally learning from work in a community of workplace practice that may have no experience of formal learning through work?
- Support – how can academic, practical, central and local arrangements enable students to learn and represent their learning effectively?
- Assessment – what would count as adequate and efficient assessment arrangements with students widely dispersed across a varied range of workplace settings?

Clearly, if part-time students are to have the same opportunities to capitalize upon their higher education to enhance their employability, then part-time and corporate providers need to address these issues, formidable though they are.

### Advice on the design and operation of work-based learning

In the code of practice for placement learning (QAA, 2001d), there is a section which provides a set of precepts, with accompanying guidance, on arrangements for placement learning that typically takes place outside the institution and that has the support and co-operation of a placement provider. The code emphasizes the need for clearly defined aims and intended learning outcomes that are understood by all parties, and for an explicit specification of responsibilities of the higher education institution, placement provider and student. There is a view, though, that it would be helpful to produce a good practice guide for work-based learning to supplement the code of practice. There is advice available from the Association for Sandwich Education and Training and the National Centre for Work Experience (Work Experience Group, 2002) and guidance from the

University of Cambridge Programme for Industry (2000), which is directed at higher education staff and employers, especially SMEs.

There is a need to help employers appreciate what is involved in successful work experience. The UK Association of Graduate Recruiters publishes *Work Experience – An Employers' Guide to Success* (2002), which makes the case for employer participation in work experience and advises on establishing links with universities, setting up and running work-based learning programmes, attracting quality applicants, and supporting and assessing students during placements.

Smaller and 'micro' businesses find it difficult to engage in planning for, and providing, work experience for students, since their staff resources are often too stretched to permit the commitment of time that such work requires. Particularly at the 'micro' end, there is a reluctance to become involved in the bureaucratic paperwork that can accompany work experience. Micro businesses in the areas of, for example, design and 'the media' find it easier to provide institutions with project briefs to which students can respond in the institutional environment, or at home. Some small organizations in these areas have taken up the concept of 'tele-working', arguing that it can contribute to functional efficiency and that it replicates some working practices. Where they engage with academic programmes, the engagement may take the form of consultation at the programme design stage and, later, when the students' responses to the project briefs come up for assessment. This form of work experience, however, highlights the ethical problem of benefiting from student work at relatively minimal cost, especially should the students produce work of a higher standard than that of the business's own staff or of the staff of an agency.

It is easier to concentrate on the learning that should come from placements, volunteering and part-time work if students, mentors, employers and teachers have a language to use that identifies likely learning outcomes and ways of mapping them onto a university's or college's awards system. The framework can exist in a prototype version, which is available to departments interested in work-based learning and which identifies common outcomes, how they might be highlighted, assessed and mapped into the awards structure. Some customization by departments and programme teams is then needed to adapt the framework to their particular learning intentions. Alternatively, Glasgow Caledonian University has developed a framework for Work-Based Learning awards which is based on individually negotiated learning contracts (Chisholm, 2002). On grounds of economy, the programme-specific approach is to be preferred, although individual learning contracts offer greater flexibility.

### Ensuring that subject matter is relevant

A common response to claims that there are skills shortages or gaps has been to set up programmes that directly address those gaps by, for example, increasing the number of undergraduate places in nanotechnology or web engineering. There is an obvious appeal to bringing the subject matter of higher education closer to what employers want, although it is not easy for higher education to be sure what will be needed in five or six years time, when the first graduates emerge from a programme (which is one reason for the over-supply of graduates with ICT strengths at the turn of the last century); it is not easy for HEIs to recruit high-quality staff in these 'leading edge' areas; and sometimes they get it wrong by, for example, all joining the scramble to produce MBA graduates.

Within established courses, subject relevance is often assured in normal classroom practice, as when students learn procedures, theories and practices that are directly related to workplaces. It is also quite common for teachers in some applied and vocational areas to teach through case studies and other materials that require academic understandings to be brought to bear on workplace issues. In other subjects, such as history, teachers sometimes find opportunities to set tasks that require students to think about workplace problems, as when they are asked to plan a museum exhibition on *Ourplace* fifty years ago. There still seems to be steadily growing interest in problem-based curricula, in which 'academic' content is explored through consideration of practical problems that are often representative of workplace practices.

The graduate apprenticeship scheme sponsored by the English government created degree and diploma level programmes, targeted at specific economic sectors. These apprenticeships should enrich the work-based learning elements of programmes and link them more securely with the 'academic' elements. Students would also be developing 'key skills', typically leading to the award of a National Vocational Qualification, always given suitable evidence of achievement from both the workplace and university study. A common feature of graduate apprentice-ships is 'a self-managed and reflective Personal Development Summary' (EMTA, 2000: J-1), which resembles what is now called 'personal development planning' in England.

The national training organization for engineering manufacture, EMTA, supported work in a number of universities, including the University of Luton, where the Work Based Learning Unit organized

> a stand-alone modular course providing training and development for graduates to practise their skills in the workplace. It has been likened to a form of 'finishing school' to prepare graduates for possible future work within a SME.
>
> (EMTA, 2000: 8)

Loughborough University reviewed the 45-week engineering work placement to integrate it more fully with the overall academic package.

## Project work and other 'contextualizing' activities

Difficulties in providing workplace learning opportunities have stimulated an interest in work-related activities, such as projects, lifelike case studies, authentic assessment and other context-rich work. Queen's University, Belfast, reports on a project-based learning programme developed in the mid-1990s 'to foster closer links between employers and higher education through the development of joint employer-academic tutor projects ... [to] offer a range of realistic projects ... [that] may be taken as an alternative to conventional dissertations or projects suggested by tutors' (Brown, 1999: 4). There were not only projects in the 'obvious' areas of science and engineering, but also in history and social science. Although one large employer estimated that each project had incurred around £250 in direct costs and about 40 hours of company personnel time, 'the benefits to the company outweighed the investment costs' (O'Neill, 1999: 75). That is not the whole story, though, because there were significant costs to the university, including the appointment of a dedicated project-based learning officer, a working group, a network and staff development workshops.

As one-offs, projects tend to be expensive and there is an appeal in cheaper ways of engaging learners with realistic problems. Some teachers at the University of Leeds have developed case studies that engage students with lifelike problems through which academic material can be mastered. This 'context' work (School of Geography, 2003a) has some resemblance to problem-based learning, although it is on a smaller scale and can be incorporated into many existing courses in a way that problem-based learning cannot. The School relates this to 'intrapreneurship', which it defines as 'the art of working within an organization to effect change, by developing new ideas, procedures or products, by innovating practice and thereby enhancing business' (School of Geography, 2003b: 1). Context materials are intended to stimulate this 'intrapreneurship', which can easily be associated with the development of good claims to employability.

### Skills enhancement

Surveys show that informants are prepared to identify sets of skills that make for employability. In auditing employability development activities in Wales, Harvey (1999: 4) collected information about embedded employability-skills development on modules/courses, defined as courses that include 'the *explicit* and transparent development' of any of fifteen named 'skills', 'which may be formally assessed'. Little (2000) reported that analysis of work-based learning case studies found the following skills were generally emphasized: personal and social skills, communication skills, problem-solving skills, organizational skills and creativity. The Keynote project aimed to 'identify, disseminate and develop the key skills of textiles, fashion and printing students, thereby enhancing their employability' (D. Allen, 2002: 2). Noting some disagreement over what these skills are, he also said that 12 out of 14 institutions surveyed reckoned that key skills were fully embedded within curricula. Although Harvey (2003) shows that there are a number of skills development schemes running in higher education, this agreement on the significance of skills of one sort or another is qualified by Allen's note that '... in the majority of the institutions, there was no explicit tracking of skills development', and in a department which had a good system in place 'very few students availed themselves of the opportunity to gain key skills accreditation' (D. Allen, 2002: 2). One explanation may be that there are costs involved in adding 'extras' to mainstream curricula which students and institutions may be equally reluctant to incur.

### Other awards

Believing that skills are not enough, some higher education providers have developed broader employability programmes. The Graduate Employability Award (Hopkiss, 2001: 4) aims 'to help you to evidence the transition from student to effective graduate employee'. The award is validated by the OCR[9] national awarding body, which means that it has national recognition. It comprises five units: the reflective practitioner; customer service; workplace safety; working with others; improving one's own learning and performance. After induction, allocation to an assessor or mentor and completion of a learning agreement, students concentrate on gathering evidence to satisfy the requirements of each of the five units. Assessment is by portfolio and a 'professional discussion' with the assessor.

Other, more local, examples of awards being made outside degree structures include the Work Experience Award developed as part of the JEWELS (Joint Systems to Enhance Work Experience Levels of Service and Satisfaction) Project run jointly by the Universities of Plymouth and Exeter, and the York Award which is a certificated programme of transferable skills training and experiential learning, offered by the University of York in partnership with a number of public, private and voluntary sector organizations.[10]

### Visits, work shadowing and mentoring

Staffordshire University introduced a mentoring scheme in 2000 which matched 18 students with disabilities with a mentor, 'that is an individual with professional experience who can open up a window of opportunity to an undergraduate with special needs' (G. Allen, 2002: 25). Both mentors and students said they gained from the relationship. The IMPACT project,[11] administered from the University of Bradford on behalf of a consortium of institutions, is 'targeted primarily at UK minority ethnic students to enhance their employability skills and increase employment opportunity' (IMPACT publicity flyer). It provides one-to-one discussions, employer events, mentoring, access to work-shadowing and work experience, mock interviews and a variety of workshops to support the job application process.

### Enhancing an entrepreneurial disposition

Small and medium-sized enterprises (SMEs) are recognized as sites of innovation and wealth creation. One line of thinking is that for growth there needs to be a greater supply of graduates with an entrepreneurial disposition. This makes the promotion of entrepreneurship an interesting way of contributing to employability. This is quite well established in some subject areas, especially – and predictably – in Schools of Business, such as the Audencia Business school in Nantes and ESC Grenoble, although it is more likely to be an MBA-level concern than an undergraduate one. In England, though, where self-employment and small-scale enterprise are quite common in some economic sectors, such as those served by the Art and Design subject area, many Art and Design departments make some entrepreneurial elements available in their programmes.

Harvey (2003) describes initiatives including:

- 'Westminster Business Consultants' is a junior enterprise organization that provides a commercial service and is run, managed and staffed by Westminster University students.
- The Business School at The University of Newcastle has developed a business enterprise module as a way of embedding an array of attributes in the curriculum.
- At Liverpool John Moores University, there is an optional one-day course for arts students on self-employment that has been in operation since 1997 and had 89 participants last year. It is now attracting attention from graduates in other disciplines.

In some subject areas, a curriculum concern for entrepreneurship would be a significant contribution to graduate employability, given what is known about employment patterns (Blackwell and Harvey, 1999). In others it might broaden students' career planning. Brown and Puddick (2002) report on a Cambridge University scheme, based on the assumption that

> ... if students could be exposed to the realities of entrepreneurial businesses through working in them, their awareness of the necessary conditions for success would be enhanced and their fear of the unknown would be reduced ... Such exposure might persuade more people that learning can be used to create wealth rather than just to get a job.
>
> (Brown and Puddick, 2002: 50)

The programme comprised induction packs, placements, projects, lectures and workshops. At a money price of about £500 per graduate, the programme was good value for money, although there were substantial hidden costs and it is not easy to see how it could be *substantially* extended beyond the 50 students who had participated in the first year. Donnelly (2003), describing an established 'enterprise' programme at Heriot-Watt University, which attracted more than 500 volunteer participants in 2002, is very clear about the substantial costs, logistical problems and compromises. He concludes that

... there is clear evidence that enterprise can be learned by large numbers of people and that they can produce ideas capable of commercialization, given the help of the university. Whether universities themselves are capable of addressing this challenge remains to be seen.

(Donnelly, 2003: 43)

As with work-based learning, a difficulty is getting commitment from SMEs. Remarking on data showing that in 1998 less than 3 per cent of them claimed to have collaborated with higher education, Brown and Puddick comment that

... even in the Cambridge area where the existence of the University was assumed to be a major reason for their location, the companies had generally never taken a student on work placement.

(Brown and Puddick, 2002: 52)

Ball (2001) said that art and design graduates need self-confidence, which might come from independent learning, business awareness and a better understanding of entrepreneurship. The University of Brighton has responded by providing fashion and textiles design students with 'a group assignment that raises awareness of how and why businesses succeed or fail' (Ball, 2001: 17), which is supported by 'five interactive workshops designed to raise students' awareness of issues for small businesses, why they are started, why businesses succeed or fail, aspects of business management, such as finance, costing and pricing and the skills required by owner-managers' (ibid.). Copies of students' reports were sent to owner-managers, who appreciated their insights and involvement. Students too appreciated this applied entrepreneurship course. Although Ball did not address issues of sustainability and scale, this approach looks to be generalizable since it is not customized (there were 50 students in the first presentation) and it appears to stand in place of more traditional final year projects.

An alternative is to consider how entrepreneurship might be an option within the mainstream curriculum, even available to such as philosophers and historians. While it is unlikely that work placements could be offered, much could be done to foster an entrepreneurial cast of mind. Gibb (2002) encourages the creation of environments conducive to learning and entrepreneurship. The goal is to promote entrepreneurial behaviour, 'the ability to cope with uncertainty and complexity' (p. 135) by designing learning environments that 'enhance the capacity of individuals to practise such behaviour in a way that will, hopefully, enrich their lives and help their organizations to perform better' (ibid.). When he later says that '... much of this [entrepreneurial] way of life can be rehearsed by use of appropriate pedagogy' (p. 137), we see a connection between his view of the development of entrepreneurship and ours on the promotion of employability.

## Learning from part-time work

Although it has been traditional for North American students to work to pay their way through college, it is a newer phenomenon in the UK. Most students in the UK now have part-time work and it is being appreciated that there is an opportunity here for strengthening student claims to employability. Noble comments that some universities and colleges

> See extra-curricular and off-campus activity through, for example, part-time employment, student union activities ... as a means of developing employability. Students are sometimes given the opportunity to gain an additional qualification as a part of this work ...

(Noble, 1999: 125)

*Insight plus*,[12] run by the Careers Research and Advisory Centre (CRAC), helps students to develop claims to achievement on the back of their part-time work. In the 2001/2 academic year it was run at eleven UK universities and was planned to grow fourfold in 2002/3. The programme comprises workshops, mentoring and support materials. Three leading graduate recruitment companies support it and will use it in their recruitment programme. Student Volunteers UK, a partner in *Insight plus*, helps students to capitalize on their voluntary work and participation in the funding council's active community scheme. The University of Wolverhampton, finding that traditional mechanisms for providing student work experience, notably industrial placements and projects, were operating at full capacity, developed structures to help students to convert part-time and casual work into course credit through a level 2 module that exploited a transferable, computer-based self-assessment tool (Sidhu, 2000). Watton *et al.* (2002) summarize the experience of several such projects, finding that reflective learning logs or portfolios are the main means by which *ad hoc* work experience is converted into academic credit or other forms of recognition. Despite these initiatives, the Work Experience Group considered that 'where institutions assess learning derived from such *ad hoc* work experience, the take-up by students is low' (WEG, 2002: 7).

Students' part-time work could be turned to stronger account if it were to provide the 'life experience' enrichment of a programme of academic study which might be termed 'Work-related Studies'. This could form one component of, say, a joint programme in Subject X and Work-related Studies which might be attractive to *some* students, not least because it could help them to deal with the problem of the debt that typically arises as a consequence of pursuing a qualification in higher education. To be credible, the Work-related Studies component would need to be solidly grounded in academic disciplines, and there is considerable potential for the inclusion of material from individual and social psychology, organizational sociology, human resource management, finance and accounting, and so on. If the student then wished to extend their studies in Subject X alone up to degree-level, then this could be undertaken on a post-experience basis.[13]

## Learning from volunteering

In England there is a new stream of funding from HEFCE, known as the Active Communities Fund (HEACF), which is intended to encourage students to engage in voluntary work. Every HE institution has substantial funding, which could aid the enhancement of employability: recent research amongst 200 of the UK's top businesses shows that three-quarters of employers prefer to recruit candidates who have undertaken voluntary work experience and that over half think that voluntary work can be more valuable than paid work (TimeBank, 2001). Another form of external organized work experience is voluntary work through Community Service Volunteers, Millennium Volunteers or Student Volunteering UK. There are about 25,000 student volunteers across the UK working in community-based projects in over 180 further education and higher education volunteering groups. The case studies of 'The Art of Crazy Paving' research project (Speakman *et al.*, 2001) showed that volunteering promoted an organic learning process that honed continuing personal development planning and self-reflection.[14]

## Better careers guidance

Commenting on students' career planning, the Work Experience Group (2002: 10) observes that, 'Those who need most guidance are least likely to consult the Careers Service'. Rowley and Purcell (2001) reviewed data on users' perceptions of careers service quality and concluded that

.... The scope of provision differed widely between institutions ... There appeared to be a need for a more pro-active service during a student's course of study, that would, for example, publicise the services on offer, and arrange work placements ... Students at post-1992 universities, those following 'minority subjects' or highly specialised courses, and students over 25 were less likely to be satisfied with provision ... in those groups of students that appeared to be most in need of the service, significantly lower proportions were likely to have used it ... Although the majority of students *had* used the careers service and rated the information and guidance useful, it appeared that the majority of *those* did not visit until their final year, by which time it was often too late for those inadequately prepared for the labour market ...

(Rowley and Purcell, 2001: 419–20)

They advised careers services to give more attention to the development of career management competencies in all students, and to refocus resources in order to target those groups of students that have been consistently identified as failing to receive an acceptable threshold quality of careers advice and guidance (Rowley and Purcell, 2001). The Harris Report (DfEE, 2001) reviewed higher education careers services and made a series of recommendations designed to raise standards and improve performance and to integrate careers services into the organization as a whole. A Joint Implementation Group has addressed the six Harris recommendations and has published guidance on core services for students, graduates and employers in a report entitled *Modernising HE Careers Education* (Universities UK/SCOP, 2002). It is not clear whether funding will be available to help careers services meet these ambitions, although work commissioned by the higher education Careers Service Unit (CSU) explores ways of targeting resources so that those students most in need of advice are encouraged to seek it.

One of the outcomes of the Enterprise in Higher Education initiative of the late 1980s and 1990s was the inclusion in curricula of contributions from institutional careers services. This recognized the significance, for students' development, of a relatively early engagement in thinking about what they might need, over and above their formal qualifications, to succeed in employment. There continues to be interest in bringing careers services into closer relationships with subject departments, notably by

> ... integrating the skills of career management into the curriculum. They cover institution-wide and discipline-based approaches involving a range of activities including open and distance learning, computer-based learning materials, involvement of employers in curriculum delivery and the development of career management modules ... A major problem facing institutions is, however, one of resources to support this kind of development.
>
> (Noble, 1999: 123)

The Careers Research and Advisory Centre (CRAC) runs the *Insight* conferences for students which prepare them for the transition to work and also contribute strongly to their ability to get a graduate job.

### Personal development planning

In Chapter 8 we comment on the place of personal development planning (PDP) in a differentiated approach to assessment, so we only remark here on its potential to be integrative by encouraging students to reflect on their learning, needs and developmental plans *as a whole*. It is seen as a student-owned process that will often involve the creation and revision of a portfolio.

However, it is not something that higher education is finding it easy to address, although a great deal of work has been co-ordinated by the Centre for Recording Achievement (CRA), encouraged by the Generic Centre of the Learning and Teaching Support Network, and undertaken through projects in universities and colleges around the country.

## Responding to disadvantage

We have observed that certain groups of graduates do not fare as well in the labour markets as their degree classifications might have led us to expect. There have been some projects to enhance their employability. Amongst them are the following:

- The AGCAS MERITS (Minority Ethnic Recruitment, Information, Training and Support) Project (see Booth, 2002), which worked with Black and Asian students and graduates, who tend to be disadvantaged in the job market. The programme involves careers services at half a dozen institutions. Brunel university has extended the MERITS Project, piloted a proactive mentoring approach and offers free Career Planning Resources – hard copy, ring-bound versions of a 'Tutor Pack' and a 'Mentoring Pack'.
- The IMPACT project, designed to support ethnic minority students in various ways, was noted above.
- The Leicester Employment Skills within an Accessible Curriculum (ESAC) project[15] is creating and disseminating materials that will ensure that students with disabilities and specific learning difficulties are provided with opportunities to develop key employability skills through inclusive approaches to academic curricula.
- *Deaf and Creative* is a web site aimed at young deaf people looking for the next stage in their education or career.[16] There is information about going to university, getting a job, starting a business, doing further qualifications and getting funding. It lists job vacancies.

Despite the obvious appeal of such initiatives, we know that authorities on special educational needs provision in schools have often argued that the starting point must be good educational practice for all. Their view is that addressing many special needs depends, first and foremost, on good practices: any special provision depends upon a bedrock of good general practice, hence the title of Ainscow's (1991) book, *Effective Schools for All*. There is some support for this in research evidence that effective schools tend to be effective for *all* children (Mortimore *et al.*, 1988). That line of thought has influenced our approach to employability, which has been concerned with designs that can help all students, not just those willing or able to participate in the co-curriculum, or those who happen to have chosen subjects in which there is a plentiful supply of jobs, such as initial teacher education. Of course, it is still reasonable and possible to enhance student employability in many ways: within the mainstream curriculum and without; systemically and individually; inclusively and selectively. That general agnosticism is still our basic position, although we have views about what it is best to do in the different settings in which we have worked.

Yet there is a powerful case for identifying and targeting those who are likely to be at risk in the labour market. Without coming down on one side or the other, we draw attention to three issues attaching to decisions about targeting provision at those likely to be the most disadvantaged in the graduate labour markets. We comment on practical, educational and political-economic issues.

Regarding the practical issues, Brennan and Shah say

> The case for targeting support to students in greatest need is recognised but in practice it is very difficult to achieve. Only with regards to mature students does there seem to be successful experience of targeted support for

employability. The problems are partly ethical – institutional staff are nervous about treating students differently – and partly practical, how to identify those most in need. The way forward seems to be through some process of self-referral and student awareness raising. Better information for first year students on employability is [one area to address] ... [T]he very success of some institutions in widening participation may create difficulties in enhancing employability ... the development of an institutional culture that reflects the cultures of the majority student groups (ethnic minorities) ... [makes it] difficult to respect the diverse cultures of students and to extend their horizons and awareness beyond those cultures.

(Brennan and Shah, 2002: 3)

The educational issue is whether special provision can make up for an indifferent curriculum, which echoes earlier comments about the importance of basing special educational needs provision on good general educational practice. Issues of political economy follow: which is the best investment – curriculum enhancement for all (which is likely to preserve patterns of disadvantage), or disadvantage-busting projects?

Many of the initiatives described in this chapter are undoubtedly excellent, yet they are constrained by the quality of the mainstream curricula that students experience and they often reach those who choose to be reached by them. There is a view that employability would be best served by fuller curriculum integration, which is the line that Skills *plus* took. However, before describing the project's work in Chapters 9–12 and then returning to systemic issues in Chapter 13, we need to consider the assessment implications of locating employability in the mainstream curriculum, rather than relying on the co-curriculum for its enhancement.

## Notes

1 There are conditions. 'Typically, students must maintain a B-minus average, mentor with professionals and complete their internship' (*USA Today*, 29/9/97).
2 Further information can be found in:
   * The journal *Industry and Higher Education*, published six times a year, is dominated (70 per cent of papers) by empirical reports which typically take case study form (Valentin and Sanchez, 2002).
   * Oakland's (2002) *Directory of Employability Resources* also contains summaries of curriculum developments, work experience and extra-curricular activities.
   * *Enhancing Employability, Recognising Diversity*, published by Universities UK and the Higher Education Careers Service Unit (Harvey *et al.*, 2002) contains a further sixteen case studies of UK practice, ranging from a programme helping students from ethnic minority backgrounds (the *IMPACT* project) through the development of progress files and associated personal development planning to the development of a learning at work framework at Liverpool John Moores University.
   * Harvey's *Transitions to Work* (2003) is a substantial account of projects and initiatives that enhance higher education's contribution to employability.

3 Conversations with colleagues from universities across the European Union suggest that there are countries in which employability is conceived principally in terms of raising student achievement (better grades), updating the curriculum (ensuring content relevance) and, sometimes, developing skills (although there is some resistance to the term and government interference in higher education). There is also a lot of attention being paid to the Bologna Process, which is about harmonising the structure of first and second cycle higher education in the EU and ensuring that transcripts from one country are easily readable in others. Important though this is, the process is, as yet, indifferent to the quality of what lies behind those transcripts – to level of demand, process standards and learning intentions.

4 *The Future of Higher Education* (DfES, 2003) refers to 'work-focused' learning, which we equate with work-related learning.

5 Explicitly excluded from this summary are work with former students, postgraduate programmes, further professional development work, other adult continuing education and life-long learning. They are important but peripheral to our concern with first cycle higher education.

6 Brennan and Little (1996: 129–30) identified six approaches to the recognition of achievement in work-based learning. Some more recent examples are given in Watton and Collings (2002: 33).

7 http://www.step.org.uk/.

8 See http://www.wmg.warwick.ac.uk/SME_MTC.shtml.

9 The acronym is a welcome alternative to 'Oxford, Cambridge and Royal Society of Arts Examination Board'.

10 For details of the JEWELS Project, see Watton *et al.* (2002), www.jewels.org.uk/finalreport.htm and associated papers. For details of the York Award, see www2.york.ac.uk/admin/ya/.

11 See www.bradford.ac.uk/admin/impact.

12 See www.insightplus.co.uk.

13 An extended discussion of this suggestion can be found in Yorke (2003b).

14 This paragraph is based on Harvey, 2003.

15 See http://www.le.ac.uk/eu/ESAC/project.html.

16 See www.deafandcreative.ac.uk/.

# Chapter 8

# Assessing for employability

## The problem of warranting achievements

We have insisted that many of the achievements that employers value resist reliable assessment. Even if we devise and can afford to use tolerably-reliable ways of judging complex achievements, there are still difficulties in warranting achievement – in affirming that someone *is* fit to practise, first class or competent. One way of explaining this caution about warranting can be based on the claim that 'skills' are better understood as social practices and that their interpretation demands situationally-sensitive judgement. This raises questions about the degree to which it is wise to generalize from situationally-specific judgements – any generalization from just a few judgements would be suspect. But warrants are exactly that, generalizations from some instances of practice to future performances. They are also plainly high-stakes, which means that they must also at least be *tolerably* reliable. The problem for the assessment of those achievements that make for strong claims to employability is that many of them defy measurement. The more complex the achievement, the harder it is to assess it without over-simplification, on the one hand, and afford sufficient, tolerably-reliable assessments to make generalization reasonably trustworthy, on the other.

## The importance of assessment for the promotion of employability

> The single, strongest influence on learning is surely the assessment procedures ... even the form of an examination question or essay topics set can affect how students study ... It is also important to remember that entrenched attitudes which support traditional methods of teaching and assessment are hard to change.
>
> (Entwistle, 1996: 111–12)

Assessment, as Entwistle says, affects how students study; for example, encouraging them to take 'deep' approaches to tasks, thereby discouraging them from 'surface' approaches, or *vice versa*. Assessment identifies what is to be taken seriously and what is not. And the assessment standards, which are often expressed as criteria or indicators, tell students what they need to do in order to succeed and, in good courses, they are the basis of improvement-centred feedback to students.

There are many interesting assessment methods (Knight and Yorke, 2003b, summarize fifty-one) and there is no shortage of books on how to use them (for example, Brown and Knight, 1994; Banta *et al.*, 1996; Hounsell *et al.*, 1996; Brown *et al.*, 1997; Walvoord and Anderson, 1998; Heywood, 2000). However, in order to decide which methods are best for a course (we are leaving programme assessment aside for the moment) there is a need to have a fairly well-formed sense of what the assessment tasks are intended to achieve in respect of learning behaviours, the understanding of content and performance standards. Which methods are best for an employability curriculum geared to the development of student understanding; subject-specific and general skills; efficacy beliefs and malleable self-theories; and strategic thinking or metacognition? We are going to argue that the more complex learning goals cannot be captured by the high-stakes assessment routines, such as examinations, that are in common use. Those routines may be suited to the assessment of subject understandings (although some would argue that they are really only good for assessing the retention of information) but not helpful in judging the 'E' and 'M' of the USEM account — and they are arguably not very good for the SEM. Since it is agreed that things valued enough to be stated as course learning outcomes should be assessed, we have a problem. How to assess complex learning if summative assessment is scarcely fit for the purpose? We will offer some solutions, first at course level and then at programme level (and we are convinced that with learning, teaching and assessment cultures, the programme level is the one that really matters). First, we take a brief look at some basic assessment concepts.

## Summative and formative: high-stakes and low-stakes assessment

Assessments are frequently used to sum up a person's achievement. In these cases, there is a *summative* purpose behind the tasks learners are set. Summative assessment provides 'feedout', in the shape of a warrant to achievement or competence (such as a degree certificate), and in the form of information that can be used as performance indicators in appraising the work of teachers, departments, colleges and national systems of education. Assessment for summative purposes is high-stakes assessment.

One implication is that those being assessed are likely to do all they can to conceal ignorance and suggest competence. That is in tension with another implication, namely that when the purposes are summative then the assessment should get it right – should be accurate, objective and reliable. In summative assessment there is a conflict between the intention to find out what learners understand and can do and the learners' interest in hiding their shortcomings. There is a further difficulty because reliable judgements of achievement are based on the *repeated* use of carefully tested tasks, which are judged by more than one assessor using low-inference assessment criteria. The problem is that what should be and what can be afforded are not necessarily the same. There are also serious technical difficulties, not reviewed here, with the idea that complex achievements can be captured by reliable assessment procedures (Knight 2002c). But high-stakes assessment has to be done because stakeholders expect grades and classifications. The question then becomes how best to do something that is inherently problematic.

Some achievements, especially those connected with understanding and the more straightforward skills, can be fairly reliably assessed in much the same way they are currently assessed. Practice might be improved by:

- Refining the assessment tasks.
- Writing programme assessment plans to ensure that these learning outcomes are repeatedly assessed throughout the programme.
- Developing assessment criteria which students have and understand and which assessors use.
- Making resources available for double marking of all summatively-assessed work, with the exception of work where there are clear right/wrong answers.

These actions will help to optimize the capacity to warrant or certify some achievements. The important point is that there will be many achievements for which an appropriate level of reliability cannot be reached (because the learning outcomes are inherently fuzzy), or where the department cannot afford the expense of getting reliable judgements that also preserve the integrity of the complex achievement in question.

Assessments are also used to identify what learners need to do in order to improve their work. This second approach to assessment, which is intended to inform students about how to do better, is often called *formative* assessment. Any task that creates feedback to students about their learning achievements can be called formative assessment. Diagnostic assessment, which involves using carefully-designed tasks to try and identify barriers to learning, can be seen as a type of formative assessment that is little used in higher education. Notice that formative assessment, with its emphasis on providing useful feedback, is more helpful when learners are open about their limitations and do not try to conceal ignorance or bury mistakes. Whereas summative assessment purposes discourage learners from being open, formative assessment purposes thrive on disclosure. Furthermore, with formative assessment the stakes are not so high – no-one's future rides on the accuracy of advice about continuing to improve one's work – which means that we need not worry so much about reliability. Reliability is obviously good if you can get it or can afford to get it but it is not central to formative assessment in the way that it must be central to summative assessment. That is very useful because there are some things which we want students to learn that cannot be reliably assessed, or cannot be reliably assessed *with the resources available*.

In a substantial meta-analysis of studies investigating the effectiveness of formative assessment, Black and Wiliam (1998) concluded that formative assessment was a powerful influence on learning. The effect size was around 0.7, placing it on a par with the effect sizes that Marzano (1998) found for the self-system and metacognition (loosely, the 'E' and 'M' of USEM, respectively). The studies in these meta-analyses related largely to school pupils, and those relating to post-compulsory education were not separated out. However, it is plausible to infer that 'what works' for school pupils ought to apply, *mutatis mutandis*, to higher education. The inference is strengthened when note is taken of the effectiveness of formative assessment as it is used at Alverno College in the US (Mentkowski *et al.*, 2000).

Advice on giving feedback with due care for efficacy beliefs was offered in Chapter 6. Here we consider the general conditions under which feedback is likely to contribute to learning.

### Conditions favourable to low-stakes assessment for formative purposes

Some colleagues have been sceptical about the power of creating enough good feedback, the evidence notwithstanding.

One line of criticism is that, as research clearly shows (Black and Wiliam, 1998; Torrance and Pryor, 1998), teachers may intend to create good feedback but it often does not work: the learning potential remains unrealized. The conclusion is that providing good feedback is no small undertaking. Six main conditions for success, in brief, are as follows:

1    Sufficient tasks are provided
2    Students engage with these tasks
3    There are criteria or indicators of achievement
4    Learners and assessors know and understand the achievement indicators
5    Good feedback is provided on submitted work
6    Feedback is received and attended to.

### Sufficient tasks are provided

This is obvious, but programme assessment reviews often show that some programme learning outcomes get scarcely any attention – the 'key skill' of numeracy is a case in point in many Arts and Social Science programmes. The failure to cover learning outcomes can also be seen at the course or module level where it is quite common to find that there are not enough tasks to create decent opportunities for getting feedback on all course learning outcomes. In some cases that is because there are too many learning outcomes. (We found a course of 30 contact hours and a further 170 student learning hours which had 19 learning outcomes. Needless to say, most were neither addressed nor assessed.) We tend to see this as a programme design failing more than something to blame on the course team. In other cases the problem is that teachers are so busy telling, that there is no time for tasks that get students thinking and doing.

### Students engage with these tasks

This can be understood as a point about motivation, which means designing tasks that students recognize as important and worthwhile. It is also a point about the teacher's authority, indicating that teachers need to require students to participate in *all* learning activities.

### There are criteria or indicators of achievement

Many teachers have spent too much time trying to write unambiguous statements of learning outcomes that can then be objectively used in the measurement of achievement. We have already said that this is philosophically suspect, psychologically misconceived and practically impossible. However, it is very useful to have some indicators, even 'fuzzy' indicators, of the sorts of performance that could be considered as evidence of appropriate achievement. Without indicators it is hard for students and other assessors to have a sense of what could be counted as evidence of achievement. Indicators do not replace skilled judgement; they support it by providing a rudimentary language in the form of broad-brush reference points for all to cite in arriving at and justifying assessment judgements. Without them students have little idea of what acceptable performance looks like and assessors rely on their individual experiences.

### Learners and assessors know and understand the achievement indicators

Where criteria exist they are usually published in programme and module handbooks and posted on the web for good measure. This is not enough.

First, students have to realize that these indicators are the name of the game, that they describe what is going to be valued and that it might be quite different from what they expect to be valued. Knight was always disturbed to get final year students wailing, 'I hadn't realized that I'd get a third [class honours degree] if I didn't cover those two criteria'.

Second, they need to understand what the indicators *mean*. Small group discussion helps, especially if it precedes as well as follows attempts to apply the criteria to make judgements on examples of student work. It also helps to get students to look closely at marked work that has been anonymized. Ideally, they would first see it without knowing the grade and comments, try to judge its quality themselves and then reflect on the indicators once the grades and comments had been disclosed to them.

*Tasks are appropriate to (matched to) learners*

Matching means having a sense of pacing so that there is time for consolidation as well as for new learning. It is not a science. The psychological literature is full of reports of tasks that logically ought to have had certain levels of difficulty, yet which turned out to be psychologically quite different from expectation. In general, though, tasks are easier when learners are given more scaffolding or guidance; when they are asked to work with a restricted amount of information; when concepts, problems and solution strategies are both well-formed and well-known; and when others contribute. Good feedback helps learners to understand what they will have to do in order to succeed as they go on to tackle tasks that are less well-defined and relate to larger amounts of less well-organized material.

## Good feedback is provided on submitted work

Feedback should be:

* Purposeful. Purposes might include correction of errors, development of understanding, promotion of generic skills, development of metacognition, maintenance of motivation.
* Related to the achievement indicators. Some work calls for comments that lie outside the criteria associated with a task but, when learners have been working with indicators in mind and where teachers want to give advice about future improvement, it is likely that the criteria will set the boundaries within which most comments lie. Criteria-referenced comments can also help learners to see the goodness of fit between judgements and their work. By the same token, they can help teachers to be fair and consistent in giving feedback.
* Timely. Feedback needs to be fast so that students can respond to it with the work fresh in their minds and in time to act on it before tackling another task of a similar sort. Higher education practices are often dilatory compared to the same day turnaround common in many primary schools and the one week turnaround in secondary schools.
* Appropriate, in relation to students' conceptions of learning, knowledge and the discourse of the discipline. This point is intended to indicate that good feedback can only be effective if learners and teachers share the same underlying ideas about the rules of the game. Some good feedback fails because the teacher has not spotted that students are playing the academic game by different rules.
* Developmentally useful. This is the most important of these messages about good quality feedback. Many teachers take pride in the amount of content-related feedback they give and in the number of errors they correct. Yet the whole idea of formative assessment is that learners get good suggestions for improvement. Since they are seldom likely to do the same task again, the implication is that feedback should be general, directed to similar but different

problems in the future, not specific. The most useful advice gives concrete advice about *getting better*.

• Understood. This essentially repeats the last point. However well-intentioned the teacher's advice, if students do not understand it, then the potential of formative assessment gets lost.

### Feedback is received and attended to

There are plenty of stories of students checking the mark and then ignoring all the carefully-crafted feedback that goes with it. This may be less likely with peer and self assessment that produces comments but not marks. When grades are involved, some tutors return the work and feedback but withhold the marks for a couple of days. Students are probably most likely to attend to feedback when they work within a programme-wide learning culture that has convinced them of the power of low-stakes, formative assessment and of feedback in all its forms.

Even if these conditions are met, it is not true the students will not take seriously something that is not graded. They may be compelled to do ungraded work for formative purposes (it is a condition of being allowed to do graded work); they may be induced to do it (as when formative work prepares for demanding, authentic, high-stakes tasks); and they may be persuaded that they will benefit from it (when they have become 'knowing students', who have enrolled in a learning culture unlike the ones to which they will often have become accustomed). There is a double point here: programme designers need consciously to devise 'rules of the game' that value formative assessment and students need to know the rules and why they are good rules.

## The need for knowing students

Students come to a class with learning histories that have shaped their beliefs about the rules of the academic game, particularly about what learning is and what teachers do. Many innovative teachers have found that students resist academic practices that do not conform to those expectations, partly because they do not understand the thinking behind them and partly because some firmly believe that they have paid to be instructed and then graded on what they remember. If low-stakes assessment is made a central feature of a course it is necessary to explain at least four things very clearly:

• Why there is such an emphasis on formative assessment. Students need to appreciate that the idea is that all learning outcomes should be assessed, even though it is not feasible to assess them all summatively. Formative assessment is a way of paying serious attention to those that escape high-stakes assessment. There is also compelling evidence that it can be very good for learning, which is why some learning outcomes that are summatively assessed are also formatively assessed. A course assessment plan shows how formative and summative assessment are dovetailed to give sustained attention to all course learning outcomes. There is more about plans in the next section.

- Why students should expect to do peer and self assessment. Formative assessment works well when teachers give thoughtful feedback on improving performance, especially when feedback is related to assessment criteria that are known, understood and used. (They might, for example, be printed on assignment cover sheets that are distributed when assignments are set.) The habits of judgement learned through assessing other students and then through evaluating one's own achievements contribute to student employability and are a basis of life-long learning.
- That teachers cannot be the only judges of all achievements, nor is assessment just about grades. Teachers design learning sequences that contain plenty of opportunities to create and get comments related to course learning outcomes. Then they encourage everyone to engage fully with the learning opportunities in the course, sometimes lecturing but sometimes expecting students to work independently; sometimes grading but sometimes expecting students to appraise themselves or each other. This is not idleness and dereliction of duty, as some students suppose, but necessary behaviour if learning is to happen on the intended lines.
- That formative assessment will not work unless students and teachers take it seriously. Obvious though the point is, students need to be told that low-stakes assessment is not to be treated lightly. Indeed, in some online learning environments, participation in discussions, which could be understood as creating feedback, is compulsory for course credit. Teachers might want to extend the principle to face-to-face work as well, perhaps requiring students to provide evidence that they contributed criteria-related feedback to others on $x$ occasions during the course.

## Implications for courses, modules or units

What might this concern for formative assessment and need for summative assessment mean at the level of a single course or module?

A starting point is the obvious point that not all learning outcomes are judged in the same ways. Some (such as giving references in good style, or using English grammatically) only attract attention when background assumptions of competence are violated. In other cases formative assessment is used, while others are subject to direct high-stakes assessment for summative purposes.

It is helpful to distinguish between learning that is

- directly assessed, for high-stakes purposes, as when we use multiple choice tests to make sure that students recall information;
- indirectly assessed with high-stakes in play, as when we say that good displays of critical thinking betoken analytical and synthetic performances as well;

- directly assessed, with low-stakes intentions, as when students get feedback, often from other students, on their contribution to group work;
- indirectly assessed for low-stakes purposes – production of a portfolio could be taken as indirect evidence of other achievements that are subject to low-stakes assessment, such as perseverance, willingness to learn and time management;
- presumed to be satisfactory unless contrary evidence is compelling, as when students do not follow referencing conventions.

The advantages of taking a differentiated approach to assessment are that it makes better theoretical sense, that it is a route to stopping teachers from trying to do the impossible,[1] and that it allows fair assessment of complex, 'fuzzy' learning outcomes.

There are decisions to be made about which outcomes are most suited to which assessment mode. These are easiest to make when a module has been designed with the following in mind:

- It does not have too many expected learning outcomes – a manageable number lies in the range from five to eight.
- Most, if not all, of these learning intentions come from the programme specification.
- A few – perhaps three – learning outcomes are identified as those that will get sustained attention in the module.
- Assessment tasks provide direct evidence of attainment in terms of the two or three learning outcomes that are module priorities.
- It is clear which learning outcomes are addressed by direct assessment with high-stakes, summative purposes, either because the outcome lends itself to high-reliability assessment or because sufficient investment has been made to get tolerably-reliable assessments of a less amenable outcome. In those cases, the assessment data can contribute to an eventual programme-level judgement of achievement: the assessment can be used for warranting purposes.
- It is clear which learning outcomes are addressed by formative means, when the public stakes are lower. Assessment data, in the form of feedback for improvement, may feed into students' portfolios and any personal development planning.
- Learning goals or outcomes that are indirectly assessed get direct attention in other modules.
- Most *programme* learning outcomes will then get direct assessment attention in more than one module, although some will be dealt with by the presumption of competence (see above).

A strength of this approach is that students and teachers alike can concentrate their learning and judgements on a few things at a time. Over-assessment, the bane of many modular programmes, is reduced because modules do not have too much to do, i.e. they have five or so outcomes to address, and have fewer as a module priority. It might almost be possible to say that the more outcomes to which a module is committed and the more that it tries to assess directly, the worse the module.

The distinctions and suggestions made so far imply having course (and, by extension, programme) assessment plans. Points to consider include the following:

1    Many course learning goals are a selection from programme learning goals. The link between course and programme learning goals should then be quite explicit. There are difficulties if the programme specification is inadequate, although university statements, such as Hong Kong's City University description of the ideal graduate,[2] provide useful pointers.

Some learning intentions will be course specific. It is helpful to limit the number of learning goals a course has and to avoid writing inflated outcome or goal descriptions.

2    Establish a course assessment plan or review the existing one for goodness of fit with the aim of developing student employability. The plan should relate major assessment activities to course learning goals, showing how each goal is addressed through assessment and sketching the rubrics or criteria to be used to judge achievement. Writing an assessment plan sometimes shows that goals need to be modified or that rubrics and criteria could be improved. Useful ideas can be had from the QAA's benchmarking site[3] or by contacting your LTSN subject centre[4] to see whether there are any subject-specific indicators you can appropriate. It may also be helpful to consult the National Qualifications Framework (QAA, 2001e).

3    When writing the assessment plan, keep it in mind that a range of learning intentions demands a variety of learning and assessment methods. The books mentioned at the beginning of this chapter describe many ways of assessing achievement. Where employability is concerned, there are reasons to prefer 'authentic' assessment methods, i.e. methods that deal with complex and life-like situations.

4    Draw on expertise in networks. LTSN subject centres, professional bodies and subject associations in the UK and elsewhere are good sources of ideas to borrow and customize.

5    Reconsider the balance between formative and summative assessment purposes.

6    Do a reality check. Can all this really be done in this course? Why not elsewhere?

7    Hold on to the idea that many assessment problems are either (i) not solvable or (ii) most sensibly tackled at programme level, possibly with support at institutional level.

It becomes clear that to take assessment seriously is to make a commitment to look closely at the whole instruction→tasks→assessment sequence. Here it should be understood that the workload involved in reappraising instruction→tasks→ assessment sequences can be considerable, although in good departments this design work can be a collaborative venture, spread over an academic year and supported by educational development professionals. In fact the need to design assessments at programme level makes such collaborative work a necessity.

## Implications for programmes

It is well understood that the complex learning achievements that employers and academics value – understandings, skills, efficacy beliefs and metacognition – tend to take time (what Claxton, 1998, calls 'slow learning'). Plenty of reinforce-ment and practice are needed. Programme-wide planning for learning, teaching and assessment is necessary. Course-level actions are neither sufficient to produce reliable judgements of complex achievements,[5] nor when we expect student development to take place across a whole programme. Clearly, many of the suggestions made for course assessment apply to programme assessment planning but there are also specific programme assessment principles. Those developed in the Skills *plus* project are shown in Box 8.1.

It is important to check that the course assessment plans, taken as a set, do show that those things valued by the programme are picked up by assessment practices. This could be based on an audit and lead to a programme-level spreadsheet similar to the one showing the distribution of learning and teaching methods and to the one showing how the main curricular pathways taken by students contribute to the development of the programme learning outcomes.

Some teams and departments use audits to provide programme-level 'maps' showing:

- The learning outcomes that were *particularly* addressed by each module and how this came together as a coherent and progressive[6] programme[7].
- The teaching and learning methods used by each module in pursuit of the two or three target learning outcomes. There is a check here that the methods are appropriate to the learning intentions and that no methods are over- or under-used.
- The assessment methods used by each module in pursuit of the two or three target learning outcomes. It is assumed that these priority outcomes will be directly assessed and the map shows whether the purposes are formative and low-stakes or summative and high-stakes. There is a check here that the methods are appropriate to the learning intentions and that there is sufficient variety across the programme.

The Skills *plus* project described the work that followed the creation of these maps as 'tuning' work. Maps show areas of over-attention (essays were over-used

---

*Box 8.1* The Skills *plus* programme assessment principles

Entitlements for students' assessment encounters across a programme and in any one year of it should be compatible with their teaching and learning entitlements. That implies, for example, encountering a variety of assessment methods and modes and getting good feedback from a variety of sources. In addition:

- Summative assessment has the important function of providing trust-worthy grades for significant learning achievements. However, by no means all achievements can be affordably and reliably graded with validity. This means that some achievements *should not* be summatively assessed by academic staff.
- Most assessments will be 'low-stakes' assessments, which are intended to improve understanding, or skills, or reflection, or the development of self-theories that sustain achievement.
- Learning criteria should be available at programme and module levels. In many cases these will be 'fuzzy' criteria that guide assessment conver-sations in low-stakes assessment.
- There should be plenty of occasions to get feedback on performance, which will tend to be conversational feedback.
- Peers (other students) will often provide feedback.
- As the programme progresses, students will learn how to become more adept at self-assessment.
- Opportunities and support should be provided to help students create learning portfolios that document their claims to educational and employability achievements. For some achievements, this is the best alternative to more traditional forms of summative assessment.

This entitlement should be explicit in a programme-wide teaching summary.

---

in Knight's History department), under-attention (a Social Science department found that no one made numeracy a priority), and poorly-sequenced attention (as when 'communication' is tackled in year one only, or electronic data handling appears only in the final year). The programme leaders then negotiated with colleagues to adjust the balance. Some historians introduced presentations; a programme leader asked a group of colleagues who were already using a lot of numerical data to declare it a priority and drop, as a priority, *their* concern to promote critical thinking, since this was being tackled elsewhere; electronic data handling was introduced in the first year and declared a priority in an existing second year course; and writing in a variety of forms and for different audiences, already a feature of one second year course, was declared a priority. And so on.

'Tuning' needs programme leaders who know their programmes well and who can use the idea of priority learning outcomes to persuade some colleagues that they can continue to develop critical thinking, which is a priority in some other courses, but that everyone would be helped if they could make it a priority to do so with numerical data, which would allow numeracy to be identified as one of the two or three target learning outcomes for the course. This concept of priority/ target outcomes and 'background' outcomes is very useful because it recognizes that good academic practice necessarily touches many desirable outcomes but, by requiring that two or three priorities be identified, it gets a sharpness of focus that helps teaching, assessment and student learning. Being largely a matter of wheeling and dealing between two or three colleagues at a time, it also avoids the public team-level wrangling that quickly turns into deadlock.

## Implications for teacher workloads

There is a great danger that efforts to improve the range, scope and authenticity of assessment can create enormous amounts of work for teachers who are already busy enough juggling multiple calls on their time. For example, teachers and learners gain from grade indicators or criteria that point to the sorts of things that will be rewarded in a given task. Again, peer and self assessment have great potential. Yet it can be a long, frustrating task to develop useful and concise grade indicators and a lot of work is needed before students become easy with peer and self assessment.

It is no less difficult to persuade colleagues to adopt practices that are based on sound enough educational reasoning but which challenge other values. For example, colleagues often say that assessment is becoming a time monster, depriving them of space to do other important things. We are not the only ones to have suggestions about ways of taming the monster. Twelve of them are:

1   Do not mark long, complicated, authentic assignments. Do make sure that there are plenty of opportunities for students to get feedback on them but do not mark them. For example, require the submission of a portfolio and then assess student learning by means of an in-class assignment – a 500 word critique/analysis/evaluation.
2   Look for opportunities to use formative self and peer assessment instead of summative tutor assessment.
3   Set short tasks. They're often harder. A 500 word essay demands no less reading than a 5,000 word one and a lot more thought, as any academic who has written a short article for a newspaper knows.
4   Set tasks requiring the production of posters, charts and concept maps. They can be quick to mark.

5   In good learning cultures, ones in which they know the 'rules of the game' and understand the criteria to be applied, students are less likely to make a complete mess of assignments, meaning that there are fewer occasions when massive feedback and coaching are necessary.

6   So too when students have worked collaboratively on projects and conversed with one another about drafts.

7   In good learning cultures, students know the grading criteria which are printed on assignment cover-and-feedback sheets. Again, this helps to reduce the incidence of badly-wrong work.

8   Cover/feedback sheets can speed up feedback when students have to identify the indicators that best describe their work (when they have to assess themselves). Sometimes the teacher need write little more than, 'I agree'. Having an idea of the student's judgement of an assignment can also make it easier to give feedback because it precisely identifies any gap between the teacher's and the student's judgements: feedback can be concise because it is targeted. Of course, this does not absolve teachers from giving two or three well-chosen pieces of advice for improving future work of a similar sort.

9   Limit what you say. Most people find up to three major suggestions enough to deal with. Cover/feedback sheets can encourage concision by restricting the space for comment.

10  Consider creating a bank of the feedback statements that you frequently use and then draw on it when you give feedback.

11  If there are lots of errors, mark the first page or two and then return the work for correction.

12  Rather than explaining what is wrong, direct students to sources so that they can find out for themselves.

Teachers often resist these and similar suggestions on the grounds that some involve compromising their beliefs about learning, teaching or what it means to assess well. Evidence of their efficacy is powerless, as is the argument that, in the face of overwork, some compromise on less important beliefs is necessary. It is more important, we argue, to give way on some assessment practices than to persist in using dry and contrived tasks that hardly engage with the ambitious learning intentions of lively academic work and the development of good claims to employability.

## Communicating achievement

Figure 8.1 suggests that assessments lead to warrants or claims, which need to be accompanied by some explanation of the circumstances under which the performance occurred, which we call 'process standards'.

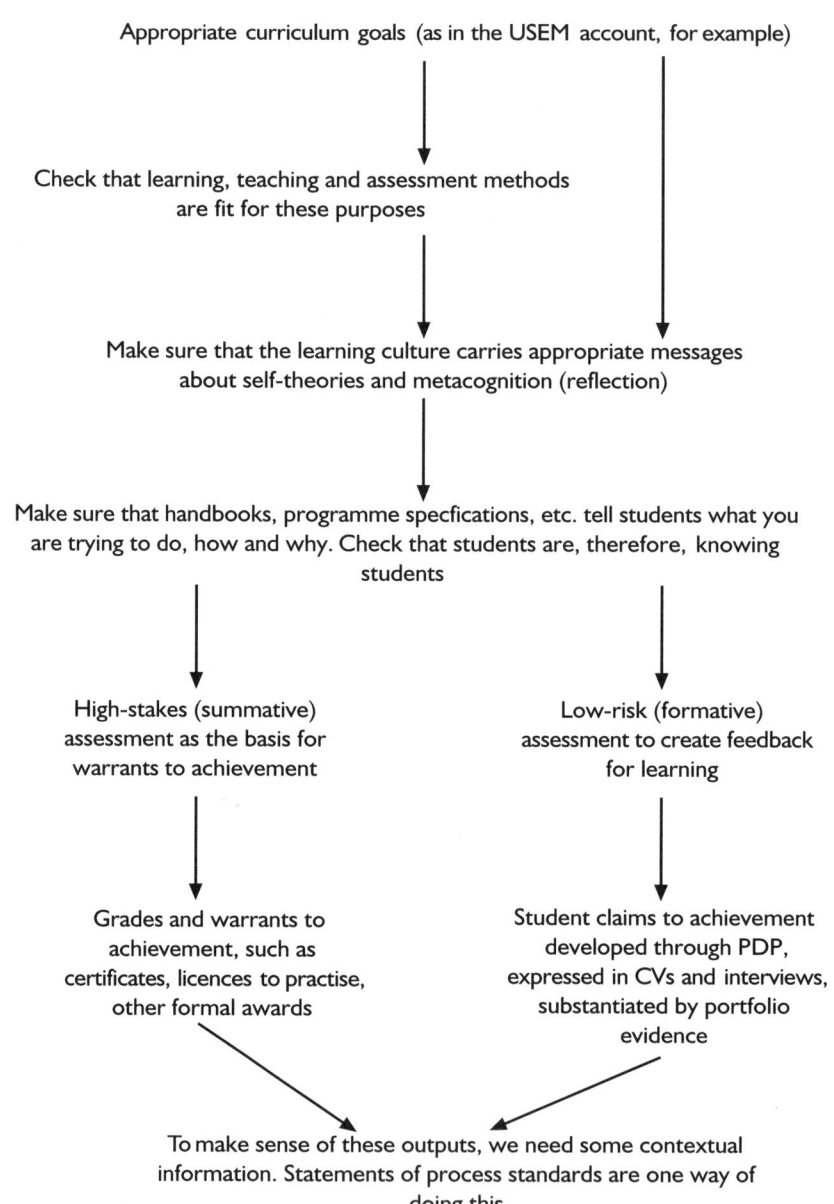

Appropriate curriculum goals (as in the USEM account, for example)

Check that learning, teaching and assessment methods
are fit for these purposes

Make sure that the learning culture carries appropriate messages
about self-theories and metacognition (reflection)

Make sure that handbooks, programme specfications, etc. tell students what you
are trying to do, how and why. Check that students are, therefore, knowing
students

High-stakes (summative)
assessment as the basis for
warrants to achievement

Low-risk (formative)
assessment to create feedback
for learning

Grades and warrants to
achievement, such as
certificates, licences to practise,
other formal awards

Student claims to achievement
developed through PDP,
expressed in CVs and interviews,
substantiated by portfolio
evidence

To make sense of these outputs, we need some contextual
information. Statements of process standards are one way of
doing this

*Figure 8.1* A programme overview of assessment for employability

## Process standards

'Process standards' is a term that invites us to appreciate that the same achievements can come from quite different learning processes. A well-written report might be the product of an individual's unaided engagement with a task, or it might be presented by an individual who has worked with others on a well-defined and pre-structured task. The observer judges the products or claims based upon them, without appreciating the different process standards behind them. Why, though, should this matter? We return to ideas about transitions and translations, introduced in Chapter 1. 'Employable' graduates are more skilled at both, which means that they have the robustness of achievement that comes from tackling 'far transfer'[8] tasks and authentic problems, and from doing so with relatively little 'scaffolding'.[9] Unless employers have some idea of the process standards at work, they are short of information they need to interpret warrants and claims. We suspect this may help explain employers' preference for graduates of some older universities over graduates from lower-status institutions[10] – we have heard of a presumption that Oxbridge graduates, for example, are not spoon-fed, although graduates of some other higher education institutions are.

The relationship between warrants, claims and process standards is sketched in Figure 8.2. However, there is no tradition of describing process standards. While it would not be hard for departments writing references or letters of recommendation for their graduates to append a description of their process standards, we see little prospect in the medium-term of there being satisfactory ways of describing process standards. The problem is not that it is difficult to write statements about the process standards but that it is not possible to authenticate them. Unless accrediting bodies or quality assurance agencies played a part in discouraging inflated claims, the danger is that, like mission statements and other presentational activities, they would be bland, exaggerated and useless.

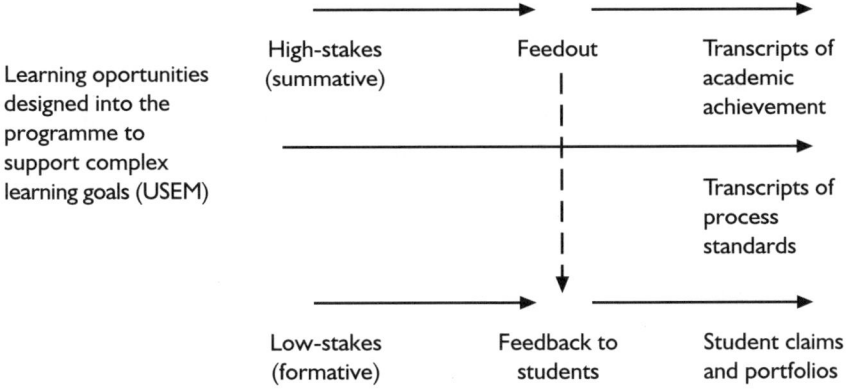

*Figure 8.2*  Three faces of reporting achievement

## Warrants

Certificates, such as those attesting that a student has achieved an upper second class degree, are extremely uninformative. Not only do they say nothing about the achievements that have been recognized with this 2:1 degree, but a series of papers from the Student Assessment and Classification Working Group (SACWG) has shown how similar module mark profiles can lead to rather different degree classifications (Yorke *et al.*, 2000; Bridges *et al.*, 2002; Yorke *et al.*, 2002). In some awards there is an element of norm-referencing.[11] In others, where awards are supposed to be criteria-related, there is evidence that they are used inconsistently (for example, Hornby, 2003). Even if we might presume consistent and reliable application of the criteria, the criteria are not routinely disclosed to employers; sometimes not to students. And even if we did know the sorts of attainments a first class degree represented, we would know nothing about the composition of 'first class-ness'.

The 2002 SACWG conference heard a series of critiques of degree classification practices in England which could be extended to most systems that take marks from a variety of sources and combine them by some formula or another to get a summary, most commonly expressed as a grade point average (GPA) or degree class. While GPAs may look more informative, they simply replace a broad categorization such as 'upper second class' with a number (GPA = 3.4). The same objections apply. Some US business schools – Harvard and Wharton are identified by Minder (2003) – forbid students from disclosing their grades because of fears that recruiters place more weight upon them than they can bear and that it leads students to concentrate on maximizing scores which can be at the expense of learning.[12]

However, the problem as presented at the SACWG conference was not pointing to the weaknesses of these approaches to reporting achievement but identifying alternatives.

Award transcripts are supposed to be more informative. They usually name the modules taken, identify their level and credit rating, and record the grade or mark awarded. Of course, it is not obvious what a mark signifies. Writing of grading practices in Canadian schools, Bercuson and colleagues (1997) complain that the absence of national examinations and standards means that it is impossible to know whether a good mark represents real achievement or low standards. So too with higher education marks. Nor are transcripts normally written in terms of learning outcomes, so that, apart from what can be inferred from the module title, they can be uninformative about what has been learnt (Adelman, 1990).

## Claims, portfolios and personal development planning

Figure 8.2 suggests that students' claims of achievements (and hence to employability) be reported in two ways: through academic transcripts, which would be part of a student's progress file and which describe achievements that the institution is prepared to warrant or certify, and through portfolios derived from personal development planning. Statements of process standards would, ideally, provide contextual background for these two reporting routes.

It is intended that, amongst other things, personal development planning (PDP) will be integrative by encouraging students to reflect on their learning, needs and developmental plans *as a whole*. It is neither a pastoral process nor an academic one, but a synoptic one. This is usually represented by a dossier or portfolio, which comprises

- A store of evidence that can be used to support claims to achievement.
- An indexing system to identify which claims can be supported by which essays, certificates, letters of appreciation, products, software, etc.
- Claims to achievement, which are often adapted to particular purposes, such as making different job applications and applying to graduate school.

All or part of the portfolio may be in electronic form and many universities are exploring online systems, such as RAPID, which is mentioned in Chapter 10. In England, PDP, which is supposed to be available in 2005/6 to all undergraduates, is usually seen as a process of:

- Reviewing achievements, which can be in-class, out-of-class or out-of-college achievements, whether specific (achieving more 'B' grades than ever before) or general (being more creative in academic work).
- Identifying learning needs, which can involve others, such as tutors or advisors, in choosing courses and careers, or identifying areas of weakness – written communication, for instance – upon which to concentrate in the next semester.
- Planning how to address these needs, which operates at several levels: how to improve performance on assessed tasks, how to improve performance on particular learning outcomes, choosing courses, career planning and job seeking.
- Representing achievements, typically for employability purposes, usually through a portfolio.

PDP is a set of processes that are valuable in their own right and a product – the portfolio – that can help to secure employment, especially when the portfolio is explicitly presented as a *curriculum vitae*-building process. It follows that a PDP scheme must ensure that:

- There is guidance that addresses generic learning and study needs.
- There is guidance on how to address subject-specific learning needs.
- There is guidance on career planning and job seeking.
- There is support for and guidance on making and maintaining portfolios that will sustain strong claims to employability.

- Students have a language, which might be based on the programme specification, in which to represent their achievements; and they are familiar, particularly through formative assessment, with the practice of making and supporting claims to achievement.

Plainly, it is in everyone's interests for departments to integrate guidance and support provided by specialists in generic learning and study practices, careers specialists and subject staff. PDP also takes staff and student time; it can look like a bean-counting activity; it can resemble school records of achievement, which are widely ignored; it is likely to be optional, and optional activities are taken up by a minority; it will rarely be embedded in mainstream programme design, except in programmes leading to professional registration. In short, unless PDP is integrated, well-designed and cleverly organized, it risks being either a time-eating monster or a mere curiosity, inspected by a few enthusiasts. Klenowski (2002: Chapter 4) has a useful summary of such difficulties.

Yet, in terms of employability, portfolios and the supporting processes are invaluable because how else are the complex achievements that higher education values, but cannot (afford to) warrant, to be represented?

## The demand side again

Even if we could have confidence in universities' judgements of students' achievements, recruiters will not necessarily pick the best. In subtle ways all sorts of factors lead some graduates to experience disadvantage. In part this is due to the methods used to select new graduate hires and in part to underlying assumptions. Assessment centres, for instance, are widely used by big firms hiring graduates, but Sternberg (1997) has argued that assessment centre judgements do not correlate well with career success – those who did best in assessment centres are by no means those whose careers flourish the most. Other firms prefer to appoint from students doing work placements or other co-curriculum activities with them: 'test-driving your next employee' as it is called in an article in *Graduate Recruiter*, April 2003. While their reasoning is impeccable – they have seen what the student can do in context, with real tasks – the difficulty is that students who get and who can afford to get placements with these firms are not always a representative sample of the cohort.[13]

There are also difficulties with the underlying assumption that the best person for the job can be identified. Assessment and selection procedures cannot be so precise. Instead of basing judgements upon absolute achievement, it would be better to recognize that any one of a number of people could do the job well and that those who have made strong progress during their degree studies might have the greatest potential for further learning. Even if this is too radical, this reasoning challenges the invalid practice of using school leaving grades as a criterion in graduate recruitment.

## The challenge of assessing for employability

Only by adopting differentiated approaches to assessment – not all high-stakes, not all direct – and by *planning assessment across programmes* can we sensibly promote employability through assessment and really help students to represent their achievements to employers. This is a more challenging statement than it might seem at first sight. After all, how widespread is programme assessment planning? And how can higher education institutions let go of the belief that the learning outcomes that they take such care in specifying need to be assessed summatively?

## Three accounts of work undertaken during the life of Skills *plus*

The following three chapters describe the work three departments undertook within the Skills *plus* project in order to improve the contribution their existing programmes made to student employability. None was able to do a 'green field' job and construct a curriculum from first principles and none had the time to get as far as they would have liked with 'tuning' their programmes. We present these accounts because they show what was done in circumstances that are probably fairly representative of higher education in the UK.

We then set out in Chapter 12 some principles of procedure, based on the ideas developed in Chapters 6–8 and the following accounts of experiences with Skills *plus*. We believe that these principles are useful to others who want to enhance the help that their programmes can give to students in making good claims to graduate employability.

## Notes

1    A lot of 'key skills' assessment is based on the mistaken proposition that it is possible to assess them with high reliability in a single module and without significant investment of resources. Teachers may feel inadequate because they know that something is amiss but do not realize that what they are trying to do is simply not possible.
2    See http://www.cityu.edu.hk/op/plan_part2.htm.
3    See http://www.qaa.ac.uk/crntwork/benchmark/benchmarking.htm.
4    There is an index to subject centres at www.ltsn.ac.uk.
5    This is because reliable judgements should be based on evidence from different judges, made at different times on the basis of different tasks and, perhaps, in different settings.
6    'Progressive' refers to progression in student learning across a programme. What arrangements are made to ensure that students at the end of the programme have achievements that are qualitatively different from those that they had on entry? Just graduating with more information would not speak well of a programme's arrangements for progression.
7    For many programmes, where there is high choice and many electives, this mapping may be restricted to core courses or to the most popular sequences of courses. A large general programme may have hundreds of associated modules, but most students will follow one of several broad pathways. These can be identified by analyzing student transcripts. Assessment maps can then be made for the most significant ones.

8　Tasks that ask us to apply understandings or practices to fairly familiar, well-defined (or 'tame') problems are 'near transfer' tasks. 'Far transfer' tasks are better tests of understanding and application.

9　'Scaffolding' refers to the degree to which tasks are 'tamed' for the learner: for example, to the degree to which they are near transfer tasks, the clarity of the task specification, the degree of task structure provided, and the amount of help from others designed into the activity.

10　There are other reasons for this, of course, including graduates' higher academic scores when they entered the more elite institutions, tradition and the greater prestige of older institutions. It is also quite possible that graduates from older universities have more 'social capital' and present themselves more easily as the sorts of people employers want. Anthony Hesketh of Lancaster University has described this as 'the aestheticization of the self': employability is a matter of presenting oneself attractively in terms of employers' preferences.

11　Norm-referenced awards are based on the candidate's position in the class. The quality of the class is an unknown factor, as is the quality of the candidate's performance.

12　Dweck (1999) would perhaps see this in terms of a bias towards performance goals at the expense of learning goals.

13　Although some university departments are careful about this. The Department of Building and Construction at City University, Hong Kong, provides a lot of employability-enhancing activities in the co-curriculum (as supplementary options). They use their teaching excellence award money from the university to make sure that all students get some co-curricular experience.

# Chapter 9

# The Skills *plus* project and nursing

*Geraldine Lyte*

## Introduction

This chapter presents some of the continuing educational developments in the School of Nursing, Midwifery and Health Visiting, University of Manchester, arising from the School's involvement in the Skills *plus* project. The project's key aim has been to build curriculum, learning, teaching and assessment (LTA) practices that enhance students' employability. It might be asked why a School of Nursing should want to become involved in a project to fine-tune curricula, with the purposes of enhancing students' employability, when the professional component of all nursing programmes is designed to prepare students specifically for employment in the healthcare sector. The project was, in fact, timely for nursing because it was initiated at a time when nursing education was considered to be too theoretically driven to prepare its students adequately for the workplace (Glen and Clark, 1999). Our curriculum planning teams felt that the adoption of the USEM framework to support curriculum development would have both professional and academic benefits. For example, by focusing on the development of subject (in our case nursing), research and key transferable skills, all of which the USEM framework embraces, it could contribute to an individual's employability at the point of registration, as recommended by the English Department of Health (DoH, 1999), the United Kingdom Central Council for Nursing, Midwifery and Health Visiting (UKCC, 1999), the Dearing Report (NCIHE, 1997) and the 2003 English White Paper (DfES, 2003). Our Nursing School wanted to use its involvement in the project to evaluate existing LTA practices and undergraduate achievements in preparation for the development of a new programme for 2002.

The case raises half a dozen issues of wider interest:

- It shows that the USEM account of employability is compatible with the need to educate nurses to high academic and professional standards.
- The account can be applied beneficially to existing practices.
- Incremental change is a feasible strategy for enhancing the contribution that curricula make to employability.
- USEM is a convenient formula for directing attention to the range of achievements that a professional programme needs to consider.

- USEM assumes that LTA approaches will be orchestrated with the intention of stimulating employability. This study shows that problem-based learning is one route to alignment.
- As Figure 9.2 suggests, USEM can help to integrate the disparate concerns of programmes with diverse aims and pathways to the award of a degree.

The programme concerned is a Bachelor of Nursing (Hons). The BN consists of a foundation period for all students, who can then choose in the second part of the programme to specialize in adult general nursing or mental heath nursing. It was selected for the Skills *plus* activity because it is a well-established programme for prospective nurses that was preparing to expand its provision to include a child health pathway and increase its number of available places. The BN traditionally recruited 40 high calibre students annually from across the country; this rose to approximately 70 students in 2001 and is set to rise again to help meet workforce requirements in the National Health Service (NHS).

Our School also offers a full-time Diploma in Professional Studies in Nursing (DPSN), which recruits several hundred students per annum. During the initial activity involved in the Skills *plus* project, the DPSN was already undergoing a major re-validation to revise its provision and to offer its students the opportunity to transfer to advanced diploma or degree pathways, depending on their academic progression. Although it was felt unwise to involve that programme directly in Skills *plus* audit and interviewing activity, the work on the BN has helped to inform DPSN development, which has used the USEM framework for its new curriculum, most clearly to support its newly proposed pathways.

Two Skills *plus* audits, focusing first on learning, teaching and assessment practices and then on the outcomes they promoted, were completed within the BN programme. Six newly qualified BN graduates and their employers were then interviewed about employability issues. Finally, a survey was done with first and final year students, using the USEM framework to explore the development of key skills, nursing skills, research skills and students' overall personal and professional development. The findings were fed into the main Skills *plus* project and into curriculum development in the School's pre-registration undergraduate programmes – the new BN and the DPSN programmes – as it was considered an ideal approach to meet the academic and clinical requirements for undergraduate nursing programmes. The distinctive attention to efficacy beliefs and metacognition sat well with our professional emphasis on reflection and on personal qualities and attributes.

This chapter now reviews what the undergraduate programme team concerned has learnt about employability and curriculum development from its involvement in the Skills *plus* project.

## Auditing and reviewing the 1997–2001 Bachelor of Nursing (Hons) programme

Prior to re-validation in 2002, the BN programme offered a series of subject-based units of learning within five core modules that were designed to help students acquire a broad base of knowledge and skills for clinical practice. The first Skills *plus* audit assessed the range of learning, teaching and assessment activities used by lecturing staff, within all five core modules. This constituted a range of units of learning to promote academic, clinical and research skills (Table 9.1).

Lecturers identified their LTA activities for each unit of learning (a sample of one unit's LTA activities is provided in Table 9.2) and the data were collated for each academic year. The tables showed that students and their teachers used a wide variety of activities to develop nursing, research and core skills. Research skills development was strongly in evidence throughout each module and it was judged important to build on this strength in the revised BN programme by increasing the focus on the relationship of research and evidence-based healthcare. Activities that encourage self directed learning, experiential learning, teamwork and clinical skills development appeared to be scarce in parts of the programme. Research in nursing education has advocated the use of such activities, principally through the adoption of enquiry-based approaches such as problem-based learning. The intention is that such activities will make students better prepared for employment in today's health service (Frost, 1996). The BN applied problem-based learning in parts of its programme and planned to extend this application for both the existing and future curricula.

The second audit enquired about the skills promoted by the five core modules of the BN programme. The point of reference was the list of 39 aspects of employability that are shown in Box 2.1. Ten of the BN teaching team, selected because of their particular knowledge about and/or strategic involvement in the programme, participated in the second audit. Each identified qualities and skills from the list of 39 aspects that were stimulated within their core modules. The findings suggested that many important aspects of employability for nursing practice were addressed in the BN programme, in that most of the 39 were explicitly developed. However, just as the LTA audit, although broadly reassuring, showed some gaps, varying degrees of development were in evidence in this second audit: for example, there were qualities and skills that students were expected to develop without there being a specific curriculum emphasis upon them, including self-confidence, problem-solving, awareness of international health issues and the ability to work cross-culturally.

In sum, although many aspects of employability appear to be addressed by the BN programme, a greater emphasis on the development of certain personal qualities, core and process skills was identified as a priority for fine tuning in the existing programme and then for development in the 2002 curriculum. The 2002 development has also had to take account of demands arising from changing political and professional expectations of what constitutes an 'employable' newly qualified staff nurse. These expectations are illustrated most clearly in two recent

Table 9.1 Core modules and units of learning in the BN programme

| Core modules | Units of learning | | | | |
|---|---|---|---|---|---|
| Biological Sciences | Anatomy | Physiology | Pharmacology | Pathology | Microbiology |
| Social and Behavioural Sciences | Sociology | Psychology | Health Psychology | Social Policy | Health Policy |
| Nursing Theory and Practice (Adult) | All Clinical Practice Units | Nursing Theory and Informatics | Adult Nursing Theory Level 2 | Theoretical Framework of Nursing | Organization and Management of Care |
| Nursing Theory and Practice (Mental Health) | All Clinical Practice Units | Nursing Theory and Informatics | Mental Health Nursing Theory Level 2 | Theoretical Framework of Nursing | Organization and Management of Care |
| Health Studies | Neighbourhood Study | Health Promotion | Epidemiology | Family Study | Specialist Practitioner Units (Yr 4) |
| Professional Studies | Communication Skills | Teaching and Assessing | Counselling Skills | Information Technology | All Research Units |

*Table 9.2* Range of learning, teaching or assessment activities in one mixed theory/ practice unit of learning

| | |
|---|---|
| Lectures | X |
| Seminars | X |
| Tutorials | X |
| Work on standard problems/case studies | |
| Work on less structured problems | |
| Structured work in peer groups | X |
| Self-directed peer group work | |
| Structured independent study | X |
| Self-directed learning | |
| Clinical work/visits | X |
| Team work | |
| Practicals (lab. or IT) to learn skill | |
| Practicals (lab. or IT) to solve problems | |
| Workshops | |
| Web searching for materials | X |
| Set reading books/articles | X |
| Reviewing literature | X |
| Use of original sources (e.g. archives) | |
| Make video or tape-slide presentation | |
| Essays | |
| Examination | X (summative) |
| Group project | |
| Critique | |
| Multiple-choice questions | |
| Self assessment | |
| Peer assessment | |
| Oral presentation | X (formative) |
| Poster or web poster | |
| Experiential learning | |
| Research dissertation | |

X indicates learning, teaching or assessment activity identified in this unit.

English Department of Health documents, *The New NHS: Modern, Dependable* (DoH, 1997), and *Making a Difference* (DoH, 1999) and the UKCC's Peach Report (UKCC, 1999). The 1997 DoH document made recommendations for extending the skills base of nurses' roles, whilst the 1999 DoH document and the Peach Report provide more detailed proposals to strengthen the nursing, midwifery and health visiting contributions to healthcare. For example, the 1999 DoH document outlines measures for new ways of working for nurses in healthcare that require a greater emphasis on extended competencies and skills development, in the context of a changing NHS. Our curriculum planning team was keen to embrace such proposals to help our students to develop further skills for clinical decision-making and care, leadership and innovation.

Before the findings from the audits could be widely used to inform curriculum planning for the BN, student and employer inputs into Skills *plus* were sought.

Six BN graduates and their employers were interviewed. This offered another and sometimes critical perspective of the quality of the BN programme, especially in relation to how ready new practitioners felt for their role, and how employers rated their skills and competencies. The interviews were analyzed and considered alongside reports of interviews done elsewhere within the Skills *plus* project. There were also distinctive nursing-specific elements which concerned the BN team. For example, whilst both the new graduates and their employers were largely positive about the utility and quality of the BN programme, there was less enthusiasm from students about the ways in which practical nursing skills were being developed:

> things that you get asked as a health visitor all the time ... I mean the basic things like ... everyday sort of development, things like that, I think we did learn at university, em, – but apart from that, like, there was quite a lot that was missed out, I'd say.
>
> (BN graduate working as a health visitor)

> Em ... practical things like that you're not allowed to do as a student, and that's sort of, I think it worries a lot of newly qualified nurses, that you know, they've never done, they've watched things being done ... hundreds of times during their training, but they've never been allowed to do it, so, so I think it's something that worries.
>
> (BN graduate working as a hospital-based nurse)

This illustrates a familiar issue in nursing education, whereby a division can exist between the planned curriculum and what students perceive they learn. Conversely, both students and their employers highlighted some of the theory and practice components of the programme which they felt were really integrated with the reality of clinical work:

> They're [the new graduates] quite confident ... they speak out, em, and are able to sort of argue your point and not be intimidated at all by other people who might be on the working party.
>
> (Employer)

> I would hope doing the degree they [new graduates] would have some sort of insight into other issues that are going on, wider issues, sociology issues, whatever the latest White Paper is, and targets and some audit skills and, em, – yeh – it's what I'd expect to see.
>
> (Senior ward manager)

> It seemed to come when you were on the placements because you did, say, em, a lot of, say, anatomy and physiology whilst you were at university, and then you saw it in practice.
>
> (BN graduate working as a hospital-based nurse)

These interviews, although not representative of the total population of our students and employers, highlight issues that have also been identified in routine evaluations of the BN programme.

Finally, the perspectives of students, both beginning and nearing the end of the programme, were sought. All first year (n = 71) and final year (n = 34) students were asked to participate in a Skills *plus* survey to rate their skills attainment and general beliefs about life as undergraduates. Students were asked to respond to 24 closed questions and four open questions. Forty-six (65 per cent) first year students and twenty-one (62 per cent) final year students participated. There were some interesting comparisons between the two groups: for example, 91 per cent of first year students agreed that the amount of work they invested in their studies was reflected in their assignment grades, whereas only 62 per cent of final year students shared this opinion. This may reflect the difference in the demands and complexity of assignments between the two groups. In another example, 57 per cent of first years agreed that they liked learning in situations in which they could frame learning activities, and this figure rose to 75 per cent for final year students. This difference is consistent with findings from both written and oral evaluations of the BN programme, where students appear to benefit from more structure and teacher support in the earlier parts of their studies. This was a very important consideration for preparations for the new programme for 2002, in deciding the extent to which the BN would adopt problem-based learning as its main learning–teaching strategy. This will be discussed in more detail later in the chapter. In other parts of the survey, responses from the two student groups were more similar. Eighty-seven per cent of first years and 90 per cent of final years stated that they were stimulated by the challenge of difficult problems, and all respondents from both groups regarded employment as a good opportunity to learn new things. These findings offered significant insight into students' motivations for learning and meeting the demands of clinical problem-solving.

## Skills *plus* and the 2002 Bachelor of Nursing (Hons) programme

The findings from the audits, interviews and survey, carried out as part of the wider Skills *plus* project, were very influential in the design of the new curriculum for the Manchester BN programme. Analyses that were supportive of the existing programme highlighted strengths that could be continued into the new programme, such as the development of research skills. Analyses that indicated where there was scope for improvement, for example, for further development of problem-solving skills, provided part of the rationale for making changes, particularly for the learning and teaching strategy. In the past, several traditional curriculum models have been used, with mixed success, for the development of nursing programmes in England (for example, Lawton, 1983). However, nursing education has had continuing difficulty addressing a so-called theory/practice gap (Spouse, 2001), which is a practical and ideological difference between students' classroom, placement and employment experiences. It is therefore understandable that recent reviews of nursing education provision in the United Kingdom (UKCC, 1999) say that newly qualified staff nurses do not always have the necessary and/or appropriate skills for their practice roles.

In order to address this in the 2002 BN programme, the curriculum planning team opted for a unitized framework in which each unit would focus on the development of nursing knowledge and skills for employability, lifelong learning and personal development (Figure 9.1). This tackles one set of problems but the concentration on courses/units makes it harder to achieve the programme coherence which was so valued by the Skills *plus* project.

The team aimed to provide students with a stimulating and facilitative learning environment, to enable them to acquire the in-depth understanding of multicultural health and of causes of ill-health that underpins nursing and multi-professional healthcare in primary, secondary and tertiary settings. Other aims for the new programme included the development of students' insight into clients' needs and the development of the nursing and generic skills necessary to deal with different practice situations and to participate fully in the effective management of client care.

**Year one**
Common foundation programme

| **Year two** | | |
|---|---|---|
| *Semester one* | *Semester two* | *Extended semester two* |
| Care of people with common mental health problems | Acute care of individuals with mental health needs and their families | Elective unit (students choose a placement) |
| **Year three** | | |
| *Semester one* | *Semester two* | *Extended semester two* |
| Care of individuals with serious and enduring mental health problems in the community | Care of older people with mental health needs | Management and consolidation of practice |
| Dissertation | | |

*Figure 9.1* The BN curriculum framework, showing the mental health nursing option

## The BN curriculum model

The BN curriculum model combines professional and academic criteria. The main points of reference were:

- United Kingdom Central Council for Nursing, Midwifery and Health Visiting[1] (UKCC) nursing competencies (UKCC, 2001);
- Quality Assurance Agency for Higher Education (QAA) Academic and Practitioner Standards for Nursing (QAA, 2001b);
- The USEM framework from Skills *plus*, adapted for undergraduate pre-registration nursing education;
- The literature on problem-based learning, which was chosen as the major learning and teaching strategy.

## UKCC nursing competencies and QAA standards for nursing

The UKCC nursing competencies and QAA standards for nursing represent statutory requirements for inclusion in nursing programmes. They represent the basic range of skills and knowledge that students need to demonstrate in order to register as a nurse and seek employment.

## The Skills plus USEM framework

The USEM framework for the BN programme was appropriate because of the project's declared concern with graduate employability and – crucially – with the 'low pain, high gain' strategies for shaping undergraduate curricula to enhance it. Unlike curriculum models previously used, USEM offered the BN a framework adaptable to the outcomes associated with professional practice and with higher education. In particular, efficacy beliefs and metacognition together facilitate the integrated development of practice skills through the curriculum when they are combined with a concern to develop knowledge, understanding and skills. The task was then to design into units of learning, practice-based learning and classroom teaching, a good range of opportunities or *affordances*. This was to stimulate individuals to develop the range of achievements described by the programme specification, and to explore beyond their immediate goals and consider what they might become in the longer term in their chosen profession. In such ways USEM combines a concern to ensure students' fitness for practice (competence) with the higher order cognitive skills required for the University of Manchester's academic awards. Figure 9.2 illustrates how the USEM framework was applied for the BN programme. It outlines what core knowledge and skills are to be developed for nursing employability, in tandem with personal development and reflection.

| *The USEM framework* | |
|---|---|
| **Understanding**<br>Nurses should acquire understanding of the subject areas they study. Evidence for employers that an individual has passed a threshold of competence in under-standing complex nursing subject matter will be demonstrated by the academic qualification they receive in tandem with their professional registration. | **Skills**<br>Competence to practise as a graduate nurse will be demonstrated using three types of interrelated skills.<br>Nursing-specific skills that meet the competencies set out by the UKCC (2001).<br>Research skills required to engage in evidence-based healthcare and/or to conduct further systematic inquiry into nursing and healthcare.<br>Key transferable skills that relate to the ability to do things that are widely valued, but which are not tied to any particular situation or subject area. |
| **Efficacy beliefs**<br>Efficacy beliefs are the set of ideas that people have about themselves: their efficacy and scope and self-confidence that can make a difference in nursing practice or other given situations. | **Metacognition**<br>Metacognition is concerned with reflecting and capitalizing on one's own learning and actions to best effect. In nursing this means being ready and being able to think about the best way to act in a situation. It is a necessary component of self-directed learning, about planning for future situations and for promoting life-long learning. |

*Figure 9.2* The USEM Framework from Skills *plus* adapted for undergraduate nursing

## A matched learning and teaching strategy

The teaching and learning approaches for the BN programme had to be designed to promote the development of the outcomes implied by the USEM account and appropriate for nursing practice and leadership. 'Authentic' learning and assessment arrangements were needed, on the assumption that students will benefit from 'authentic' learning and tend to be more employable because they learn better when goals, learning and assessment methods are in alignment. This emphasis on 'deep' approaches to learning was consolidated in the BN by adopting problem-based learning, which is reported to facilitate a more student-centred approach to learning and to encourage a closer relation of theory to students' clinical work. Problem-based learning is noted for its focus on the student's experience of learning through analysis, intervention for and evaluation of problems, situations or circumstances that are posed within a programme of learning (Wilkie and Burns, 2003). It is characterized by small group learning in which students direct their own learning process, supported by a lecturer who takes on the role of facilitator. The problem, situation or circumstance is designed to emulate real-life situations for students to work with. For nursing students, problems can be developed from a range of different learning environments they may find themselves in during the course of their programme, such as a short stay hospital ward, a GP (general practitioner) practice, or a visit to a mother and newborn baby at their home. The process usually begins when students are provided with a brief scenario, from which they have to clarify terms and identify key issues to address. Once this is achieved they consider possible explanations, develop learning outcomes, agree rules for group process, collect evidence, arrange periodic meetings with their facilitator for feedback, support and further information, and finally, present their findings and conclusions. This latter component is sometimes used as an assessment strategy for problem-based learning-based curricula (Boud and Feletti, 1997).

Problem-based learning was initially introduced into the BN programme in the mid-1990s. The nursing theory and practice module piloted the approach for a number of years and was subject to formal evaluation in 1999. Drawing on the accounts of students and facilitators, it highlighted strengths of, and disadvantages with, problem-based learning. A particular strength was that students found that they used more evidence from research to support their decision-making. However, they also reported that the facilitator role was ambiguous and that there was insufficient time to meet in groups due to the demands of the other, teacher-led units. Facilitators experienced difficulties in supporting group learning, especially in determining what support they should offer. The findings were used to improve the learning and facilitation process on the existing programme, including proposals for staff development for facilitation (Barrow *et al.*, 2002). Several units of learning in other modules subsequently applied problem-based learning, although there was little or no co-ordination between units and/or the problems that were presented to students. However, problem-based learning in the 2002 programme was designed to integrate subject matter within units of learning, focusing on a core of professional practice, and sharing aims and learning outcomes. The new curriculum also aimed to foster the development of positive efficacy beliefs and metacognition by promoting student-centred learning through group experiences and individual learning and reflection. Evidence of learning could come, for example, by referring to developing competence in making clinical judgements and decisions, and to skill in identifying clinical practices in need of further research.

While appreciating the likely benefits of problem-based learning, the BN team recognized the value of more traditional systems to support learning. This hybrid approach (i.e. problem-based learning and traditional teacher-led input) was considered a strength for the new BN curriculum for several reasons. The audits, interviews and survey findings from Skills *plus* demonstrated the existing strengths and rigour within the theoretical components of the programme, particularly in the development of research knowledge and skills. More traditional teaching approaches also offered the facility for lectures and other presentations from academic and practice-based experts who are the current innovators and leaders within healthcare. It was considered essential to maintain these strengths by continuing to include material and approaches that had been very positively evaluated by students, lecturers, practitioners and external reviewers. For example,

*Table 9.3* Problem-based learning applied in the Manchester BN programme

| | |
|---|---|
| Year 1, Foundation Studies | In the foundation year, the emphasis is on a combination of teacher-led subject-based units of learning and application of subject-based material within clinical problem-based situations. During this time students are also prepared for more self-directed and small group learning techniques, with particular emphasis on classroom/clinical interaction and interpersonal relationships and group learning processes. |
| Year 2, Branch Year 1* | In year one of the branch, students will still be guided by pre-set modular learning outcomes and facilitator guidance for small group work. However, the emphasis will switch to student-led small group work, based on real client case studies. |
| Year 3, Branch Year 2 | In year two of the branch, students will be expected to take increasing responsibility for developing their own learning outcomes and for managing the small group learning process with the support of a facilitator. |

* Branch studies relate to the options for specializing: children's, adult or mental health nursing.

a core unit of learning in the final year of the BN programme involves writing a dissertation. This unit had benefited from a project internally funded by the university, to develop core content and standards for undergraduate dissertation students and their supervisors. In addition, it had been our experience that beginning students seek more support and structure within a programme of learning. A hybrid model of problem-based learning was therefore agreed and the model designed for the BN programme is presented in Table 9.3. It illustrates how the first year focuses on orientation to learning and working, both in groups and individually. The problem-based learning process described above is still applied, except the facilitator provides more structure and support by developing learning outcomes for students, setting meeting times and joining in group discussions. In year two and particularly in year three, the process of learning will become more student-focused. They will be encouraged to be more independent in problem-solving and decision-making, in preparation for their initial employment.

## Monitoring the impact of the new BN programme

The revised BN programme started in September 2002, six months before this chapter was written. The first year students and their facilitators evaluated the first semester and early indications suggest that the skills focus of the USEM framework, applied through problem-based learning, is having a positive impact on students' development. In particular, problem-based learning appears to foster closer relationships between students and their facilitators because of the emphasis on interaction within the classroom. However, it is too early in the programme for a robust evaluation, especially because students have not had sufficient problem-based learning-based learning or work-based experience to measure attributes such as a positive self-efficacy.

In addition to the internal monitoring mechanisms for the BN, a research-based evaluation has been proposed. The key aim of this evaluation will be to explore the assimilation of USEM, applied through problem-based learning, and employability. The evaluation will be conducted using case study research of students' development, employability and initial employment. In carrying out this research it will be possible to demonstrate the extent to which the curriculum model, and application of USEM in particular, have equipped students with the necessary knowledge, skills and qualities to fulfil the aims of the programme and meet the current and future needs of employers.

## Concluding comment

Since the Skills *plus* project began in August 2000 it has had a big impact on both new and existing undergraduate nursing curricula at the University of Manchester. The project has been particularly influential because USEM offers a user-friendly design to help higher education providers and their partners (in our case, NHS trusts) to focus on developing and fine-tuning their curricula; in the School's case, it has been able to draw on the work that has been produced from the main Skills *plus* project to support BN curriculum development. The methods used (for example, audits) have been a particular strength, especially for helping nursing to challenge the usefulness of curriculum frameworks that were, perhaps, too theoretically driven. They have also helped to highlight existing good practices in learning, teaching and assessment from key stakeholder perspectives.

Most importantly, involvement in the Skills *plus* project has promoted cross-fertilisation of ideas between participating institutions and across the different disciplines represented in the overall project. This has further informed curriculum planning in our School and brought to our educational research and development the benefits of inter-disciplinary collaboration.

## Note

1   It became the Nursing and Midwifery Council (NMC) in 2002.

## Chapter 10

# Skills *plus* and the Construction Management programme at Liverpool John Moores University

*Aled Williams*

### The context of education for the built environment

Currently there is much discussion of curriculum issues within the construction and surveying bodies, which has led to divergent positions because of differing perspectives on professional accreditation. The Chartered Institute of Building (CIOB) has for some time maintained its course accreditation criteria and entry standards. The rationale of the CIOB favours a largely 'inclusive', output-oriented approach. This reflects the added value to student capabilities that derives from the completion of a programme of study, evidenced through the assessment outcomes and abilities as defined by the CIOB syllabus. At the time of the work reported in this chapter the CIOB required that modules had to be evidenced against a prescriptive mapping document, their *Educational Framework* (1995). This makes certain areas of study compulsory for all students, thus putting a limit on flexibility.

In contrast, the Royal Institution of Chartered Surveyors (RICS) has developed annual threshold standards for the accreditation of courses in 'partner institutions' (RICS, 2001). Each individual university partnership course is expected to meet four threshold measures which comprise: entry standards, research quality, teaching quality and employment of graduates. The recruitment policy adopted by the RICS aims to attract 'high flyers', by working to a threshold that requires that 75 per cent of the cohort at each level have an average of 17 points at 'A' level (230 UCAS points) or equivalent. This gives rise to an 'exclusive', input-oriented, stratified intake and stratified profession.

The alignment of teaching, learning and assessment with the requirements of professional bodies, industry *and* universities is of paramount importance. Consequently, designers of built environment courses have to try to strike an appropriate balance between education and training. Even though the emphasis of the vocational courses in the area of the built environment is discipline-specific, the courses also incorporate a grounding in general management, legal matters, economics, finance and team building. In other words, on programmes in the built environment, students learn both discipline-specific and generic skills (including 'soft' skills).

Biggs (1999), following Leinhardt *et al.* (1995), makes a distinction between 'professional' knowledge and 'university' knowledge:

- *Professional knowledge* is procedural, specific and pragmatic. It deals with executing, applying and making priorities
- *University knowledge* is declarative, abstract and conceptual. It deals with labelling, differentiating, elaborating and justifying

(Biggs, 1999: 41)

Biggs suggests that, when teaching for the professions, the integration of different fields of knowledge has tended to be left to the student. However, his position does not describe very well an overtly vocational programme, such as a built environment degree, in which the intention is to blend the declarative and procedural forms of knowledge at lower and higher levels. The implication of Biggs's suggestion for this chapter is that the learning that takes place on built environment courses (the acquisition of knowledge, skills and understanding) is differentiated from that integrative learning that occurs within the construction industry. To complicate matters, the construction industry is in a state of flux and there is an increasing emphasis on developing its professionals to be reflective practitioners.

## Background to the BSc (Hons) in Construction Management

The School of the Built Environment (SOBE) at Liverpool John Moores University participated in Skills *plus*. My role in this involved looking at how employability skills interact within a construction curriculum, taking a programme perspective. The course chosen for the School's involvement in Skills *plus* was the BSc (Hons) in Construction Management, which is vocationally-based and accredited by the Chartered Institute of Building (CIOB).

Learning outcomes for the Construction Management programme are driven by industry requirements and can to some extent be altered over time in order to meet the requirements as they evolve. The School's Industrial Liaison Group, sandwich 'year out' employers, and professional body requirements inform the course content. The CIOB *Educational Framework* (1995) is quite prescriptive as to the recommended modules/elements to be included within the course syllabus, although this has recently been revised (CIOB, 2002). The practice has therefore been for the Head of Studies to map the course modules and compare them against the CIOB core competencies for each academic level in order to secure professional accreditation for the programme.[1]

The Construction Management course is a four-year sandwich degree where the third year is the professional training element. Currently, there are approximately 24 students at each level. The selection of this programme for engagement with Skills *plus* took into account the following:

- This long-standing course has a good employment track record and is highly regarded within the industry.
- Participation would, it was hoped, inform any developments in the Construction Management programme.
- The School's Teaching and Learning Co-ordinator was formerly the Head of Studies for this programme.

The Skills *plus* project involved analyses, or audits, of the expectations of the individual core modules within the Construction Management programme. Auditing took place at each of the three levels in order to identify gaps or duplications in provision and to highlight areas of the programme where further, more detailed exploration might be required. The analytic work involved an examination of the programme handbook. Contributions to the analysis were made by the Teaching and Learning Co-ordinator and Head of Academic Programmes.

Another engagement in Skills *plus* was an investigation of the contribution that Built Environment courses in higher education make to graduate employability. Structured interviews were carried out with graduates, line managers and human resource managers at contrasting construction organizations. These were intended to elicit understandings of how employability and skills development were understood in the workplace, which, in addition to contributing to a wider set of interviews for the project, would inform the Built Environment curriculum.

## Skills *plus* analyses of the Construction Management programme

The first audit involved mapping teaching, learning and assessment activities against the outcomes in the programme specification. It was found that lecturers used a range of different teaching methods and activities in order to develop the variety of skills expected by the CIOB *Educational Framework* (1995). However, some kinds of activity appeared to be under-used – for example, the development of skills for the dissertation module and the need for 'less structured' problems.

The second audit involved mapping the 39 Employability Aspects suggested by Skills *plus*, and described in Chapter 2, against the curriculum of the Construction Management programme. Once these employability aspects were mapped against the learning, teaching and assessment activities, the data gathered were collated into tabular format for each level. The presence of each of the 39 aspects in the modules was coded as: 'Explicitly', 'Implicitly' or 'Not at all'. An analysis of this tabulation was subsequently carried out focusing upon the following areas:

- Main qualities and skills that were explicitly developed over time;
- Qualities and skills that students were expected to develop over time, although there was no explicit focus upon them;

- Aspects of employability that appeared not to be being developed in the programme, either explicitly or implicitly.

The principal outcomes of both audits are given below.

### Too few 'unscaffolded' problems

The audit revealed that there were plenty of structured and 'scaffolded' problems throughout the programme, but little emphasis on the more open-ended, 'unscaffolded' problems that reflect the complexity of those that are met in the industry. The programme was not progressively removing the 'scaffolding' from the problems it set and was therefore not maximizing the chances of students developing autonomy.

As suggested in Chapter 8, formative assessment is critically important to learning. The sequence of learning tasks could benefit from a greater emphasis on formative 'low-stakes' assessment in the early stages, since this would emphasize the importance of the learning as students worked towards meeting the summative assessment expectations. Learning could be better developed through the use of mini-projects and/or practice tasks that would not necessarily be formally assessed (if summative assessment were required, then the weighting could be sufficiently low that a student could retrieve any initially weak performance). A consequence could well be 'deeper' learning, supported by better and more timely feedback from lecturers, tutors or peers.

### Development of skills for the dissertation module

At Level 3 (final year) it was found that the dissertation module required students to have previously developed a range of skills. However, preceding modules at lower levels (Levels 1 and 2) showed no explicit preparation for many of them. The dissertation module expects students to use the following skills which were not evident at lower levels:

- Critical Commentaries
- Making a Bibliography
- Concept Mapping
- Literature Review
- Research Design.

Thus, there is a need to make these skills more explicit at lower levels so that they are progressively developed and nurtured over the duration of the programme.

### The need for interdisciplinarity

Traditionally, Built Environment courses in higher education have tended to operate in separate 'silos' in which the various subject disciplines are seen as discrete.

Although many Built Environment programmes now have a largely common first year, when students work in teams they still tend to be grouped by discipline. The outside world involves problem-working, often without complete information, which requires a multidisciplinary approach and understanding. A key question to consider is how the School should seek to build interdisciplinarity into the construction curriculum. The *Accelerating Change in Built Environment Education* report believes that interdisciplinary education and teamwork is an area that needs to be addressed:

> Many current learning and teaching programmes are focused on single discipline subjects that exclude multi-disciplinary understanding and team-work experience. These reinforce rather than break-down the silo mentality that exists between the built environment professions and within the industry itself.
>
> (Coulter, 2003: 7)

In recent years, the School's curriculum has moved slightly towards inter-disciplinarity. This has largely been due to 'one shot' activities such as the final year joint project. The joint project involves students on the four professionally accredited final year degree programmes in Building Surveying, Construction Management, Quantity Surveying, and Real Estate Management. Normally, it takes place over an intensive one-week period with a common theme bringing the various disciplines together. The main aims and objectives relate to the undertaking of effective group work within a multidisciplinary team. The joint project enables students to develop a greater awareness of other disciplines' roles, skills and problems. Also, the individual student experience is enhanced through reflection on the set of skills that have been developed during the module. The project is assessed in two parts, reflecting the need to assess both the end product and the process through which that product has been developed.

Even though there is some interdisciplinarity within the final year, as a result of the joint project this is not foreshadowed earlier in the programme, and it is evident that there is a need to provide more opportunities for the progressive development of students' capacity for interdisciplinary working over the duration of the course. Further, feedback has indicated that students want integrative projects at earlier levels in order to help them to contextualize their studies by exposing them to the full range of professional work in property and construction.

There is a divergence of views between the academic staff, professional bodies and employers regarding interdisciplinarity and teamwork. Employers argue that there is not enough work on 'real world' problems, which are ill-structured and 'messy', within a true interdisciplinary perspective. This was corroborated from interviews conducted for the Skills *plus* project where it was said that students learn team-working skills throughout their period in education, from school to university. However, as one human resource manager pointed out, the teamwork that is organized in university is different from the kind of teamwork needed in professional practice:

[The] concept of team-working is different in university compared to the 'real world'. At university this tends to be peers [whereas] at the workplace this tends to have different levels, which can be a quite difficult adjustment to make for graduates.

However, common to both university and employment is the need to fit in and co-operate with others, although in professional practice this applies to a hierarchy of people at different levels within and outside an organization, including work colleagues, clients, consultants and contractors (who have diverse requirements). There may be the need to re-shape the notion of teamwork at university so as to overcome the traditional 'flat' student teams. One approach could be the inclusion of external practitioners or administrative staff and technicians as well as academic staff and students in order to increase the hierarchical element in teamwork.

The increased use of interdisciplinarity and unstructured problems embedded within the curriculum would help in the achievement of the following:

- The development of graduates who can deal with ill-structured problems.
- The gaining by professional bodies of graduates with enhanced professional capability.
- Graduates who are able to 'hit the ground running' in employment.

One of the main aims of the sandwich 'year out' is to enable students to acquire the 'tacit knowledge' which is necessary for them to be effective in the workplace. The Skills *plus* interviews strongly confirmed that the sandwich 'year out' was an important vehicle for the development of employability, in that it helped the students to relate theory to practice. However, students are increasingly omitting the sandwich year and progressing directly into the final year from Level 2. The Chartered Institute of Building takes the view that industrial placements are of importance for the construction profession and has expressed concern at

> the relatively low numbers of students taking sandwich placements. Further investigation is needed … into the possibility of sandwich training becoming mandatory.
>
> (CIOB, 2003: 14)

If the sandwich placement is not to be made mandatory, then it would seem that there is a need for some curriculum development to mitigate the effects of losing the sandwich year and to help these students to get the most from their final year studies. The curriculum may need more explicitly to prepare students (or prime them) for the situations they can expect to find when they get into the workplace. Would, perhaps, an alternative approach drawing on 'non-sandwich' student experiences (such as block vacation work experience within a construction firm or university summer school integrative project) develop the 'tacit knowledge' that is desired of a graduate?

## Main qualities and skills that were explicitly developed over time

The main qualities and skills developed over time, as identified by the audit based on the 39 aspects of employability, were:

- Independence (reference A4 in Box 2.1) – which ties in with self-confidence
- Adaptability (A6)
- Self-management (B15)
- Commercial awareness (C24)
- Teamwork (C39) – mainly discipline-specific group work.

## The need for a 'rounded graduate'

As a provider of higher education, the School aims to produce a 'rounded person' on graduation. The interviews that were conducted for the Skills *plus* project with six professionals in the construction industry showed that personal qualities and attributes were seen as essential for graduate employability. Interviewees said that, when they were appointing for graduate positions, the main personal qualities needed by individuals were high levels of motivation and a willingness to learn. A human resources manager stated that it was not just academic ability that made a graduate employable:

> When we're looking specifically to appoint people we're looking for the more rounded person, not just the qualification, and it's everything that goes with having a mature attitude and disciplined approach to the way they deal with problems, and not just relying on the education that they've had. We like to think there's a bit of lateral thinking going on as well; able to think a little bit differently ... and they need to be already showing those seeds of a thinker ...

Brown *et al.* (2002: 11) in a paper about employability in a knowledge-driven economy refer to the notion of an 'employable and productive person'. This raises the issue of whether the job-specific technical skills are taken as given, with construction employers looking at what extra the graduate can offer. Brown *et al.* quote a human resources manager to the effect that academic qualifications were taken for granted and also as saying:

> Judgements about one's drive and commitment, communication skills, team-working and self-management skills have become more important alongside any consideration of paper qualifications. The value of an individual to an employer is no longer represented by the denomination of academic currency but the economy of experience.

> (quoted in Brown *et al.*, 2002: 19)

## Getting students to deal with new situations

In the Skills *plus* interviews that I conducted, a recurring theme was how students grapple with new situations. This is relevant both within the higher education sector and to the wider issue of preparing students for employment. The students pick up signals from the syllabus (and especially the assessment requirements) regarding the need to deal with the challenge of new situations. If they perceive that they are being faced with routine problems with a 'right answer', then they may not make the leap to tackle situations 'in the wild'. They may remain reactive in their approach. The programme therefore needs progressively to support the development of students' capacity to deal with the complex, often not clearly defined, problems that they will face in employment. This would mean working with them, from an early stage in the programme, on the development of their own individual cognitive learning strategies. Developing students' capacity for 'learning how to learn' is an important curriculum aim, as it is desirable that students become autonomous learners as soon as possible in the programme.

The construction employers who were interviewed perceived the set of skills possessed by graduates as lacking some aspects of knowledge of professional practice. The argument was made by one human resources manager that there needed to be more bias towards the everyday working practices that graduates had to implement as construction professionals. However, there is something of a 'Catch 22' in operation, in that the employers believe that many of these skills are only acquired through experience in an employment role! One human resources manager who was interviewed acknowledged the point when saying:

> There is no substitute for experience, and the technical knowledge required can't be taught; it can only be gained by experience. I would expect universities to be able to direct their students to know where to find information, but the actual detail of that information just can't be taught as there is too much there.

In other words, the university could provide the framework for students to develop their technical abilities, whereas the workplace could provide the opportunity to refine them.

Graduates, too, acknowledged that the demands of their programme and of the workplace differed. When interviewed about the skills they had had to acquire since graduation in order to remain employable, they tended to focus on job-specific knowledge and skills, which were not taught in enough depth at university. It is not obvious how universities can respond to any calls that they should prepare students for the specific demands of many different workplaces.

A fundamental problem on a vocational course, such as construction, is the gap between acquiring discipline-specific knowledge and applying it in practice. For example, statutory legislation is subject to change (sometimes quite rapidly) and hence when graduates draw on the knowledge that they have gained whilst at university, the information they have is sometimes dated. Of course, it is recognized that graduates are expected to carry out continuing professional development (CPD) or life-long learning, implying strongly that the acquisition of skills such as data gathering and handling should have formed a significant part of the students' university experience.

### The development of qualities and skills without specific attention being given to them

Whilst it may be assumed that reflection is automatically a component of a vocational construction programme, the audit of the Construction Management programme revealed that reflectiveness (A10) was under-represented. There was only one module at Level 1 (Management and Organization) and two modules at Level 3 (the dissertation and Project Analysis and Synthesis) which explicitly developed reflection at the time of the audit. Hence it was acknowledged that there was a need to review the relationship between Levels 1 and 3 and to discover how the identified gap might be bridged.

One of the main problems making claims for employability is the problem of dealing with certification of personal qualities and discipline-specific skills. Following the Skills *plus* auditing, the RAPID (Recording Academic, Professional and Individual Development) Progress File[2] software was adopted by the school, initially within a module at each course level. The web-based RAPID Progress File software is used as a vehicle to support reflection and as a tool for auditing and recording the development of student skills and competencies within a module. This can be accessed both internally and remotely via the university intranet, which gives flexibility in respect of student access. The RAPID software provides a framework for the self-auditing of Key Skills, Personal and Professional Skills, and discipline-specific Technical Skills and it also acts as a resource for the production of a short reflective essay. This review is expected to include a summary of the development and achievement of the skills expected as an outcome of the student's engagement in each module, and an identification of areas of strengths and weakness. The students have an opportunity to acknowledge any aspects of their progression that need further development through the incorporation of an action plan within the reflective essay.

The adoption of the RAPID Progress File software and its subsequent embedding within the Construction Management programme have provided a vehicle for students to evidence claims to employability. Also, RAPID has served to raise student self-awareness through the benchmarking of their own personal progress and development over the whole degree programme. As a 'carrot and stick' encouragement towards the completion of the Progress File, this element is assessed, and attracts 15 per cent of the total marks available for one module at each of the three levels.

The use of RAPID aligns with the expectations from the QAA that each student will, by 2005–6, engage in compiling a progress file. Student feedback and staff experiences have led to a belief that the use of RAPID will result in greater reflectiveness on the part of students, and their increased capacity to demonstrate it.

The audit also showed that resolving conflict (shown as C36 in Box 2.1) and negotiating (C38) appeared explicitly, and hence were assessed, but only at Level 3 – though they might appear less prominently at earlier levels in the programme.

### Aspects of employability that appear not to be developed, explicitly or implicitly

Whilst most of the 39 aspects of employability shown in Box 2.1 are incorporated into the Construction Management programme, some of these may be so on an implicit, rather than an explicit, basis. Skills *plus* has enabled the programme team to think about the relevance of the following areas which, on the face of it, do not appear within the programme:

- Malleable self-theory (A1)
- Creativity (B17)
- Political sensitivity (C25)
- Ability to work cross-culturally (C26)
- Ethical sensitivity (C27)
- Acting morally (C31)
- Influencing (C34).

### Conclusions

The key issues from Audit 1 (teaching, learning and assessment activities) helped the programme team to reflect on the related issues of interdisciplinarity and the need for 'less structured' problems in leading up to the dissertation module. The need became apparent for better-sequenced learning encounters through the provision of 'scaffolding' at lower levels, which would be progressively removed in the interest of developing autonomy in students. There was a recognition that more 'low-stakes' assessment was required to encourage students' learning, since the current emphasis on relatively short-term assessment outcomes may be distracting from the development of the individual in the longer term. Mapping the 39 employability aspects (Audit 2) raised a number of pertinent issues about the programme's contribution to the development of students' personal qualities and skills.

The construction employer interviews imply that job-specific skills are taken as a 'given', but that employers were looking at what the graduate could offer in addition. They also gave a perspective on teamwork that contrasted with that held within the university – in employment, teams often involve members from different levels in the organizational hierarchy. It was recognized that it would be desirable to include an element of hierarchy in the Construction Management programme as a result. There was a general acknowledgement that the sandwich 'year out' developed students' 'tacit knowledge' regarding employment situations. However, there was a need for the programme to seek to build-in opportunities for students not taking the sandwich route to develop 'tacit knowledge'.

The recognition of personal qualities and discipline-specific skills has been facilitated through the use of the RAPID Progress File software. The main benefit of using RAPID is that students have reflected on the 'tacit skills' they have developed before they make their job applications.

The rethinking stimulated by Skills *plus* does not necessarily mean wholesale curriculum re-design, since much can be done by making adjustments to the existing curriculum. Some of these adjustments may concern the teaching/learning *process*, rather than programme content. As well as teaching students the skills and knowledge that they will need if they are to become competent construction professionals, their university education should also serve to develop other personal qualities such as the ability to become 'reflective practitioners'.

## Notes

1   Further information on the CIOB *Educational Framework* and developments can be found in Platten (2003).
2   Further information on the RAPID Progress File can be found in Maddocks and Sher (2003) and at http://rapid.lboro.ac.uk/.

# Chapter 11

# Employability and social science

*Margaret Edwards and Chris McGoldrick*

## Issues

This is a report on a local investigation of issues that pervade this book. Liverpool John Moores University's School of Social Science (SSS) was interested in questions such as: is there any truth in gibes about the relative unemployability of social science graduates?[1] How employable are social scientists from new universities, in comparison with those from older universities? Are curricula in the School keeping pace with workplace change?

Small-scale enquiry produced material to guide reflection on ways of maximizing the School's contribution to undergraduates' employability. The evidence reported here was collected precisely because employability is of immense current concern and involves difficult reflections about values, curricula, management and resources. Attention focuses mainly on the work of Sociology, the programme within the School which participated in Skills *plus*. It is instructive to compare this with the position in another discipline that is also far removed from being a vocational study (Chapter 5). The question that both chapters address, albeit at one remove, is whether employability is mainly a concern for 'vocational' and 'applied' subject areas, or whether there is something enriching here for Arts, Humanities and Social Science as well.

### Employability and the School of Social Science at Liverpool John Moores University

For many social scientists, 'employability' is a social construct, in respect of which the education system, the structure of class relations and the labour market closely interact (Bourdieu and Passeron, 1977). Rhetoric at national and international levels equates employability with economic competitiveness (Blunkett, 2001), yet universities in the UK suffer substantial resource shortfalls (NCIHE, 1997; Universities UK, 2002). Likewise, the UK's lowly productivity position within the G7 group of countries has been attributed to weak skill levels in the employment-age population, but factors such as relatively sparse investment in research and development by government and companies are also implicated (DTI, 2000). Emphases in much of the employability literature are on supply-side features (such as the size and 'skills' of graduate populations); there is less recognition that demand for graduates can fluctuate with economic conditions, and changing organizational structures and cultures (Brown *et al.*, 2002). Furthermore, graduates from new universities may find graduate employment more difficult to achieve than those from older universities, since some employers appear sceptical of new university credentials (Harvey *et al.*, 1997). 'New university' students may have fewer family, financial, social and cultural resources upon which to draw than students from older universities. At the time when the government's intention is to widen participation in Higher Education (HEFCE, 2001), employers increasingly appear to be looking for the very characteristics, such as social confidence, which are more likely to be part of middle class social capital (Brown and Scase, 1994: 142–3).

So, we have an under-theorized concept and loaded dice. Neither is a reason for passive acceptance of structural disadvantage, however. The following sections trace developments in thinking about employability within SSS.

## Social Science at Work: a study of employability issues

The School commissioned a small-scale study (McGoldrick, 2001) which tracked the post-graduation experience of a sample of 46 of the School's 1997–2000 graduates, stratified by discipline (Economics, Geography, History, Politics and Sociology). Seventeen employers were consulted about their recruitment criteria for graduate-level jobs or jobs in which there was progression to this level of work. The graduates reflected upon features of their personal histories, their undergraduate curricula and post-graduation experience which had been helpful or unhelpful in achieving and retaining employment, particularly at graduate level. The employers mainly represented companies which were typical SSS graduates' destinations and aspirations.

The work was impelled by two main concerns. The first was to raise the profile of employability within SSS. The second was to use the information as encouragement to curricular reflection, particularly because there was uncertainty within the School about the compatibility of 'employability', as expressed in many key skills analyses, with the School's values. At the same time, there was recognition that social science curricula needed to keep pace with workplace changes.

Graduates have always left for a job market which has changed since their tutors graduated, but there are indications that the generation and work experience gap may now be more pronounced. Research by the Open University suggests that between the late 1980s and the mid-1990s, changes in higher education curricula increasingly had 'not been keeping pace with changes in the workplace' (Brennan, 1999: 4). Graduates particularly reported some lack of preparedness in oral communication and ICT (information and communication technologies). ICT competence is required even at early stages of graduates' job searches since a high proportion of job advertisements and applications are now organized online (Prospects, 2002).

There may be other areas where workplace preparation is needed. Feedback from SSS graduates suggested that beliefs in 'a job for life' persisted, most markedly among first generation graduates. There is still a core of work, mostly in the upper reaches of the occupational hierarchy, which offers a measure of security, financial reward and prestige. Many graduates now entering the labour market, however, are more likely to experience flexibility – of work functions, numbers employed, and hours worked. The reasons for labour market shifts have been examined elsewhere (for example, Lechner and Boli, 2000). The 'time pioneers' (Hörning et al., 1995) may relish flexibility. Other graduates, especially those without family resources and networks, may find flexibility problematic. Several studies including those by the Association of Graduate Recruiters (Hawkins and Winter, 1995), Harvey et al. (1997), and Skills plus itself, illustrate how employability goes beyond the first post-graduation job, important though this is. The development of attributes such as self-awareness, adaptability, confidence and a willingness to tackle new learning are identified by Skills plus as important preparation for life and a changing labour market.

The SSS study was small-scale. The stratified random sampling of graduates produced broad convergence with most characteristics of the social science graduate populations as recorded in the university's student information system, but the findings reported here are tentative. Nevertheless, the study was a useful catalyst in prompting academic reflection on the employability perceptions of the School's graduates rather than on those of 'graduates' in general.


## Some key issues raised by *Social Science at Work*

### Graduate employment destinations

In interview, the graduates showed a clear awareness of the importance of study following degrees in less-obviously vocational disciplines. For a good number, however, especially those without family financial resources, earning a living and paying off debts were imperatives. There has been a reduction in the proportion of Liverpool JMU students, and SSS graduates in particular, undertaking further study as a first destination. In 1997, 22.5 per cent of SSS graduates entered directly into further study but by 2000 the proportion had fallen to 17.5 per cent (see Table 11.1).

It appears that for an increasing proportion of SSS graduates, first degrees carry a greater weight of preparation for life and work. Careers guidance emerged as a key feature of this preparation. Graduates who had been unemployed for some months after graduation typically had not consulted the Careers Service

*Table 11.1* Liverpool JMU: first destination returns to the Higher Education Statistics Agency, for the year 2000

| First destination | SSS (%) | Liverpool JMU (%) |
|---|---|---|
| Permanent employment | 60.4 | 66.4 |
| Temporary employment | 5.8 | 4.6 |
| Further study | 17.5 | 15.4 |
| Unemployment | 11.7 | 9.2 |
| Other | 4.6 | 4.4 |

independently or gone to arranged talks. As one unemployed graduate, who had ignored Careers talks, ruefully commented: 'I thought that if I concentrated on my degree, it would all work out'. The workplace was tougher than he had thought. Among the sample, several months' post-graduation unemployment meant a weaker record in achieving graduate work, a finding which follows the results of larger studies (for example, McKnight, 2003).

### Influences on graduate employment

There is evidence that employers use degree class and further study as 'filters' in order to process the increasing volume of graduate applications following the massification of HE, particularly in the 1990s (Nove *et al.*, 1997). Degree class and further study were the most significant predictors, at the 90 per cent confidence level, of graduate employment within the SSS sample. In summary, the likeliest achievers of graduate employment were: male; aged 18–19 on entry; and holders of an upper second degree (there were no Firsts in the sample). They had also: often undertaken further study; had graduates in their families; hunted for jobs; and sought careers advice.

Family history was important in that those who had a graduate parent, partner or other close family member seemed to have an edge: more respondents with this experience had achieved upper second class honours degrees, undertaken further study and consulted careers advisers. Some explanations of this were: 'It was an uncle [a graduate] who helped me most with my CV'; 'My parents pushed me to the careers service ... it was good advice'; 'They [graduate parents] agreed to support my MA'.

Graduates without family graduate experience and resources were more likely to refer to the 'different world of uni', to mention financial difficulties which could mean the imperative to 'take any job' upon graduation, and to identity other factors that led to over-modest job aspirations. The relationships between social class, the education system and job aspirations have been explored, for example, by Bernstein (1975) and Bourdieu and Passeron (1977).

Nevertheless, there were female graduates with lower second class honours degrees and no further study or family graduate experience who had progressed to successful, graduate employment. An important factor here appeared to be purposeful work experience, either through SSS's work experience modules or during vacations on the advice of the university's Careers Service. In interview, it was clear that employers used the good quality work experience 'credential' as an alternative, or an additional, filter to a good degree and further study. One employer spoke for several, however, when she observed: 'they [the students] have a degree to get'. The quality of the work experience, including reflection upon it, appeared more important to these employers than the length of the experience.

## The Social Science curricula and employability

The traditional academic skills of critical analysis and synthesis were considered helpful in gaining and surviving in graduate-level employment by nearly 98 per cent of the graduates. Most employers claimed that a key reason for employing graduates was that, as one expressed it: 'graduates generally learn faster ... they have been trained to think ... to find out'. The capacity to learn and a willingness to adapt in the changing workplace were highly valued attributes among the employer sample. Graduates and employers shared the perception that critical thinking was, as one graduate commented, 'at the core of the degree'. Another said 'this is *the* transferable one'. Disciplinary knowledges were helpful to nearly two-thirds of graduates, but all recognized the need to adapt to changing circumstances.

The following sections will mainly focus on work within Sociology, the SSS programme which participated in the Skills *plus* project.

## Sociology's contribution to employability

The British Sociological Association summarizes Sociology's contribution to employability in the following way:

> Studying sociology involves continuous interplay between matters of concern in society and concepts and theories of society. The requirement to reason and critically analyse the workings of society makes sociology an effective medium of intellectual development in the course of an undergraduate degree or other programme of study. Employers recognise this.
>
> (BSA, 2002: 1).

The QAA subject benchmark statement for Sociology (QAA, 2001c) makes similar points about a 'characteristically dynamic discipline' which is both 'theoretical and evidence-based' (p. 4). However, the benchmark statement goes further and specifies that programmes should include opportunities for the development of 'transferable skills' in seven main areas:

- learning and study
- written and oral communication in a variety of contexts and modes
- statistical and other quantitative techniques
- information retrieval
- ICT
- time planning and management
- group work.

(QAA, 2001c: 5)

Within the small *Social Science at Work* sample, Geography graduates were most likely to obtain graduate jobs; Sociology graduates were the next most likely. *In both disciplines, however, there were accounts of failed attempts to achieve graduate-level jobs.* Graduates' perceptions were that curricular differences would have encouraged earlier progression to graduate-level work, especially in more prestigious areas of work, and better survival 'on the job'. This is consistent with findings from a small study of unemployed graduates reported by Knight and Knight (2002).

Sociology graduates remarked upon the following contributions their undergraduate programmes made to their employability and personal development:

- Curricula which had given them 'more understanding' (of clients in difficult circumstances). Reflection was encouraged: 'I am more sympathetic … I know where people are coming from better'.
- Analytical approaches to social issues and policies: 'It was a maturing process to come across new ideas … and dissect them'.
- Supportive academic staff.

There is a notable difference between these reflections on the contributions made by undergraduate work and the reports from the main set of Skills *plus* interviews with new graduates and their co-workers (see Chapter 4).

There were requests from this sample of SSS graduates for:

- A wider range of written work, such as reports and summaries, although the strengths of the academic essay as an opportunity to explore in some depth and develop arguments were recognized.
- More applications of theoretical perspectives in case studies.
- Higher-level ICT, numeracy and statistics.
- Further guidance in giving presentations.
- More group work.

This 'wish-list' is more consistent with the main Skills *plus* findings. So too is the finding that graduates who had not sought advice from the Careers Service were, in retrospect, likely to regret it.

In summary, Sociology offers insights and approaches which are valued in the workplace, as the graduates and several employers who had recruited sociologists to their companies testified. Nevertheless, graduates and employers recognized that there were gaps in the curriculum which could limit work opportunities. It was felt that ICT, numeracy and statistics could be particular weaknesses among social scientists.

Sociology benchmark statements and reports, for example by Dearing (NCIHE, 1997) and Harvey and colleagues (1997), give very general indications about what ICT competence, numeracy and statistics involve, so the employers and Sociology graduates were specifically probed on this point. They identified the following as helpful in achieving and retaining graduate-level work:

- Competent email use and the ability to locate and use information and opinion from a variety of sources, including Internet.
- 'Ability beyond the basic level in all areas of standard software such as Microsoft Office … including spreadsheet, database … word-processing we take for granted … PowerPoint can be a very useful plus' (Employer).
- Numeracy and statistics. Graduates and employers felt that weaknesses in these areas were more likely to hamper social scientists, including Sociologists, than graduates in some other disciplines. As one graduate – now in marketing – commented: 'there's hardly a job now that doesn't demand the ability to handle numbers with confidence'. Employers said that they were not generally looking for high-level competence from social scientists in these areas. One added: '… but we are looking for an ease in reading and constructing tables ($n$ and %); the ability to spot trends … basic statistics – such as mean, median, mode – up to … correlation (a word which is often used loosely) … basic stuff. Can graduates spot "iffy" statistics – is too much being claimed for too little – are visual representations misleading?' Another employer welcomed 'SPSS (Statistical Package for the Social Sciences) – even at basic level on the CV … if they've done that, they are likely to have a nodding acquaintance with key statistics'.

## Representing and enhancing Sociology's contribution to student employability

The focus of this section is on representing employability to prospective Sociology students, undergraduates and academic staff. Key issues are who is representing what to whom, and at what stage in the progression from university entry to graduation? Are there stages in the undergraduate career when an explicit approach to employability may be counter-productive? Might a more coy approach, however, do students a disservice?

There are reasons other than those already identified in this chapter why 'employability' can be a slippery concept to represent to school students and to Sociology undergraduates. There may be misperceptions arising from careers advice prior to university about what 'Sociology' involves and where a degree in the discipline might lead. There can be, as one graduate expressed it: 'the naïve view that if your heart's in the right place ... and [if] you have done [your] best', graduate work where you can 'make a difference' will be achievable. The majority orientation amongst these predominantly female students was one of 'social commitment' (Brown and Scase, 1994: 91) in which financial rewards tended to be regarded as secondary to the rewards of 'making a difference'. This social commitment led some Sociology graduates to successful jobs in the public sector. In other cases it led to more tenuous work in the voluntary sector. The choice of Sociology itself may be associated with a pre-higher education belief that social/ community orientated work does not require the abilities, for example, to structure policy, give professional presentations and cope with ICT and quantitative data analysis.

Now that further study immediately following graduation is becoming harder for a number of social scientists to afford, however, there is a more pressing need – in sympathetic and realistic ways – to give more direct focus to some undergraduate thinking about post-graduation. Sociology undergraduates were less likely than other SSS undergraduates to seek Careers Service advice, in spite of encouragements from academics. Women graduates in SSS were generally more likely to express diffidence in aiming for graduate-level work. Students from non-graduate families appeared less likely to plan for post-graduation, hold misperceptions about where a first degree could lead and to express diffidence that 'Careers were only concerned with high-fliers'. The commitment of SSS to social justice could extend still more actively to raising the aspirations of some students.

## How does Sociology 'represent' employability to undergraduates?

In addition to outlining the programme content, resources and student support, the Sociology student handbook identifies key features of the programme as the development of confident, effective and independent learning, time management, communication and presentational skills, the ability to work with others and to undertake problem-working and ICT. The work-based learning module stresses the need for applied work, the enhancement of personal qualities such as intellectual maturity, initiative and independence of thought, and increased understanding of how organizations work.

That group work, discussion and presentations, for example, provide experience which is valued in the workplace is not, at the moment, spelt out in official module or programme documentation. Other important practices, such as oral presentations, ICT and work in numeracy and statistics (typically unpopular with a number of social scientists) are developed when students work on some mainstream curriculum topics which are also presented as the sort of activities that students will encounter upon graduation. The priority is building confidence, especially for students who may have unhappy experiences of these types of work from schooldays. So, the programme contributes to employability in an apparently incidental, but purposeful way.

It is important, though, that students appreciate what they have learned, know that many features of the undergraduate curriculum, including those which they may initially find more difficult, are valued by employers, and understand how to represent their achievements. The 'embedded' approach may not sufficiently pinpoint connections between undergraduate learning and employability. The School is developing learning contracts which include student reflection upon learning and making more explicit connections between undergraduate curricula and employment. Another approach is to encourage students to reflect on achievements in order to draft *curricula vitae* a few months before they apply for first long vacation work, when there is a powerful extrinsic reason for reflection and claims-making (Kneale, 1997).

## Representing employability to academic staff

Staff in the Sociology programme were involved in four main ways with work designed to enhance the contribution their activities make to student employability:

- Feedback was received from Sociology graduates and employers.
- The programme participated in Skills *plus*, which encouraged a more subtle view of employability than some previous key skills discussions within the literature. An important message of Skills *plus* is that 'intelligent' employ-ability is compatible with, and may well enhance, the academic learning of the programme.
- It was suggested that undergraduate employability could be enhanced by a mix of 'tweaking' the existing curriculum and some wider changes. This was done by illustrating the potential contribution of existing learning and teaching approaches to student employability.
- Staff were involved in an Away Day for the Sociology programme which included discussion of employability and key issues from Skills *plus*.

One member of the Sociology team, reflecting on this set of activities, said that they 'helped [us] to reflect on what we do – across the programme … we have a good record at looking at the programme overall … but this [Skills *plus*] helped to pinpoint … strengths and gaps'. The mapping of methods of learning and teaching and forms of assessment across programme levels (see Chapter 12) had shown how certain methods of learning and teaching at particular levels were bunched. For example, students need to develop critical writing in extended form, but the mapping suggested a heavy reliance on academic essays which tended to

*Table 11.2* Curricular development in Sociology which was encouraged by *Social Science at Work* and Skills *plus*

| Actions | In progress, 2002 | Developing from 2003 |
|---|---|---|
| **1 The curriculum**<br>Enhancing case studies and problem-working<br>Increasing use of study visits | Student feedback favourable<br>Student feedback: 'enjoyable and facilitated learning' | Enhanced work-based module at School level |
| Reducing curricular content (level 1) and increasing study of learning | 'Situating Sociology' option introduced | Positive feedback: 'Situating Sociology' to become core techniques |
| Enhancing existing ICT familiarization work | E.g. Improved email and wordprocessing techniques; embedding e-information search (e.g. Internet, e-journals, Blackboard); chat room analyses; basic Excel | Diagnostic ICT testing at level 1. Some students, including standard-age entry, lack basic ICT |
| Developing Excel work to include own analyses | Student lack of ICT confidence and resistance to ICT learning has inhibited development in this area in the past | Prior ICT enhancement and focus on problem-working within sociological context should assist |
| Introducing SPSS and further statistics | Cross-disciplinary pilot | A cross-school approach |
| Enhancing more formal oral presentation work | A difficult area for some students. With high student/staff ratio; it is time-consuming to assess | Year-long modules will allow time for more development of this work |
| Embedding the above more widely across levels of the degree | In progress | |
| **2 Assessment**<br>Reviewing assessment methods within programme | Substantial academic essays retained but reduced in number. More assess-ment based on e.g. reports, pamphlets, précis | |
| Enhancing student self-assessment and diagnostic, summative and formative assessment | Enhancing self-assessment and formative assessment | Changes in university's modular framework will facilitate wider range of assessment |
| Enhancing assessed group work within the programme | An area of difficulty for some students, especially in short (semester-long) modules | More year-long modules will assist here |
| **3 Other**<br>Encouraging closer contacts with Careers Service | In progress | |

exclude more varied forms of writing, especially at levels 2 and 3, and to create a considerable assessment burden for academic staff.

### Actions contributing to employability and work in progress

Table 11.2 summarizes the work that was encouraged by *Social Science at Work* and by Skills *plus*, and that was facilitated in part by a changed modular structure. There has been a great deal of wide-ranging work to enhance the existing provision, principally by making explicit things that were implicit and by bringing more coherence to the programme.

### The impact of Sociology's work in the enhancement of employability

Although it is not possible to produce valid numerical data, feedback from SSS Sociology graduates and employers, and the findings of the Skills *plus* project, suggest that recent changes in the Sociology programme are likely to be helpful in further assisting Sociology graduates to obtain and succeed in graduate-level work. At the time of writing, the main outcomes of the programme's deliberations on employability were as follows:

- *Social Science at Work* reinforced programme leaders' ideas about curricular change. Sociology agreed to participate in Skills *plus* because the project combined an elaborated view of employability and a workable methodology – it called for direct reflection on what was taught and how it was assessed at programme level. Skills *plus* was felt to:
  - illustrate that employability is a much broader issue than key skills discourses had been suggesting;
  - show how curricula that encourage employability could be compatible with existing approaches within the discipline;
  - demonstrate that employability could be enhanced by tweaking and embedding rather than by complete curricular overhaul;
  - identify points where more radical re-design was needed.
- It became increasingly appreciated that embedding the knowledges and techniques of disciplines *across* academic programmes and expressing them in different contexts encourages better learning among students, especially where complex outcomes of learning are concerned (see Chapter 12). For example, developmental, formative assessment assists deep learning but it is difficult to achieve if skills are divorced from the disciplinary context or if the programme is divided into short modules. The university is moving away from a framework of semester-long modules which is a constructive development.

- Oral communication (especially presentations, including group presentations) and work in ICT and numeracy need enhancement. One advantage of embedding a variety of learning methods across the programme, including the more difficult ones for some students, is that student confidence can be built up – and avoidance is more difficult.
- Nevertheless, the embedded approach is not problem-free. As Dearing (NCIHE, 1997) recognized, the development of some employability skills among academics may take time. The School is adopting a 'semi-embedded' approach whereby cross-disciplinary working assists in the teaching of SPSS and statistics which are relevant to analyses within Sociology.

### Further advice

'Advice' may imply that SSS is expert in employability work. This section will more modestly summarize approaches which are proving helpful in our consideration of curricula and employability.

'Team-working' is often cited as a key feature of employer wish-lists and applies to academic practices as much as it does to students about to enter the graduate labour market. Protecting academic values, sifting good change from the bogus and implementing good change in higher education is, to the best of one's extent, a collaborative effort. The following advice has emerged from teamwork, mainly at programme level.

- Recognize that 'employability' is not an invasive alien. 'Intelligent' employability, as advocated by Skills *plus*, is usually being promoted by most HE programmes; the challenges are to recognize the familiarity of employability and to articulate learning in terms of life and work, to colleagues and to students.
- A review of employed graduates' reflections on their university and work experiences is rewarding, sobering and a stimulus to change.
- Try curricular mapping (see Chapter 12). These 'maps' or audits are revealing of gaps, overlaps, duplication and bunching of content and assessments.
- Consider whether you are over-teaching (content) and over-working (staff), looking particularly carefully at assessment practices. Can you release space for more variety in learning and teaching – can you increase the amount of problem-working, applied work and study visits? Is more variety of student experience needed if students are to claim the diverse achievements that employers value?
- Focus on staged curricular adjustment. A 'big bang' approach is seldom necessary. Staff and other resources are such that innovation fatigue could hinder changes that would serve students well after graduation.
- As far as possible, embed skills elements within different levels of the programme and integrate with the knowledges and analyses of the disciplines.

Staff development and some flexible realignment of teaching responsibilities may be necessary.
- Careers Advisers are allies and might helpfully contribute to some programme discussions.

Finally, keep faith in the best of academic traditions: up-to-date knowledge of the discipline, rigour in inquiry, independence, adaptability, creativity and the encouragement of student understandings. They too are highly marketable.

## Note

1   One of the more printable is: Q. 'What do you say to a social scientist in a job?' A. 'Big Mac and fries, please'.

# Chapter 12

# Principles and practices for enhancing employability at programme or departmental level

## The false promise of innovation projects

There have been thousands of projects to improve learning, teaching, assessment and the curriculum more generally in different phases of education and in different countries. The range of interventions, most with the aim of ultimately, but not necessarily directly, improving student learning, is considerable. Some, such as innovations based on formative assessment, have secure evidence that there are substantial results when they are properly implemented (Black and Wiliam, 1998); for others, such as the use of group learning methods, the evidence is more ambiguous and suggests a more limited potential (Slavin, 1996); and in many cases, such as training primary teachers to be better at task setting, delivery, assessment and planning (Bennett *et al.*, 1984), any impact seems short-lived. Our reading of this history of innovation is that the difficulty is not so much in making innovations work as generalizing them, because interventions that have short-term impact when they are in the hands of enthusiastic, well-resourced and well-informed volunteers seem to wilt when transplanted to general practice, where they compete for attention with the full press of daily life. Innovations that had some beneficial effects *in vitro* frequently falter when released into the wild of daily practice.

Is there any reason to believe that the sorts of innovation described in Chapters 9–11 will fare better? The odds are against such a belief, given a history of innovation that shows most failing to have any significant, long-term impact. Yet the USEM approach was designed in some knowledge of the forces that tend to favour what *is* over what could be. Research into change and the failure of most innovations to make a difference suggests three main conclusions:

- The first phase of innovation is atypical: it often involves volunteers and volunteers tend to be more confident and enthusiastic than non-volunteers; it usually has some extra resources; considerable attention is paid to making sure that the innovation and the thinking behind it are properly understood; and it is a centre of attention. These conditions do not always hold in later phases, yet the first phase innovation may only have 'worked' because of them.

- Although there has been some tendency to blame teachers for the failure of innovation and shortfalls from best practice, attributing to them a lack of competence, commitment, or both, an alternative view concentrates on the ecology of practice (Bennett *et al.*, 1984). Here, (school)teachers are very busy people who make thousands of decisions a day as they try to cope with the fast-moving uncertainties of practice. Faced with multiple demands on their time, having to hand practices that are routinized and generally safe, and working within established systems of expectations and possibilities, they are attracted to behaviours that may be educationally less than ideal but which, in a real sense, *work*. Although it may be necessary to change their ideas about learning and teaching in order to improve practice, these new ideas will struggle to make a difference in the face of the established cycles into which teachers' practices are attracted. We suggest that this position, that practices are created by systems of beliefs, expectations, habits, constraints, possibilities and roles, can be extended to higher education.
- Small changes that are compatible with these systems are more likely to 'stick'. If teachers themselves initiate them or have a direct part in their development, so much the better, although mandated change – change required by administrators or policy-makers – can have effects.

The *tuning* approach was designed so that:

- A set of small changes, negotiated with module leaders, would be a sufficient response, certainly in the first few years of an attempt to enhance student employability.
- Changes would be compatible with engrooved practices because they would be negotiated and intentionally small.
- Teachers did not need to learn complicated new teaching procedures, although they did have to consider the claims, set out in the first chapters of this book, that good pedagogic practices tend to promote achievements that employers value.
- Although changes make some resource demands, the *tuning* approach is deliberately not dependent on new resources for its success: the very idea of tuning the curriculum is about working with what is there.
- The approach is highly flexible. It was used across the range of subject areas in universities with research strengths, as well as with ones with other claims to distinctiveness.

There are points of difficulty as well. Reports from participating departments at the end of the second year spoke of nine in particular.

- The language issue. One participating department reported that, 'some participants found definitional problems and omissions'. An implication is that some of the dimensions of employability, and the ways in which they relate to teaching/learning experiences in existing programmes, need to be made more transparent to both staff and students.

- The need for 'knowing students'. Students need to appreciate how their employability is being developed and how the learning, teaching and assessment activities relate to its different elements.
- The Year 1 and progression issues. There is a need to introduce the dimensions of employability early in a programme and then to revisit them regularly. Curricular coherence and progression may easily be lost in systems that offer students free-ish choice from many modular alternatives.
- The assessment issue. Departments reported that their assessment methods were not always consistent with an employability-sensitive curriculum or with the rather general expectations included in those subject benchmark statements[1] that have been published by the QAA. Even if employability were not a concern, it is likely that many departments' assessment practices would give cause for concern (Knight and Yorke, 2003b). Where employability is a concern, then in addition to actions necessary to embed decent assessment practices, work needs to be done on a number of difficulties – technical, economic and ethical – outlined in Chapter 8.
- The need for more tools. One report said that the project needed to develop more 'pitch pipes', by which it meant tools to help teams with the business of tuning their curricula. Those that had been developed were useful but it would be valuable to have more.
- Dangers of overload. Curriculum overload was a problem. The enrichment of curricula with employability-related teaching/learning activities implies pedagogical substitution and rearrangement rather than addition of further content. However, some of the teaching, learning and assessment methods that need to appear in a programme to enhance employability can also be quite time-consuming – in-class presentations take more public time than essay assessment does. Where professional and statutory regulatory bodies exert control over content, the challenges are more severe, since it is more difficult to win an argument for emphasizing the *quality* rather than the quantity of learning.
- The cost of out-of-class activity. Some activities (e.g. fieldwork) which should enhance employability are becoming increasingly problematic for institutions because of safety and insurance considerations.
- Unrealized possibilities. Many students have part-time employment to finance themselves through higher education. This situation has some potential (as yet little tapped) to enhance claims to employability. The CRAC *Insight plus* project and others show how this sort of work can be translated so as to support good claims to employability.
- The evidence of success issue. Although there is a demand for evidence that this *tuning* approach works, an issue to which we return later in the chapter, some resistance was reported to the language of social science when it was used to explain the good research sense of what is proposed. There were

some reports of academic impatience with the work of Dweck and with the term 'metacognition'.

Nor can it be said that the project had managed in two years what might be better seen as a six to ten year task. In the June 2002 reports from participating departments, colleagues referred to the need for further funding for research, networking and development; head of department and team leader training; more sponsors; embedding; and extending from project departments to other parts of universities. Above all they pointed to the limits to what projects can be expected to do. The external evaluator, Alan Wright, who is director of first cycle (undergraduate) education at the University of Quebec, was enthusiastic about project achievements and asked a dozen questions about the project's work once funding ceased (Wright, 2002). There was, he considered, more to do.

In being open about difficulties reported at the end of the second year of these departments' engagement with the project, we are putting aside the overwhelming reports that Skills *plus* is an effective way of working on these and other problems, as indicated in Box 12.1. However, the reports lead to two important conclusions: first, that the *tuning* approach implies a need for sustained attention – it is not a two-year fix; second, that attempts to tune curricula to enhance employability fall foul of endemic problems with the quality of curricula in higher education, the most obvious of which is the dishevelled state of assessment practice. (This is not primarily an 'employability problem' but attempts to enhance employability high-light it.) Although this approach recommends actions that should ease underlying assessment problems, it is a little hard to criticize an innovation for failing to solve a problem, namely incoherent assessment practices, that should have been addressed anyway through general quality assurance and quality enhancement procedures. The enhancement of employability is not the only ambition that will come to nothing if fundamental issues to do with curriculum (for example the issues of coherence, progression, amount of demand on students, and assessment) are not tackled.

## *Tuning* – the approach in outline

The project was about:

- Working with departments on undergraduate *programmes*
- Infusing programmes with *entitlements*
- *'Stocktaking'*
- *'Tuning'* existing curricula.

Participating departments needed to agree with this agenda and to identify one person to liaise with other teachers and with the project. The project contributed 'low cost, high gain' methods of tuning the curriculum to enhance both its educational power and students' employability. It supported developments with modest funds, research-based practical support, on-demand in-service events,

*Box 12.1* Departments' favourable comments on Skills *plus*, June 2002

1.  'Although on their own such changes may be marginal, they should have an overall cumulative effect. [Changes in 2002 included:]
    *   Sandwich placement year
    *   Graduate enterprise module
    *   Re-vamping an existing study skills module around USEM
    *   Continuing review of assessment practices.'
    *   '[We have made] several modifications to modules across the four years without altering the existing curriculum plan and design:
    *   Student self-identification of achievement
    *   Fourth year self-assessment and reflective workbook
    *   Two students each did a project that provides baseline evidence of student skills achievements.
    The concepts proposed by Dweck influenced my own thoughts ... a paper is in preparation.
    Value for quinquennial professional accreditation review.'

2.  'The concept was well worked out and consistently applied:
    *   Concept and interpretation flexible enough to accommodate difference
    *   The concept seemed to "grow" but without losing its base consistency
    *   The "background" which was supplied and the discussion at colloquia were interesting
    *   I was happy with the emphases ... which are mostly not explicit within key skills discourses.
    A good move to involve practising teachers at the grassroots, rather than at the "centre".
    Reporting instructions have been clear.'

3.  'A useful model.'
    'The model is seen by the programme team as particularly helpful in providing a simple concept of "graduate skill".'
    'In contrast [to some benchmark statements], Skills *plus* offers a much more coherent notion of what constitutes undergraduate education and its relation to personal development.'
    'Skills *plus* was the approach I was seeking. I was deeply dissatisfied with key skills curricular approaches ... [in contrast, Skills *plus* gives] "to airy nothing/A local habitation and a name".'
    'The cross-disciplinary approach is valuable.'

4.  Commonly reported influences on curriculum development processes:
    *   New discussions amongst staff, course, programme and School teams

    continued...

Box 12.1 continued

- More thinking about *learning* – e.g. a new interest in problem-based learning
- Curriculum audits
- Curriculum tuning, consolidation, clarification and innovation
- A greater emphasis on metacognition/reflection/'knowing' students
- Explicit documentation for students and reviewers
- Some increase in personal development planning, the keeping of learning portfolios and counselling students about their choice of modules and pathways
- Achieving the maximum, 24 points, in Quality Assurance Agency Subject Review.

5. Miscellaneous project benefits
   - Has stimulated research, including student research: surveys of students, their achievements and the contribution made by their degree programmes; and research with recent graduates
   - Has led to more connections with employers
   - Has led to successful bids for internal funding and scholarships
   - Has led to successful external bids and collaborations
   - Has raised awareness of the significance of activity outside the classroom (especially of part-time work and the co-curriculum)
   - Has raised awareness of metacognition
   - 'The [six] colloquia were excellent.'

colloquium meetings involving representatives of all participating departments, and the status and attendant publication opportunities that came from working in a high-profile national project.

We now describe each of the four project elements in turn.

### A programme focus

It should be clear that the concern is with complex learning, which takes years and involves plenty of practice, in which mistakes are made, judgement improves and capacity increases. If there is to be any hope of complex learning transferring from one context to another, then there is agreement that the learner needs to use that learning in different situations, *to be aware of using it, and to reflect on the sorts of situations in which it would be good to use it in future*.

One-shot approaches to skills development, such as a first year module on time management, usually fail or have little impact because complex learning is being treated as if it were pretty simple learning. It is not that the one-off module is inherently useless but rather that the key points need to be encountered repeatedly in somewhat different guises by learners who are aware that they are engaging with time management issues, for example, and who think strategically about how they could use what they are learning in the future. What is true of skills[2] is more compelling when it comes to embedded, encultured and embodied self-theories and habits of thought – when we look at efficacy beliefs and metacognition.

> Complex learning needs whole programme attention, the full three or four years of the undergraduate experience.

The learning we wish to encourage is not easily captured in the form of propositions and information. By and large it depends on repeated and diverse experiences accompanied by feedback designed to prompt strategic thinking. Agreed, students can be informed about the value of reflection or the ways in which helplessness becomes an acquired way of meeting the world. However, changing their self-theories and habits of thinking or strengthening their skills, depend, on a *sequence* of learning encounters and on thinking about them. This means that the programme should be seen in terms of its key concerns (with skills and much more besides), its key messages (for example, malleable self-theories are superior to fixed ones), and processes (the ways in which people learn, teach, assess or are assessed).

> This view of curriculum means that we do not ask departments to change the subject matter they teach. It does mean thinking about learning, teaching and assessment experiences and considering the ways in which they are distributed across the three or four year programme.

In curriculum development work with departments we need to avoid mistakes that are recognized by the literature on curriculum change in schools but which are little known in the higher education community. Four mistakes are:

* To rely too much on rational curriculum planning, which *begins* with statements of goals and learning outcomes. Learning arises from worthwhile engagements with worthwhile material. Outcomes can then be recognized and, if there seem to be imbalances at programme level, teaching, learning and assessment methods may be 'tuned' to get a better balance. It is a different matter to write content- and context-free outcomes and try to make the material and learning and teaching practices fit these abstractions.
* Scorched earth change, when the old is totally displaced by the new.
* Fast change.
* Paper changes, otherwise known as change without change.

A major implication is that we do not ask departments to *begin* by drawing up statements of learning outcomes or by signing up to someone else's list. A project view, which is derived from work on school curricula, is that learning outcomes tend to look after themselves when learners engage with worthwhile content through a variety of well-conceived learning, teaching and assessment processes that provide occasions for metacognition and consideration of self-theories.

However, outside bodies do want to see learning outcomes set out in programme specifications and they want to know where each outcome is promoted, developed and assessed. As it is, departments often do not know. A set of 'maps' (see Table 12.1) can satisfy them on these scores. So, we are clearly saying that it is necessary to explain what programmes do in terms of learning outcomes *and* that it is best to start with good content and good teaching and learning sequences, *then* identify the outcomes that they could legitimately be claimed to foster. If there turn out to be gaps then programme leaders can 'tune' the curriculum to fill them or decide that the learning outcome in question really ought not to be a part of the programme specification.

---

Project work with departments was not dominated by wrestling with statements of learning outcomes. Stocktaking and mapping led to some tuning of programmes to deal with gaps in the range of learning, teaching and assessment practices and in the outcomes that they served. The outcomes did not lead the work but the work was checked against lists of outcomes that might be associated with a programme in a subject area. Further tuning work dealt with any gaps that had been identified.

---

## Entitlements

A key principle in the project is that all students taking a programme and its constituent courses should be entitled to messages and encounters that develop understandings, skills, efficacy beliefs and metacognition. It is likely that the entitlements in different departments will have a great deal in common and it is inevitable that each set will be distinctive.

## Messages

The key messages that pervade the programme are likely to include:

- A major goal of the curriculum is to develop subject understanding, named skills, efficacy beliefs and metacognition. All four matter.
- Skills are widely valued. Students need to take stock of their achievements and create claims to having important skills; to take responsibility for identifying where their claims need development and for doing things to make

Table 12.1 Learning, teaching and assessment methods in the key modules of an undergraduate programme

| Teaching, learning and assessment activities | 101 | 102 | 103 | 200 | 201 | 202 | 203 | 204 | 301 | 302 | 303 | 304 | 305 | 306 | 311 |
|---|---|---|---|---|---|---|---|---|---|---|---|---|---|---|---|
| Lectures | ✓ | – | ✓ | ✓ | ✓ | ✓ | – | ✓ | – | ✓ | ✓ | – | ✓ | ✓ | – |
| Seminars | ✓ | – | – | ✓ | ✓ | ✓ | – | ✓ | – | ✓ | ✓ | – | ✓ | ✓ | – |
| Tutorials | All modules offer students opportunities to consult tutors on a one-to-one or small group basis, according to student preference. | | | | | | | | | | | | | | |
| Workshops | – | ✓ | ✓ | – | – | – | ✓ | ✓ | ✓ | – | – | ✓ | – | – | – |
| Problem-working | All modules engage students on problem-working activities, which vary within and between modules in complexity and the amount of scaffolding provided. EDS 300 is the capstone, involving complex problems that are typically identified and defined by students. | | | | | | | | | | | | | | |
| Structured work in peer groups | ✓ | ✓ | ✓ | – | – | – | ✓ | ✓ | ✓ | – | ✓ | ✓ | – | ✓ | – |
| Self-directed peer group work | – | ✓ | – | – | – | – | – | – | – | ✓ | ✓ | – | ✓ | ✓ | – |
| Group projects | – | ✓ | – | – | – | – | – | – | – | ✓ | – | ✓ | – | – | – |
| Structured independent study | – | – | ✓ | ✓ | ✓ | – | – | ✓ | ✓ | ✓ | – | ✓ | ✓ | ✓ | ✓ |
| Self-directed learning | – | – | – | – | ✓ | – | – | – | – | ✓ | – | ✓ | – | ✓ | ✓ |
| Web-enhanced teaching | – | ? | ? | ✓ | ✓ | – | ✓ | ✓ | – | ✓ | ✓ | ✓ | ✓ | ✓ | – |
| Web searches | – | ? | ? | – | – | – | ✓ | ✓ | ✓ | ✓ | ✓ | ✓ | ✓ | ✓ | ✓ |
| Practical work | – | ✓ | ? | – | – | – | – | – | – | ? | ? | ✓ | – | – | ✓ |
| Critical commentaries | – | – | – | – | ✓ | ✓ | ✓ | – | – | – | – | – | ✓ | ✓ | – |

| Teaching, learning and assessment activities | 101 | 102 | 103 | 200 | 201 | 202 | 203 | 204 | 301 | 302 | 303 | 304 | 305 | 306 | 311 |
|---|---|---|---|---|---|---|---|---|---|---|---|---|---|---|---|
| Essays | ✓ | – | ✓ | ✓ | ✓ | ✓ | ✓ | ✓ | ✓ | ✓ | – | ✓ | – | ✓ | – |
| Set reading | ✓ | – | ✓ | ✓ | ✓ | ✓ | ✓ | ✓ | ✓ | ✓ | ✓ | ✓ | ✓ | – | – |
| Analyses of target documents | ✓ | – | ✓ | ✓ | ✓ | ✓ | ✓ | – | – | – | ✓ | ✓ | – | ✓ | – |
| Interpreting data. | ✓ | ✓ | – | ✓ | ✓ | ✓ | ✓ | – | ✓ | ✓ | ✓ | ✓ | – | – | ✓ |
| Student presentations | – | ✓ | – | – | – | – | ✓ | ✓ | – | ✓ | – | ✓ | ✓ | ✓ | – |
| Written examinations | ✓ | ✓ | – | ✓ | ✓ | ✓ | ✓ | ✓ | ✓ | ✓ | ✓ | ✓ | ✓ | ✓ | – |
| Making a bibliography | – | ✓ | – | – | – | – | – | – | – | ✓ | – | – | – | – | ✓ |
| Literature review | – | ✓ | – | – | – | – | – | – | – | – | ✓ | – | – | ✓ | ✓ |
| Research design/ strategy | – | ✓ | – | – | – | – | – | ✓ | – | ✓ | ✓ | – | – | – | ✓ |
| Concept mapping | – | ? | – | – | – | – | ✓ | – | – | – | – | – | – | ? | – |

Note:
In some courses learning opportunities vary according to students' choice of task.

them stronger; to know how they will publicly support their claims to skills mastery to different groups – employers, for instance. (Some students are unaware of the skills they have acquired through higher education and their wider lives. Good personal development planning practices can make a lot of difference here.)

- People tend to be more effective in what they do, the more they have the following characteristics:
  - A belief that they can often (but not necessarily always) make a difference, i.e. they have self-efficacy (Bandura, 1997).
  - They have developed learned optimism in their approach to life, rather than learned helplessness (Seligman, 1998).
  - They have 'malleable' rather than fixed self-theories (Dweck, 1999).
  - They are motivated and determined in what they do (Pintrich and Schunk, 1996).
  - They use their experiences, positive and negative, as opportunities for further learning.

### Encounters, experiences and processes

If a degree simply warranted that a person had acquired a lot of information, or that they had a body of propositional knowledge, then there would be little need to worry about how that information or knowledge was acquired, as long as it was fit for the purpose.

However, a complex account of the aims of higher education implies that the nature of undergraduate encounters, experiences and processes do matter because some sorts of learning demand certain educational encounters. Information about, say, Heidegger's *Being and Time* can be acquired in many ways but skill at oral communication cannot be developed on the Internet; reflection benefits from there being people to reflect with; and developing self-theories that give weight to effort and mindfulness demands plenty of appropriate feedback on performance, including feedback from peers.

Three things to stress are:

1   The project team's knowledge of research into student learning is behind the list, in Box 12.2, of encounters, experiences or processes to which students should be entitled if we hope that they will have an undergraduate education aligned with the Skills *plus* model. Recall that not all encounters will be appropriate to all subjects and situations, and that others may be added.

2   If a programme is planned so that students have these encounters, and if they are organized in such a way that students experience progression – their engagements become progressively more challenging – then it is probable that those students will have satisfied learning outcome requirements of the sorts found in benchmarks, level descriptors and the like.

*Box 12.2* Principles of good teaching that are consistent with the development of employability (from Knight and Yorke, 2002)

1. Students' teaching encounters across a programme and in any one year of it should:
   - Alert them to the 'rules of the game' – make them aware of what is valued and how it may be produced, both in general and in each case.
   - Use the requisite variety of media (face-to-face, audio-visual, online conferencing, asynchronous information and communications technology).
   - Use the requisite variety of methods (presentations, Action Learning Sets,[3] work experience, seminars, proctoring, tutorials, computer-assisted instruction, independent study projects).
   - Be in a variety of styles (coaching, instructing, facilitating, clarifying).
   - Meet the standard indicators of good teaching, namely, interest, clarity, enthusiasm.
   - Be structured across the programme as a whole so that they get progressively less help and guidance from teachers as they encounter more complex situations, concepts, arrangements, etc.

   *This entitlement should be explicit in a programme-wide teaching summary.*

2. Students' learning activities across a programme and in any one year of it will be largely determined by their teaching entitlement. In addition:
   - There should be opportunities for depth study.
   - Curriculum should not be so crowded that 'surface' learning is encouraged at the expense of understanding.
   - Information and communications technology should be treated as a normal learning tool.
   - Students should expect to work collaboratively, whether learning tasks require it or not.
   - Time for strategic thinking, reflection, planning and portfolio-making should be written into the programme. Students should know that, and they should know that they are expected to engage with these learning activities and involve peers, friends and tutors at appropriate times.
   - There should be plentiful feedback that is intended to help future performance (rather than identify informational lapses), especially by encouraging self-theories that value effort and mindfulness.

   *This entitlement should be explicit in a programme-wide teaching summary.*

3. Entitlements for assessment encounters across a programme and in any one year of it were summarized in Box 8.1.

3   This is a practical approach centring on what people *do*. It is much easier to tune a programme using it than it is if you begin with benchmarks or other statements of learning outcomes and then try to make the curriculum fit.

## What's new?

What is new about these claims? Surely, this Skills *plus* model is only a set of practices that have been widely endorsed in the literature and by official agencies? Yes, Skills *plus* does commend practices that are already widely admired. However, the claim that the best way of planning coherent curricula that support complex learning goals is to concentrate on learning processes – encounters, environments and messages – is contrary to a preoccupation with module-level planning, on the one hand, and to the orthodoxies of 'rational curriculum planning' (RCP) and outcomes-led planning on the other. It establishes an alternative way of thinking about employability, one that is securely located in research and theory.

The model sketched here is direct because it is about what people do, not – as with outcomes thinking – about abstractions, nor – as with RCP – about logical accounts of what they *ought* to do.

- It is realistic, because the position that many complex learning outcomes cannot be precisely specified and cannot be reliably, ethically and cheaply assessed frees faculty from the Sisyphean search for valid, reliable and affordable ways of assessing them, or from trying to crush such assessments into traditional formats.
- It is accessible because it is easier to orchestrate key messages, encounters and environments than it is to write learning outcomes and work back from them to curriculum.
- It is more respectful of academic freedom than some attempts to assure and enhance quality have been.[4]

Of course, departments and universities must continue to gather the best, most reliable evidence of student achievements in terms of criteria that are valued by employers, funding bodies and governments. It is right that they should state, as clearly as possible, what they expect students to understand and be able to do, and it is proper that evidence of student achievements should be publicly available. However, it may be easier to do these things if we *start* by planning for entitlements to vital learning, teaching and assessment engagements that are suited to complex, important and often hard-to-measure learning outcomes.

## Stocktaking

Existing programmes will already deliver many of these entitlements, which means that most programmes could make strong claims that what they do is educationally good and enhances students' employability.

These educational and employability claims would be strengthened if programme leaders knew where and when students got these entitlements and had these encounters. For example, it is common for oral work, such as presentations, to appear in professionally- and vocationally-oriented modules in the first and final years. Programme leaders need to know this in order to judge whether students are getting sufficient and sustained engagement with oral communication for them to have a reasonable chance of becoming proficient in it. Conversely, programme leaders need to know which entitlements are absent from the programme, rarely appear, or are not evenly distributed across the programme. Finally, leaders need to know whether the people teaching first and final year courses, say, deal with the same skills or learning processes in suitably different ways – they need to know about any planned progression. This 'stocktaking' or auditing is a key part of planning the curricula that are needed if the Skills *plus* approach to complex learning is to be effective.

We recommend three refinements on the obvious procedure of sending each module tutor a questionnaire.

- By all means include all teaching colleagues but it is the modules that are central to an award that matter most. If need be, concentrate on them.
- Make the enquiry in stages – (1) ask about teaching and learning methods, then (2) about module learning outcomes, then (3) about assessment methods. This does not overwhelm colleagues and also gives two points (between enquiries a and b, and between 2 and 3) to talk with colleagues about any matches/mismatches in their answers.
- Recognize that colleagues will claim to promote a myriad of learning outcomes and perhaps to use a wide range of learning, teaching and assessment methods, which is admirable. In each case, though, ask them to identify just the two, three or four that get sustained and deliberate attention or use. The reasoning is that there is a better chance of teaching, learning and assessing things that are clear priorities: other things may be fostered but will be hard to pick out of the background. Concentrate instead on three or four highlights, checking, of course, that this does not end up excluding anything truly important.

Departments will, if they broadly accept our position, wish to take stock of their programmes to establish the pattern of coverage of learning, teaching and assessment entitlements and the ways in which they are organized to promote progression.

Table 12.1 shows the edited results of the audit of learning and teaching methods in core courses on one programme. It led to an audit of the priority outcomes of learning for each of these modules and thence to an audit of principal assessment methods. Some 'tuning' or rearrangements followed each audit.

## Tuning

It follows that departments should tune their programmes so that gaps are filled or deliberately left unfilled and so that progression is planned into the sequence of encounters.

This is not a mechanical matter because it depends on judgement about, and sensitivity to, what is possible in the circumstances. The aim is that at the end of the process each participating department will be able to make a confident claim that its programme contains well-sequenced encounters and messages that, taken together, offer learners a good chance of being able to make strong claims to employability. At the same time those engagements should enhance the learning that takes place during the programme and also help undergraduates to become genuinely useful in a variety of workplaces.

This is not a simple process. That is not because we think that the Skills *plus* model is difficult or demanding – our knowledge of the research into curriculum planning in schools makes us think that 'tuning' is simpler and far more intuitive than starting with statements of learning outcomes (and project experience points in the same direction). However, the use of negotiation to orchestrate the elements of a programme into a harmonic set means that the approach can be slow.

Each department needs to have someone who has confidence and authority to work on programme-wide development. Notice the implication that employability is one facet of programme enhancement and that it ought to be given to someone who has at least an understanding of (and preferably responsibilities in respect of) student retention and success, assessment, teaching quality appraisal, course reviews, and so on. Where such quality enhancement functions are distributed amongst several people there is a considerable danger that teachers will be harassed by colleagues with different missions.

The tuning work generally comprises five major activities:

### Orchestrating

Employability co-ordinators need to ensure that the curriculum, as a whole, contains a fitting, well-sequenced blend of the messages and encounters. Their job of orchestration is crucial to the project's success.

### Negotiating

There will be continuing conversations with module tutors to encourage them to tune their modules by, for example,

- Replacing some learning, teaching and assessment practices by others, thereby helping to get a balance of encounters across the programme.
- Identifying opportunities to highlight some of the key programme messages, particularly in module handbooks and task specifications.

- Adopting new ways of marking work and giving feedback so that self-theories are addressed and key messages are communicated.
- Developing, as need be, new ways of organizing teaching and learning – for example, by setting group projects or requiring web-based inquiries to be done.

The aim of this negotiation is to get colleagues to agree to present their modules in ways that allow it to be said that the programme, as a whole, gives a good, sustained and progressive coverage of the valued encounters and key messages.

Inevitably, the specific circumstances of each department mean that what is negotiated is:

- Provisional – things will continue to change as opportunities emerge, possibilities for improvement are seen and some things are abandoned because they prove too difficult.
- The best that can be done at a time, in a place, given the circumstances.
- Nevertheless, an improvement on what went before.

### Learning

Co-ordinators themselves have learning needs, particularly needs to become confident with this approach to enhancing employability and the quality of students' learning. The Skills *plus* project was able to go some way to accommodate these needs, but in general there is remarkably little professional education in pedagogy and curriculum for heads of department, team leaders and other change agents.

### Clarifying

The project used low cost, high gain methods to make a difference, relying on clarification of existing good practice as much as on innovation. However, incremental approaches run the risk that casual observers, and even students, might not appreciate how well-crafted the revised programmes are. Of course, this is less likely if the key messages really do saturate the programme and its documentation. Nevertheless, the gains will be greatest when it is clear to all involved that the programme is distinctive because it has embedded good practice in order to enhance learning and employability.

Programmes are seriously weakened if students do not know what it is they are learning, formally and non-formally. In what sense has learning taken place if students are not able to identify it, describe it and support claims to it with evidence?

This point can be summarized by asking whether we know something if we are not aware of knowing it. If students, teachers, employers and colleagues do not know that the tuned programme is a powerful means of improving learning and employability, then in what sense can it be a powerful means?

*Sharing*

When people who lead programme reform are networking with each other and with institutional leaders who have responsibility for teaching and learning, then more can be achieved, and with greater efficiency, than if they work alone. The UK Learning and Teaching Support Network[5] offers cross-institutional brokerage and advice to departments and HEIs, and has a commitment to employability through its Generic Centre and Subject Centres.

## Targeting and a curriculum for all

This approach is concerned with the mainstream curriculum and with the sorts of entitlements that should be available to all students. However, consideration of *employment* statistics makes us wonder whether the *employability* of some students might need to be 'over-enhanced' because the labour market does not work even-handedly and certain groups of students face systemic disadvantage when it comes to looking for graduate work. However attractive the Skills *plus* approach might be, it might reasonably be seen as being misconceived, in that it could be seen as favouring those who will often already have plenty of social and cultural capital and offering little to those who may lack sufficient capital to even appreciate the significance of employability-enhancing work, let alone benefit from it. Within higher education, targeting of particular student groups is a possibility but this can be construed negatively in terms of stigmatization. However, the problem probably lies – to a greater extent – outside the boundary of higher education, in the recruitment of graduates. Though we might wish to do something to improve matters in that realm, this lies beyond our reach.

## Beyond the module

The 'tuning' approach is clearly a programme-level approach that, through the principles of subsidiarity and negotiation, touches the modules that contribute to an award – certainly the most popular ones. Some will see this as an erosion of academic freedom and although we have been at pains to argue that it is not, there is no doubt that it does require teachers to be mindful of their contribution to programmes of study. There is also a benefit.

We have often observed colleagues in despair because they have failed to assess professional competence in a module, or they cannot see how to turn students into poised writers in ten weeks, or because they cannot see how to cover the main elements of employability in their course. Hargreaves (1994) has written a good account of the ways in which schoolteachers tend to give themselves a hard time and feel guilt, shame and despair by trying, individually, to solve problems that are not soluble (the reliable assessment of some complex achievements) or which can only be solved by department or school. Teachers try to do alone things that are beyond the reach of individuals and, sometimes, beyond the reach of any wise person.

We have argued that employability and associated judgements of achievement are like that. Agreed, enthusiasts can have a great impact in the co-curriculum but it falls to programme *teams* to plan for the assessment of fitness to practise,[6] the development of slow-to-grow achievements and the presentation of well-founded claims to be highly employable. This leads us to a conclusion that is, we think, important and often overlooked: individual teachers should not be expected to rectify leadership, design and management failures. The teacher expected to assess fitness to practise in a single module is probably working in a badly-designed, supinely-led programme. We have often seen this with assessment, where colleagues ask how to solve what they think of as assessment problems but which are really design or leadership issues and therefore *not their problem* – and certainly no reason for shame and guilt.

Heads of department may, in their turn, say that they are constrained by institutional leadership and policies and we agree that some aspects of employability carry implications for whole institutions, or substantial parts of institutions, and could cause intra-institutional difficulties if programmes or departments 'went it alone'. Chapter 13, then, moves 'up a level' to that of the whole institution and considers some of the issues that have a strong supra-departmental significance.

## Notes

1  Note that these expectations have an element of piety about them, since they do not address the (admittedly difficult) question of how to assess some of the personal skills and qualities they commend.
2  The term is used for convenience. Objections have been described in Chapters 1 and 2.
3  Action Learning Sets are small co-operative learning groups that meet regularly to work on members' problems. Problem-working should lead all members to learn with each other, the underlying belief being that learning comes from action and that good actions are based on learning.
4  Although there is no direct comparison between the way government treats schools and higher education, it is salutary to hear that between 2000 and 2002 the English education ministry sent 75 official documents to secondary schools.
5  See www.ltsn.ac.uk. At the time of writing it is not clear what will replace the LTSN in 2004.
6  Recall from the discussion of reliability in Chapter 8 that such judgements should be based on repeated observations in a variety of settings (or on a variety of tasks) by different trained observers using performance indicators that are understood similarly by all parties. These technical requirements can only exceptionally be met at module level.

# Chapter 13

# An institutional perspective on employability

## Reprise

We begin this final chapter with a reminder that our view is that there is a considerable degree of overlap between the aim of supporting good learning and that of enhancing employability, and that it is a misperception to see these as being substantially oppositional. *The Sunday Times* quotes the head of the policy unit at the UK Institute of Directors, saying that

> The view of our members is that, providing that a course is intellectually demanding, it will turn out people with potentially employable skills ... Classics and medieval history turn out people with super brains and the employer can be satisfied that someone has stretched themselves.
>
> (11 May 2003: 13)

Although we think there is more to employability than a demanding course in Classics, the general position that employability is enhanced by good programmes is in line with our thinking. If we aim for the development in students of good learning in the discipline *and* of achievements that are more 'generic' in character, then success in employment (and in life generally) is likely to be greater.

However, there is a view that academic programmes can be 'diluted' by material that is not subject-specific, to the point that the organization might choose not to recruit graduates who have followed such programmes. Utley (2003), reporting on a CRAC conference, quotes David Lathbury, the Head of Process Chemistry at AstraZeneca, as saying that 'businesses were increasingly frustrated by degree programme add-ons, such as computing skills and foreign languages, that aimed to broaden course appeal but distracted from the core subjects' (p.1).

Lathbury was further quoted as saying

> This is a very worrying trend. There seems to be an emphasis on generalist skills at the expense of core subjects. But the fact is we don't mind whether someone can use PowerPoint or not. We are interested in whether they are scientifically able.
>
> (Utley, 2003: 1)

We see here a hint of the view that generic achievements are oppositional to those in the discipline. Our line is that the generic has to be located within an academic context if the student gain is to be maximized, and in subsequent correspondence Lathbury (2003) indicated that he shared this view. However, the interview data summarized in Chapter 4 show that in some employment contexts the disciplinary requirement is stronger than it is in others. There is no 'one size fits all' approach to facilitating student success, as far as curriculum design and structure is concerned. For some types of curricula the emphasis is primarily on the discipline, although it is usually said that a number of generic achievements go with developing expertise in the discipline; for others the emphasis may be more definitely on general intellectual development across one or more subject areas. The difference does not imply that some curricula are intrinsically 'better' than others for developing 'graduateness':[1] they may, however, be better in respect of some employment opportunities than others.

Let us, for a moment, reflect on what 'scientifically able' might mean. Obviously the term incorporates disciplinary understanding, the capacity to conduct investigations rigorously, and probably some capacity for innovative thinking. The scientist employee also needs to be able to communicate well with colleagues. We prefer to think in terms of graduates being 'scientifically effective', which would stretch beyond a narrow interpretation of 'scientifically able', in that our term captures something of the more generic achievements that are needed *in addition to* an individual's expertise as a scientist in the laboratory. Whilst an ability to handle PowerPoint may be useful, the more fundamental requirement is an ability to present proposals and findings convincingly to others, and in a manner that does not jar with the intended recipients' expectations (which implies some sensitivity to matters such as internal politics, and how best to handle them). Where the science is conducted on a team basis, as is often the case, the ability to work constructively with others is another important component of scientific effectiveness.

Although we have addressed the relationship of subject discipline to employability by discussing one particular disciplinary area, we believe that what we are saying has a general applicability. The challenge, as we see it, is how institutions might exploit, through their curricula, the commonalities of good learning and employability to maximize the chances of student success.

## The institutional aspect

Knight and Trowler (2001) and Trowler *et al.* (2003) argue that the department (or similar academic organizational unit) is where much change is instigated and carried through. In the UK higher education system of forty years ago, there would have been little point in making the argument, since by and large academic programmes were run in departments which had a considerable degree of independence. Departmental autonomy was the norm. Today, government in the UK[2] exercises considerable influence over an expanded system, through both policy-making and its implementation through funding and other agencies[3] (such as the Quality Assurance Agency). The same applies, *mutatis mutandis*, elsewhere in the world.

Other developments have militated against departmental autonomy. The rise of modular schemes in the UK, paralleling from the late 1980s developments of far longer standing in the US, sought to achieve flexibility in student choice and also to make more efficient use of institutional resources. This is not the place to discuss the merits or otherwise of the move (there are arguments on both sides), but the integration of hitherto freestanding programmes brought with it a need for institution-wide structures and processes. The institution developed as a corporate entity as the powers of departments became constrained.

The consequence of changes such as these is that the institutional dimension cannot be ignored. Pro-Vice-Chancellors and the like are given institutional responsibilities in respect of policy development and implementation. Contemporary policy concerns in the UK are widening participation, learning and teaching, student retention and completion, and student employability. Life-long learning was a major concern a few years ago but seems to have exceeded the politicians' attention-span. However, our view that employability has life-long implications would lead us to assert the value of an approach to institutional policy-making that would integrate life-long learning with the contemporary concerns we have listed. We make the point because some institutional structures disperse responsibilities for these policy concerns amongst various senior colleagues who may be so pressed (often by bureaucratic requirements) that they have little time to think deeply about and research the policy areas for which they have responsibility, let alone join up their thinking with that of colleagues. There is a need for senior colleagues to have time for thinking about the complex challenges facing their institutions: this may imply some reduction in the time given to 'administrivia' and committee work.

All of the five policy concerns noted in the preceding paragraph bear in some manner on the ways in which an institution approaches curriculum design and implementation. The focus of attention of this book has been employability, but there have been a number of points at which the connection with other policy concerns has been readily apparent. We seek in this chapter, therefore, to examine some of the institutional implications of engaging with employability as we have described it. Our alignment of employability with good learning makes it inevitable that we do this by concentrating on curriculum-related issues. We exemplify our concern for learning and employability by addressing four institution-level concerns.

## Four institution-level concerns

Whilst employability can be accentuated in particular curricula, we address here four concerns that need attention at institutional level: learning environments, personal development planning, assessment, and quality assurance and enhancement.

## Learning environments[4]

In Chapter 7 we described a number of ways in which aspects of employability can be built into curricula, or promoted through the co-curriculum, including:

- Employability through the whole curriculum.
- Employability in the core curriculum.
- Work-based or work-related learning incorporated as one or more components within the curriculum.
- Employability-related module(s) within the curriculum.
- Work-based or work-related learning in parallel with the curriculum.

Let us repeat our appreciation of the useful gains that can be made from free-standing modules focusing on aspects of employability and say again that gains are likely to be greater where the opportunity is taken to use the subject discipline as the site for learning of a more generic kind. We therefore concentrate on employability in core curricula, acknowledging that it is difficult to get pedagogic coherence when there are many optional and elective modules. We also acknowledge that some work-based or work-related learning frequently takes place relatively independently of the academically-driven parts of the core curriculum. Our view is that any appraisal of a programme in which employability is a priority should consider the way that employability is being fostered through the variety of learning opportunities that are available in the co-curriculum, but always with a concern that these extra-curricular opportunities should be widely taken up and not confined to a privileged minority.

As we said in Chapter 6, learning is not only tied to instruction, but develops from non-formal settings as well as from the set-piece engagements typical of higher education. This draws us to plan in terms of the total learning environment. We highlighted four areas of significance:

- Students' approaches to learning in general.
- Students' approaches to studying in undertaking a particular task.
- Whether the learning environment is generally rich in possibilities for learning.
- The degree to which the curriculum is internally consistent or, in Biggs' (2003) terms, 'aligned'.

The institution has explicit responsibilities in respect of the last two, and some implicit responsibilities in respect of the first two (in that staff are in a position to influence students in their approaches to learning and studying). However good the learning environment is, student success is influenced by motivations, perceptions, and self-theories – and hence the outcome in terms of student success is only probabilistic. As Goodyear puts it:

> … we should recognize that we cannot influence directly the learner's cognitive activity… the best we can do is help set up some organizational forms or

structures that are likely to be conducive to the formation and well-being of convivial learning relationships. Learning communities may then emerge. Thirdly, we must recognize that the learner has freedom to reconfigure or customize their learnplace.

(Goodyear, 2002: 66)

It then follows that curriculum design has to be seen as the provision of a facilitating framework for learning rather than a tight prescription (see Ganesan *et al.*, 2002). This opens up the possibility of incorporating, via devices such as personal development planning and portfolio construction, learning that is tailored to the needs of the student whilst remaining true to disciplinary expectations. In this way the challenge regarding equity that was introduced in Chapter 1 and revisited briefly towards the end of Chapter 12 begins to move towards some form of resolution.

### Personal development planning

In Chapter 8 we considered some of the implications of recommendation 20 of the Dearing Report (NCIHE, 1997), which was that institutions, over the medium-term, should develop the concept of a progress file designed to assist students to identify their achievements and to provide information to others about these. Two elements were envisaged:

- A transcript recording achievement (which should follow a common format).
- A means through which students could monitor and reflect upon their personal development, and thereby build on their achievements. This has become known as personal development planning (PDP).

The programme transcript is likely to be little more than a list of courses, levels and credit ratings. It will have the advantage of relating to the European Diploma Supplement, which is intended to create a European currency for education qualifications. It should have important implications for the portability of qualifications but, as Adelman (1990) warns, it should not be anticipated that the transcript alone will be very informative about student achievements.

As we have said, PDP is a set of processes that are valuable in their own right and also a product – a portfolio of achievements – that can help in securing employment. If it is to optimize the chances of student success, PDP is likely to require an institutional approach that brings together academic departments and student support services (particularly specialists in generic study and learning support, and the Careers Service). A fully coherent PDP scheme will ensure that the following are provided:

- Guidance that addresses generic learning and study needs.
- Guidance on how to address subject-specific learning needs.

- Guidance on career planning and job seeking.
- Support for, and guidance on making and maintaining, portfolios that will sustain strong claims to employability.

In many institutions this is a novel challenge because, although there may be informal contacts between those with an interest in PDP, and collaboration between some of them on particular projects, there is seldom a history of them coming together to see how the experience of students following particular tracks or pathways of study can be effectively supported. The demarcation of responsibilities may differ from institution to institution, although there is often a bifurcation between generic student support on the one side and programme-specific concerns on the other, which is reflected in senior managers' spheres of responsibility.

## Assessment

As we suggested in Chapter 8, and more extensively elsewhere (Knight and Yorke, 2003b), the inclusion of some facets of employability in assessment schemes is fraught with difficulty: the validity, reliability and affordability of assessing contributions to team activity – to give just one example from the many possible – are highly problematic. Some kinds of performance are not amenable to grading with the robustness that is desirable when students are to be 'labelled' with an overall grade point average or honours degree classification. Hence there is a tendency not to include such performances, or alternatively to give them a weighting that trivializes them in the eyes of students, with predictable consequences for student behaviour.[5]

Whereas a self-contained programme in a particular discipline might have the scope to revise its approach to assessment, the same may not apply so strongly in the case of an institution-wide modular scheme. However, when a student embarks on a programme involving a combination of subjects their experience of assessment is likely to be a somewhat haphazard consequence of module choice,[6] rather than the kind of structured experience it can be in the core modules of a single honours programme (which is tantamount to a self-contained programme). For an institution operating a modular scheme, then, there is a need to address the assessment of employability – and assessment in general, for that matter – at an institutional level. This attention to the coherence of assessment practices is one aspect of the need we see for institutions to pay more attention to programme coherence.

There is also the challenge of representing a student's performances (the plural is deliberate) in respect of the curriculum that they have followed. It is uninformative – to the student and to anyone seeking to infer the student's potential – to combine, in a single grading, performances that have been achieved against quite different curricular expectations. As the English White Paper on higher education (DfES, 2003) recognizes, a preferred approach to the representation of variegated achievements is a matter for national systems rather than for individual institutions, since the latter could disadvantage their students if they chose a reporting methodology that was at variance with the norm.

### Quality assurance and enhancement

On the assumption that the curriculum aims include the development of students' employability, five of the seven questions[7] that underpinned the quality audit process run by the erstwhile Higher Education Quality Council in the UK make helpful starting points. They are:

- How are you doing it [i.e. developing students' employability]?
- Why are you doing it that way?
- Why do you think that is the best way of doing it? [Presumably an inferior way would not knowingly have been selected.]
- How do you know it works?
- How do you improve it?

The fourth of these questions might better be phrased 'How do you know that you are achieving what you should be achieving?', since there is a risk that the appraiser might be satisfied if what was originally specified was believed to be sufficient and that things 'were being done right' as far as curriculum implementation was concerned. The question 'Is there a better way of doing it?' might therefore be overlooked, yet those involved in quality enhancement hold that there is always the possibility of 'doing things better' – sometimes through incremental change, sometimes through radical change:[8] however, to do things better involves critical appraisal of what is being done. We have indicated in Chapters 9–12 how some critical appraisals were conducted under the Skills *plus* project, using a finer-grained operational conception of employability than the broad definition we have given in Chapter 1. Critical appraisal, of course, leads on to the fifth question, which takes us into the territory of institutional learning and development.

### Models for the development of excellence

Two models that have gained currency on either side of the Atlantic in recent years are the Baldrige Performance Excellence Framework (latterly differentiated into business and education strands) which guides organizations towards application for the Malcolm Baldrige National Quality Award in the US, and the EFQM Excellence Model which does likewise in respect of the European Quality Award.[9] Whilst it is not our purpose to discuss in any detail these models or other quality-related processes, such as the ISO 9000 series, the models contain pointers to ways in which institutions might think about approaching the development of employability (amongst many other things).

The Baldrige and EFQM models share some common features, though the language used differs. For anyone familiar with thinking about organizational development, the list of commonalities will generate little surprise: leadership; strategic planning; an orientation towards results; the effective and efficient management of processes; staff development; and learning from experience. How might these models be applied to employability? The models exhibit considerable cross-flow between components, and our brief treatment here makes no attempt to treat each component in a compartmentalized way.

The academic leadership commitment to employability has to be associated with sufficient institutional sponsorship if it is to be taken seriously. This does not mean that a senior academic has to be 'the institutional expert' on employability, but rather that such a person has to understand enough about what it implies to take the role of institutional champion (and the role has to be sustained if it is to be effective) in respect of development and implementation. Others may well have the specialist expertise that can be drawn upon for curriculum and staff development. The view of employability that we have set out in this book carries messages about the way that student learning might best be facilitated – active learning, enhanced formative assessment, and so on. Some staff will already be well acquainted with the kinds of expectation that follow a commitment to employability; others will be less so, implying a need for appropriate staff development activity if the pedagogic processes are to be optimally effective and efficient in the development of employability. In making this point, we remark that those in managerial positions, especially heads of department and deans, may need to develop their professional understanding of what is implied in a commitment to employability, how this might interlock with other policy initiatives (such as widening participation, and learning and teaching), and impact on the pedagogic practices of other colleagues.

The Enhancing Student Employability Co-ordination Team in England (ESECT), in collaboration with the UK-wide Generic Centre of the Learning and Teaching Support Network, is making available a range of resources that support the 'employability agenda' in the UK.[10] In England, the need for institutions to produce, and act on, learning and teaching strategies[11] provides a vehicle for the enhancement of employability, broadly in the way that the Enterprise in Higher Education initiative a decade and a half earlier contracted with UK institutions to inculcate 'enterprise' in their students.[12] We anticipate that the Teaching Quality Academy[13] that has been proposed in the government White Paper on higher education (DfES, 2003) has the potential to stimulate a wide range of pedagogical development, including employability.

Institutions that draw significant funds from the state will often be under some pressure to develop a set of criteria against which their performance can be achieved. For example, Dary Erwin, director of James Madison University's Center for Assessment and Research comments that

> Nonprofits are being asked to show evidence that they're doing what they're supposed to be doing ... since we are in another economic downturn, there is even greater pressure for accountability ... every national task force report shows people in industry and business questioning the knowledge, communication skills and quality of thinking that job applicants bring to them with their diplomas.
>
> (Dolan, 2003: 24)

Institutions need to establish ways of judging the employability of their students ('measurement' may be too strong a word here, given the difficulties that exist regarding the assessment of employability). We reiterate the point that employability should not be confused with the gaining of employment, be this a 'graduate job' or otherwise. The purpose of criteria is twofold: first, they allow indexing of student achievements; second, they allow the institution to assess how successful it has been. They thus provide a basis for institutional learning, and hence an opportunity to feed this learning into future plans and processes. This kind of information provision for learning would, in the US, typically be undertaken by offices tasked with 'institutional research' (Volkwein, 1999). The notion of institutional research is, on the whole, less well developed in the UK and Europe, and this could be seen as an institutional shortcoming when juxtaposed with the expectations of the Baldrige and EFQM 'excellence' models.

If employability is merely seen as a 'bolt-on' extra to curricula, then its promotion within the institution is perhaps more a tactical than a strategic matter. Where employability is seen as suffusing curricula (which, as we noted earlier, has wide-ranging implications for learning environments, pedagogy and assessment), strategic planning becomes much more important. Without it, the development of employability-sensitive learning opportunities could become a matter of chance, depending on the extent to which particular groups of staff and individuals were actively engaged in its promotion. We repeat that a strategic approach does not imply that developments have to be identical, and that any multidisciplinary institution has to be responsive to its intra-institutional constituencies' characters and aspirations. The principle of subsidiarity is important here, with the managerial imperative being to find a balance between tightness and looseness that optimizes the effectiveness of both the overarching framework and local adaptation.

## Managing change and innovation

Fullan (2001: 69) reminds us that, whilst innovation may be technologically simple, it is socially complex. The same is true of change that might not merit the label of 'innovation'. In other words, it is relatively easy to design responses to challenges, but considerably less easy to implement them in any system that requires the co-operation of others. The problem of staff engagement probably has a lot to do with the 'false promise' of innovation projects that we noted at the beginning of the previous chapter.

Academics respond differentially to change, as Trowler (1998) found in his study of change in a new university in the UK. In the institution studied by Trowler, individuals' strategies for coping varied. He identified four types of response: 'sinking' fatalistically; living with the change at the expense of their performance in other aspects of their work; seeing opportunities arising from the change; and finding ways in which they could reconstruct policy relating to the change. The challenge for those with managerial responsibilities is to encourage a positive engagement with necessary change – something that requires more than merely 'talking the talk'. If a reasonably broad commitment to change cannot be gained, then implementation is seriously at risk.

Figure 13.1, developed from Klein and Sorra's (1996) theoretically-driven analysis of innovation in industrial/commercial organizations, catches something of the complexity inherent in the implementation of an innovation. A higher education institution can be represented as a matrix of disciplines and managerially functional levels (with, in some institutions, not every discipline being represented at the uppermost level – labelled F4 in Figure 13.1 – comprising, say, Pro-Vice-Chancellors and Deans of Faculty). A number of factors will influence the commitment of any segment (horizontal or vertical) of the institution:

- Perceptions of the institutional climate.
- The perceived validity of the innovation.
- The incentives or disincentives that are present.
- The capabilities of those who are expected to implement the innovation.
- The perceived advantages and disadvantages of engaging in the implementation process.
- The 'fit' between the innovation and the values of those involved.

The more positive each factor is, the greater the likelihood that commitment will be engendered and that the implementation process will be effective. If any

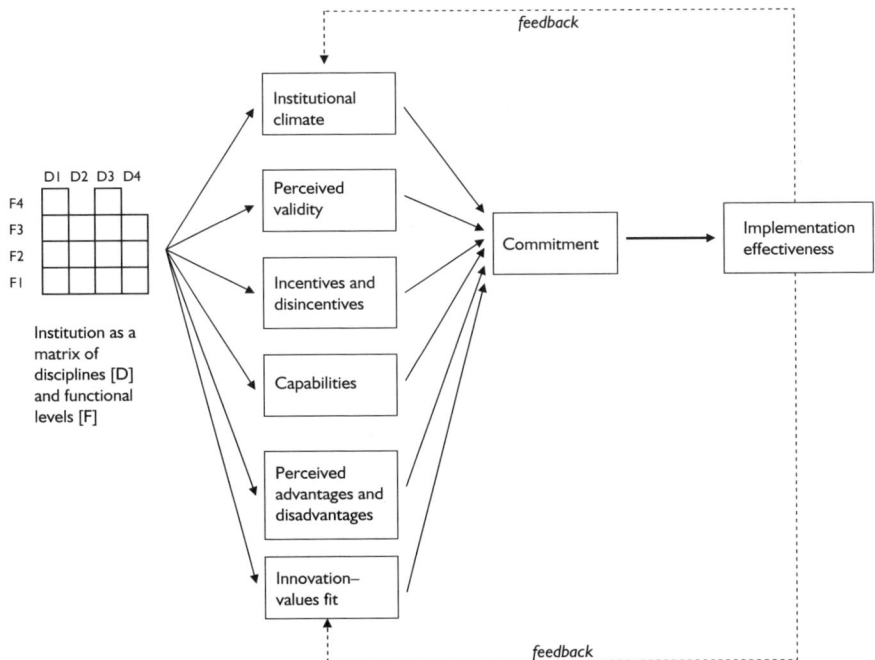

*Figure 13.1* Factors influencing the implementation of an innovation

factor is perceived to be strongly negative, then this could be sufficient to outweigh any positives elsewhere. For example, if colleagues believe (against the argument of this book) that employability has no proper conceptual underpinning,[14] or if they place their academic emphasis heavily on the subject discipline (in the sense that employability is not a significant component of their educational value systems), then the implementation of curricular initiatives designed to enhance employability may be fatally compromised from the outset. Whether the innovation 'works' or not, there will be feedback effects on the factors that govern commitment, and hence future effectiveness.

The successful adoption and implementation of innovation in an institution depend upon the skill with which staff become acquainted with the need for change, and with which change is introduced. As Elton (2003) remarks – and as the Skills *plus* project sought to do – it is sensible for senior managers to work with the grain of the culture rather than against it.

The cultures of higher education institutions are quite varied, and some approaches to the management of change that appear in the literature on organizational change may not fit well the culture of a particular institution. There are perhaps two 'ideal types' (in the Weberian sense) of institutional approach to organization and management – the top-down and the bottom-up. The top-down approach locates power at 'the centre', whence policy directives emanate for conversion into action by departments and smaller groups of staff. The bottom-up approach leaves innovation largely to departments and similar units, on the grounds that this is where the driving force for change is located, and that the role of the senior managers is to support initiatives (provided that they are consistent with broad institutional policy, according to the principle of 'subsidiarity'), and to add value to them. Some years ago, higher education in the UK exhibited a very marked polarity in management style, though latterly the gap has narrowed as governmental agencies have encouraged institutions to be corporate in their behaviour (by promoting initiatives such as the requirement for institutional learning and teaching strategies), and as strongly centralized institutions have appreciated that the liberalization of educational markets places a premium on educational innovation and entrepreneurialism.

Much of the literature on organizational change and development relates to industrial and commercial bodies in which chief executive officers exert considerable authority and power. The increasing pressures on institutions to 'behave corporately' do, however, give some of the points from this vast literature a resonance that they might not have had in earlier times, though translation into the world of higher education needs to be accompanied by plenty of caution and a preparedness to make adjustments. The following eight points, based primarily on Argyris (1990), Burnes (1992), Cherniss and Caplan (2001), Kotter (1996) and Trowler *et al.* (2003), may be helpful both to the head of the institution and to senior managers and leaders of academic organizational units, provided that they are interpreted in a manner appropriate to the context.

1   Understand approaches to change
2   Justify the need
3   Undertake groundwork
4   Establish an implementation team
5   Communicate well
6   Develop a shared commitment
7   Generate some early successes
8   Consolidate and embed the gains.

## Understand approaches to change

Trowler *et al*. (2003: 7) tabulate five theories about change: technical-rational; resource allocation; diffusionist; continuous quality improvement; and complexity-based. The tabulation is useful since it succinctly summarizes a range of considerations that apply in respect of each of the five theories. For example, the technical-rational theory uses engineering as its guiding metaphor, and assumes that a well-designed intervention will bring about the desired change. The trouble is, of course, that a change introduced 'from the top' is likely to become attenuated as it is interpreted (perhaps misinterpreted) by members of the complex human system that makes up a higher education institution.

None of the other theories probably 'works' in a pure form where institution-wide change is being sought. However, each has something to offer the change agent: the skill of change lies in knowing which theory is being called on at any particular time, knowing why it is the most appropriate for the purpose in hand, and in being able to operate in a range of ways appropriate to the circumstances in such a manner that this does not compromise the integrity of the promoter of change. Blackwell and Preece (2002) draw on Buchanan and Badham (1999) to point out that the promotion of change has a pragmatic, rather than perfectly ideal, aspect, since universal ethical principles are difficult to apply to political behaviour in organizations. Decisions (and, we would add, the consequential actions) need to be based on 'informed judgement of what is possible, what is acceptable, of what is justifiable and of what is defensible in the situation' (Buchanan and Badham, 1999: 206). Trowler *et al*. (2003: 18–19) offer some useful thoughts to those with leadership roles in respect of change.

## Justify the need

A precondition for innovation or change is that there is an identifiable need that is related to the institution's mission (or, perhaps, that might change the institution's mission). If the institution is to make a feature of employability (or any other aspiration, for that matter), there is a need to make the case for it and to explain why it has to be addressed at this particular point. The development of students' employability is a policy objective of the UK Government, and institutions are expected to respond – hence there is a strong external rationale for action, rather than an internally-focused rationale such as seeking some form of improvement in staff performance. The first challenge for the institution is to find a way of responding that is consistent with academics' expectations. The alignment of employability with good learning offers a rationale with which many academics would be reasonably content. The second, and for some institutions greater, challenge is to justify the need for action *at a particular point in time*. Kotter (1996) claims that by far the greatest mistake in seeking to implement organizational change lies in pressing ahead without having established the necessary sense of urgency.

The urgency of enhancing students' employability is likely to vary with the institution. In those in which the completion and employment indicators are high, the reaction is likely to be the question with which we began this book: 'Where's the problem? Our students are succeeding anyway.' As Hannan and Silver put it:

> For certain traditional institutions the nature of their intake has remained more or less constant, the demands of employers fairly distant and the temptations of government-advocated reforms generally resistible, despite the necessity of some minimal effort in response.
>
> (Hannan and Silver, 2000: 140)

They go on to observe that

> One of the biggest problems confronting universities ... is to convince their teaching staff, who have so far not been tempted to jump on the innovation 'bandwagon', of the desirability of the new directions advocated by senior managers.
>
> (Hannan and Silver, 2000: 141)

For other institutions, a commitment to employability may be perceived as attractive to the body of students that it sees as forming its intake. It may also be seen as contributing to institutional survival: the provisions of the recent White Paper on higher education (DfES, 2003) portend considerable upheaval in the sector (particularly for the new universities and colleges), and institutions are having to re-evaluate how they should position themselves in the market. For some institutions, a reshaping of their academic portfolios is likely to meet the criterion of urgency.

The problem with Hannan and Silver's analysis is the implicit assumption that it is the senior managers who have a superior wisdom and/or connection to external constituencies. Whilst this might have a measure of validity in some institutions, in others it probably does not, since academics have their own networks through which they can acquire understandings of what external constituencies expect. The hint of 'command and control' in the analysis does not fit well with a politicized institution whose components have considerable knowledge and power. It is less a matter of 'convincing their teaching staff', and more one of the need to discuss and negotiate with them how the institution and its components should deal with the encroaching realities. For a higher education institution, the development of a vision and a strategy through consultation is likely to meet with more success than the enunciation of them from 'the centre', because colleagues tend not to accept ready-made visions and strategies uncritically since their socialization into higher education has led them to take a questioning approach to the things that confront them. Consultation and negotiation are anathema to those who think in terms of 'action this day' and rapid results, but wise when the need is for a very varied group of staff to sign up to something that they can 'live with' even though it may not reflect their ideal preferences.

### Undertake groundwork

Someone in the institution has to have the authority (derived from their track record and personal characteristics) that enables them to champion, sustain and protect whatever exploratory and developmental work is necessary. Where employability is concerned, there may be a need for a team to establish how the various sections of the institution construe employability, how they are approaching the development of employability in their students, what they are currently achieving, and what they think they ought to be achieving in, say, five years' time. This implies some research activity in order to establish baselines, and it is wise to ascertain colleagues' feelings about what they are currently doing before suggest-ing solutions. It may be necessary to commission an existing group of staff (such as an educational development unit) or a cross-institution group to conduct this kind of work – but any such group needs to be sensitive to the need to bring the wider academic community 'into the loop', and keep them aware of what is going on.

Groundwork is always necessary, for at least two reasons:

- a body of support has to be established if the innovation is to take root; and
- whatever is to be implemented needs to be sensitive to local culture, customs and practices.

In order to ground an innovation firmly, it is generally a good idea to pilot it and to evaluate the pilot work in order to build up an internal evidence base that can be examined against whatever external evidence is available. Academics are, in general, cautious about innovations that are parachuted in – and not unreasonably, since there are many examples of innovations which have not wholly lived up to the prospectuses of their advocates (modularity/semesterization and total quality management being two rather different examples). Academics need to be reasonably convinced that any change is worth while and that they have the personal and institutional resources to make it work.

The development of students' employability is something that is essentially institution-wide. Where changing practices to enhance employability involves more than tinkering at the edges of curricula, it is likely to involve both academics and support staff since curriculum change could well involve some reconfiguring of the way that institutional resources are provided. For example, less use might be made of lecture rooms, and more use might be made of resource-based learning in conjunction with small task-defined groups (problem-based learning is one approach that demands a move away from traditional modes of engagement in lectures, seminars, tutorials and laboratories or studios). Hence institutional managers need to have a considerable appreciation of what is involved. This may necessitate, as part of the groundwork, the establishment of a senior staff development programme, perhaps involving facilitators who have a considerable understanding of the issues at stake *and* of institutional cultures.

### Establish an implementation team

A lone champion of change (even a very senior manager) is rarely able to have widespread influence across an institution, as P. Taylor (1998) pointed out in his examination of what he termed 'lone ranging' in respect of educational innovation. For any innovation to run deep and wide in an institution, there is a need for the various parts of the institution to be engaged – in other words, for a team-based approach to be adopted both to whatever groundwork is needed and to subsequent implementation. Some thought needs to be given to the composition of the team, since it needs to include not only those with formal power but also those with ideas to contribute (not necessarily the same people). Any team needs people who can work well together as professionals (they do not have to like each other greatly, but they do have to co-operate effectively).[15]

Belbin's (1981) work on management teams showed how important it is for action-oriented teams to be composed of people with complementary capabilities. During a team's life-span the need for particular capabilities fluctuates. There is always a need for a person to steer the work (who may not be the primary fount of creativity but exercises skills of overseeing, orchestrating, and making connections with developments outwith the project), and for day-to-day project management in order to ensure that things are done as closely as possible to what was intended, to time, and in a manner that capitalizes on possibilities for synergy. People in the team who have a particular creative bent may find that their contributions are particularly needed at the beginning and at intervals throughout the project – but, as T.S. Eliot might have said with reference to this context, 'Human kind cannot bear very much creativity'. Once the creative decisions have been made, the need is simply to get on with the practicalities of implementation. There is an important need for expertise in monitoring and evaluation – not as almost an afterthought in a project, but built in from the start. Educational projects almost always need to be adjusted with respect to the initial intentions as unexpected events occur (so there is always a potential need for creativity), and the monitor/evaluator should have more of a role than that of 'sweeper up' and report writer at the end.

There is often a status-differential in teams. When a team operates in a hierarchical manner the outcome can be indifferent, since the leader is implicitly assuming the role of hero and omnicompetent which their capabilities may not warrant. We recall a workshop in which groups of staff were given a puzzle whose solution required that everyone pooled the different bits of information from the cards that they had been given. In one group there was a head of department who decided that he would be the group chair and structure the problem-solving. The 'team' failed to complete the task in the (ample) time allotted, got very fractious about its failure, and became very embarrassed when its members realized that other groups had succeeded. The moral of the tale is clear: to be effective, a team is likely to need to draw on ideas from all of its members, irrespective of their hierarchical status, and the best idea should prevail. It is a distinct leadership skill to let ideas flow and to accept that someone else may have the best idea. Wise leaders see that they can use contributions to the benefit of their teams – and they are well aware that, by extension, reflected glory may accrue to themselves as well.

### Communicate well

Success in communicating widely implies the use of language that is relatively straightforward, and is preferably not saturated with 'bureaucratese' or other jargon (we note again the cautionary tale that 'metacognition', which we felt had an adequate degree of currency in higher education, proved problematic for some of our colleagues in Skills *plus*). It is necessary to have a communication strategy that goes some way beyond activities such as the circulation of newsletters and the construction of websites, since there is a tendency for newsletters to be submerged under accumulating layers of paper or to be filed below the desk, and for websites not to prove as engaging as protagonists expect. Involving others in the work implies finding ways in which the ideas can be shared, discussed and criticized. The Skills *plus* project ran a number of 'colloquia' to which participating departments were invited. At various times the colloquia involved workshop-type activities, the giving of reports on how activities had gone in the departments, and discussion of papers produced by the core team. They were generally held to have been successful in sharing understandings and to have provided common starting-points for subsequent activity, as we showed in Chapter 12.

Engagement with others lowers the risk that the intentions of the project are misunderstood. Others will bring differing perspectives to bear, and there is a need for these to be appreciated so that the need for appropriate compromises can be understood and the compromises effected. The advocates of innovations risk being so blinded by the 'rightness' of their own point of view that the existence of other, perhaps competing, 'rightnesses' is overlooked. After all, higher education institutions are political organizations (see, for example, Baldridge, 1971) with various groups fighting for their own preferred positions.[16]

It is sometimes overlooked that communication is a two-way process which also implies listening well. A place has to be made for those at the sharp end of developments to feed back their experiences and concerns. The prospect of change can be threatening and, if colleagues believe that their concerns are not being taken into account, they are less likely to make the adjustments that may be needed for the change to be successful.

### Develop a shared commitment

Higher education institutions do not fit well into 'command and control' and 'technical-rational' models of organization even when the management chart seems to suggest that this is the operational reality. In practice, groups of various sizes have considerable freedom as to how they conduct their work. Developing a shared commitment involves negotiation and compromise, and some willingness to move outside custom and practice – individual and organizational 'comfort zones'. After all, as the chairman and chief executive of Levi-Strauss once observed, one of the most difficult things to do is to unlearn the behaviours that led to success in the past.[17]

A shared commitment does not imply clone-like behaviour. Recognizing the autonomy of academics, the principle of subsidiarity should obtain, under which institutional components are permitted to interpret the broad expectations in the light of their own norms and values, but within negotiated limits so that 'ownership' is developed at the same time as coherence with the broad expectations is maintained. The possibility of a productive creative tension exists, but a balance has to be struck between cohesive advance and a tolerance for divergence and creativity. We note, in passing, a point made by Beatty and Ulrich (1991) that in mature organizations a shared mind-set can be a particular liability.

One way of developing a shared commitment is exemplified by the LTSN Engineering Subject Centre which organized a summer workshop for two senior colleagues from each of 17 Engineering departments. The five days allocated were dispersed in 1-3-1 format across a longer period in order to allow time for sustained engagement with the issues.[18] As the Skills *plus* project well understood, academics are on the whole unlikely to undergo Damascene conversions.

### Generate some early successes

As Skills *plus* demonstrated, a lot can be achieved with a series of relatively small activities – the 'low cost, high gain' approach. The managerial task is to determine where the ratio of benefit to effort is likely to be both high and worthwhile. Successes that are relatively small in scale can be celebrated and are likely to help to generate momentum for subsequent work: as the truism has it, success tends to breed success. For hard-pressed staff, this might be the optimal way of increasing the sensitivity of curricula towards employability. There is little to be gained – indeed much to be lost – by over-reaching in the pursuit of change.

If the intention is to be more ambitious, then subdividing the proposed development into manageable chunks has a similar advantage to the 'low cost, high gain' approach in that it also offers the possibility of establishing early successes. Phasing the programme of developmental activity, with markers or 'milestones' established to index progress, helps to focus attention and maintain manageability whilst moving things on.

### Consolidate and embed the gains

'Chunking' the development plan runs the risk that, once a section has been completed, the gain is left to lapse as attention shifts elsewhere. The need is for achievements to be retained and built into future phases. The history of educational innovation is littered with successes that were not embedded by the time that their funding ran out, and hence faded from view.

There is a need for the ongoing appraisal of practices and achievements, in the interests of enhancement (as all the 'quality gurus' assert). The temptation is always there to proclaim success too soon, or to take success in a few components as indicating the success of the whole development. Adopting a 'continuous quality improvement' approach minimizes the risk of resting on laurels. After all, a garden quickly reverts to a weed-strewn patch if it is left untended.

If pilot work has been reasonably successful, then the innovation has gained a toe-hold within the institution, even if adaptations have been needed in the light of experience. The 'rolling out' of the innovation across the institution requires sustained commitment, especially on the part of the person who is responsible for championing it. If the momentum is lost, then it is difficult to regain it. Many worthwhile developments in higher education have faded away because sustained commitment was lacking, and/or something else demanded attention.

### Points of leverage

The focus of the Skills *plus* project lay at the departmental level. One of the conclusions from the project was that a lot could be achieved by incorporating employability-relevant activities into routine departmental practices and by introducing new, low-profile activities. Box 13.1 identifies some of the opportunities that exist for embedding a concern for employability, and good learning generally, within a team or department's practices.

There is a sense in which the champion's task is not so much to 'sell' employability to the programme team as to infiltrate employability-enhancing activities and prompts into taken-for-granted practices. For example, the Department of Educational Research at Lancaster University added to its programme specification a set of four messages about efficacy and metacognition. Students all received the programme specification, with the messages, which were also taken up in module handbooks. Triennial module reviews asked students how far they thought the module had promoted the items in the programme specification, including the four key messages. Another innovation was a two-year course to support personal development planning (PDP) for Education majors. This was incorporated into

*Box 13.1* Opportunities for promoting employability

- Write employability into programme specifications.
- At the institutional level, ensure that new module and programme proposals are appraised in terms of their contribution to student employability, with reference to the way in which we have described it.
- At departmental and programme levels, ensure that the contribution of (a) the programme and (b) the main constituent modules to employability is spelt out in handbooks, on websites, in assessment and teaching plans, and in recruitment material.
- Ensure that there is a variety of assessment methods in a programme.
- Use auditing to make sure that modules – certainly core modules – have learning goals that are aligned with the programme specification; that teaching and learning methods mesh with the most important learning goals; and that assessment is aligned with goals and methods.
- From the beginning of the programme, use all possible opportunities to explain to students – and to teaching colleagues – what is meant by employability and how the programme contributes to its development. Talk about co-curricular opportunities as well.
- Explore opportunities for basing student projects on problems that can be represented as contributing strongly to claims to employability.
- In England, use the government's progress files initiative to highlight the complex achievements that employers value, and which have often been rather neglected because they have resisted affordable and reliable assessment. Help students to translate their achievements into employer-friendly language.
- Apply the concept of 'tuning' to existing curricula, since this has considerable potential as a powerful, low cost, high gain way of enhancing student employability.
- Use existing review and evaluation systems to highlight employability issues. For example, ask about employability in meetings of staff-student committees, in annual module reviews, in student evaluations, in (perhaps) triennial peer reviews of modules, in (perhaps) quinquennial programme reviews, and in accreditation procedures.
- At the institutional level, ensure that enhancing student employability through the curriculum and co-curriculum is evidently a concern for instructional and education development units, for careers services and other student support groups including, where possible, student unions.
- In England, institutions are expected to show how their widening participation strategies and their teaching and learning strategies are sensitive to the mission to enhance student employability. This might imply making employability a quality enhancement priority.

the compulsory dissertation module, and preparation for what was essentially a final year activity was extended back into the first half of the second year. The cost was slight, but incorporating PDP in a compulsory course brought it before all Education majors.

Whereas the Skills *plus* project spanned 17 departments in four universities, some institutions have taken up employability as an institution-wide commitment. Harvey (2003) cites the examples of the universities of Exeter and Newcastle.

> The University of Exeter is an example of an institution that has developed a strategy for embedding employability skills and attributes into curricula. The university's employability group is composed of staff from across the institution with an interest in employability and is chaired by the deputy vice-chancellor for learning and teaching. The employability group works to implement the employability strategy, which is managed by the employability co-ordinator … The university is committed to embedding employability skills and attributes within all programmes of study. To achieve this, academic schools are encouraged to incorporate team development, work experience modules and materials, work-based projects and reflective learning into programmes of study. The employability co-ordinator sits on the accreditation committee with a particular interest in the section on module description forms dealing with intended learning outcomes for 'personal and key skills'. A network of careers and employability tutors has been established with an academic representative appointed from every school. This network meets once a term and is facilitated by the employability co-ordinator. One of the duties of these tutors is to complete the annual careers and employability audit for their school, which is reported to the employability group and the university learning and teaching committee. This helps the employability group to identify which schools may need more support in certain areas.

> Similarly, the University of Newcastle sees enhancing employability as a long-term strategic challenge… The institution is moving to a strategy-led, rather than project-led, approach by fully integrating project activity to ensure 'fit' with institutional, regional and national priorities. The development of the University of Newcastle's *Employability Statement and Strategy* reflects the university's commitment, as stated in the 1999–2004 institutional plan. It places high importance, in the teaching and learning strategy on improving the employability of the students. Appropriate resources, often through pump-priming, and practical suggestions help academic staff implement the strategy. Furthermore, senior management support has created a culture that promotes and recognises innovative practice. At the school level, 'champions' with empathy for the employability agenda have helped to build an environment receptive to curriculum change. Crucial has been the embedding of project-led developments in the curriculum from the outset to overcome problems of sustainability.

> Harvey (2003: 17–18)

The significance of these two examples is not only that the institutions adopted a whole-institution approach, but also that their activities show a consistency with the eight points relating to the management of change that were listed earlier. As with Skills *plus*, there are indications that these institutions are working with the grain of departmental and disciplinary cultures.

## What next?

Colleagues participating in Skills *plus* appreciated the attempt made in the project to put employability on a sound theoretical and empirical footing. They also recognized the limitations on what could be done within the two-year period of the project's life. They considered, partly because it had been necessary to 'translate' – albeit plausibly – theory and findings from other sectors of education, that there was need for the project's approach to employability to be tested more extensively in order that more direct evidence of its potential could be gained. They suggested three directions for further work:

- Longitudinal studies tracking students into, through and out of higher education, paying particular attention to their experiences of transitions. A substantial amount of useful data could be generated through *sustained* institutional research activity. (It would be particularly useful if this work could extend into the early years of employment, so that a more distant perspective on students' higher education experiences could be gained.)
- Unemployed graduates should be studied in more depth than the pilot study (Knight and Knight, 2002) had allowed.
- There was a need to develop ways of engaging academic staff with the task of enhancing employability. This needed work at several levels: national bodies might work with educational developers to establish central strategies and approaches; there would be value in guidance for departmental champions on ways of helping colleagues to get to grips with employability (see Box 13.1 for some suggestions); and it would be useful to have straightforward, 'to the point', briefings for individual academic staff to read. These actions would be more powerful if heads of departments and deans had some research-informed professional education in the design and implementation of educational programmes.

There is also a need for employability to be studied in relation to other policy initiatives. In the UK, significant relevant and overlapping initiatives would include those relating to widening participation, learning and teaching (including assessment), retention and completion, and life-long learning. There has been something of a tendency for institutions to deal with each policy initiative from government or elsewhere in isolation, as it has come forward. This is understandable, but it lessens the chance of synergy. Charles and Benneworth point to the problem of intra-institutional disconnectedness:

Departmental structures and the legacy of fragmented funding and initiatives can leave higher education institutions with a proliferation of outreach activities and internally competing units.

(Charles and Benneworth, 2001: 70)

A major, and continuing, challenge for institutions is that of optimizing their internal loose-tight couplings – or, put another way, of 'joining up' strategies and policies and using the principle of subsidiarity to maximum beneficial effect.

Higher education is a human system, not a precise mechanism, in which causes produce a range of effects – some intended, some unintended (and perhaps antagonistic to what was intended). If we are interested in enhancing students' employability, we need to have a better understanding of how best we can mobilize educational resources to that end. This, too, points to the importance of institutional policy-making, implementation, and research activity.

## Notes

1   The multidimensionality of 'graduateness' was shown in HEQC (1997), and an argument for valuing different configurations of graduate achievements can be found in Knight and Yorke (2003b).
2   This phrase elides the differences that exist in political structure in the various nations of the UK, which do not alter the general point being made.
3   Note that the 'ownership' of different agencies varies, though government is usually in a position to exercise influence.
4   This section draws upon a fuller discussion in Knight and Yorke (2003a).
5   We acknowledge, of course, that some curricula – particularly those closely linked with professions (such as teaching, healthcare and social work) – do incorporate employability in assessment criteria since the graduate's licence to practise depends on being able to satisfy examiners that they have reached a standard appropriate to a beginning professional.
6   There is anecdotal evidence that some students choose modules on the basis of their assessment methods.
7   The first two of the seven questions are: 'What are you trying to do?' and 'Why are you trying to do it?'
8   Argyris and Schön (1974) drew the distinction between 'single-loop learning', in which the existing framework for action is accepted, and 'double-loop learning' in which the framework is subjected to challenge. There are correlations between single-loop learning and incremental change, and between double-loop learning and radical change.
9   Details of the Baldrige Award, as it applies to education, can be found in Baldrige National Quality Program (2003). Those of the EFQM Excellence Model can be found at http://www.efqm.org/model_awards/model/excellence_model.htm (accessed 6 April 2003).
10  See www.ltsn.ac.uk/ESECT.
11  Acceptance by HEFCE of these strategies results in the release of earmarked funding.
12  'Enterprise' took on different colourings in different institutions, but had to be accepted by the Employment Department and its predecessor bodies which were responsible for managing the initiative. One might say that this was an example of subsidiarity in action.

13   This involves bringing together three UK agencies focusing on enhancement. At the time of writing the name had not been finalized, nor had other structural matters.

14   Note the problem that 'core' or 'key' skills have in this respect (Wolf, 2002).

15   Argyris (1990) issues a reminder – and experience bears out – that 'the management team' in an organization is often something of a myth.

16   In his discussion of learning organizations, Senge (1992) gives insufficient weight to internal politics.

17   See Bennis and Townsend (1996: 97).

18   This is reported briefly in Trowler *et al.* (2003: 12–13).

# Envoi

We have argued that employability is a construct that is far richer than that of 'skills', irrespective of whether we are invited to believe in 'key', 'transferable', 'core' or 'generic' skills. Importantly, we align it with the kinds of achievements that are valued by academics who might reject 'skills' because of philosophical, theoretical or empirical difficulties.

The USEM (understandings, skilful practices, efficacy beliefs, and meta-cognition) account has a credible theoretical and empirical foundation – indeed, as we have been working on this book we have turned up material of which we were previously unaware yet which has buttressed the argument that we have been developing. We are therefore confident that this book does have something useful to offer to higher education systems which are increasingly being pressed by governments to demonstrate their contribution to economic prosperity.

Institutions, as collectivities, are expected to respond to the expectations of governments and their agencies. Some of that response has necessarily to be addressed at institutional level but, because of the variations that exist in disciplinary cultures, practices and expectations, there is no sense in an institution adopting a monolithic approach to the enhancement of employability – in the vernacular, 'one size does not fit all'. An analogue of the European Union's principle of subsidiarity should prevail, under which a general conception of employability is given different colourings according to the characteristics of programmes and departments, with the proviso that whatever is done must correlate reasonably well with the general conception.

The Skills *plus* project, which triggered most of the work reported in this book, was based firmly on 'tuning' – doing what could be done at relatively modest cost, whilst offering the prospect of high gain. It did not ask participants to overthrow what had been built up over a period of time; rather, it asked them to consider what could be done without the need to send programmes through a burdensome revalidation process, yet could be expected to improve student learning in ways consistent with the aim of enhancing employability. We suggest that this modest approach to innovation and change may turn out to have been more acceptable and influential than some of the other, more dramatic, interventions that are envisaged from time to time.

The implications of the case we have laid out in this book are, however, more far-reaching than might appear at first sight. Curricula (and, more specifically, pedagogic practices) will need refocusing in some contexts if students are to be as fully equipped as possible to make claims for employability. The staff development implications should not be overlooked. For the institution, it would be a mistake to box-off employability from other aspects of institutional policy and practice. However their policies are determined, institutions need to ensure that there is coherence in what they are seeking to achieve in respect of widening participation, learning and teaching, retention, employability and life-long learning.

We said at the end of Chapter 1 that we saw considerable challenge in convincing our colleagues that employability was not inimical to their values and practices. Anyone who has reached this point in the book will probably have come to a view as to whether we have succeeded. We hope you agree that we have.

# References

Adelman, C. (ed.) (1990) *A College Course Map: Taxonomy and Transcript Data.* Washington: US Government Printing Office.

Ainscow, M. (1991) (ed.) *Effective Schools for All.* London: David Fulton.

Allen, D. (2002) *The Keynote Project – External Audit.* Nottingham: School of Art and Design, Nottingham Trent University.

Allen, G. (2002) 'Students with special needs and their mentors', *Exchange*, 2, 25.

Altbach, P.G. (ed.) (1996) *The International Academic Profession.* Princetown, NJ: The Carnegie Foundation for the Advancement of Teaching.

Anderson, L.W. and Krathwohl, D.R. (2001) *A Taxonomy for Learning, Teaching and Assessment.* New York: Addison Wesley Longman.

Anderson, L.W. and Sosniak, A. (eds) (1994) *Bloom's Taxonomy: A Forty-year Retrospective. Ninety-third Yearbook of the National Society for the Study of Education.* Chicago IL: University of Chicago Press.

Argyris, C. (1990) *Overcoming Organizational Defenses.* Boston, MA: Allyn and Bacon.

Argyris, C. and Schön, D. (1974) *Theory in Practice: Increasing Professional Effectiveness.* San Francisco, CA: Jossey-Bass.

Association of Graduate Recruiters (2002) *The AGR Guide to Work Experience – An Employers' Guide.* Warwick: AGR.

Astin, A.W. (1997) *Four Years that Matter: The College Experience Twenty Years On.* San Francisco: Jossey-Bass.

Atkins, M. (1999) 'Over-ready and self-basting: taking stock of employability skills', *Teaching in Higher Education*, 4(2), 267–80.

Baldridge, J.V. (1971) *Power and Conflict in the University.* New York: Wiley.

Baldrige National Quality Program (2003) *Education Quality Criteria For Excellence.* Gaithersburg, MD: US Department of Commerce. Online at http://www.quality.nist.gov/ Education_Criteria.htm (accessed 6 April 2003).

Ball, L. (2001) 'Preparing graduates in art and design to meet the challenge of working in the creative industries', *Art, Design and Communication in Higher Education*, 1(1), 10–24.

Bandura, A. (1997) *Self-efficacy: The Exercise of Control.* New York: Freeman.

Banta, T., Lund, J.P., Black, K.E. and Oblander, F.W. (eds) (1996) *Assessment in Practice.* San Francisco: Jossey-Bass.

Barnett, R. (1994) *The Limits of Competence.* Buckingham: Society for Research into Higher Education and the Open University Press.

Barnett, R. (2000) *Realizing the University in an Age of Supercomplexity.* Buckingham: Society for Research into Higher Education and the Open University Press.

Barrow, E., Lyte, G. and Butterworth, T. (2002) 'An evaluation of problem-based learning in a nursing theory and practice module', *Nurse Education in Practice*, 2, 55–62.

Beatty, R.W. and Ulrich, D.O. (1991) 'Re-energizing the mature organization', *Organizational Dynamics*, Summer, 16–30.

Becher, T. (1999) *Professional Practices: Commitment and Capability in a Changing Environment*. New Brunswick, NJ: Transaction Publishers.

Belbin, R.M. (1981) *Management Teams: Why They Succeed or Fail*. London: Heinemann.

Bennett, N., Desforges, C.W., Cockburn, A. and Wilkinson, B. (1984) *The Quality of Pupil Learning Experiences*. London: Lawrence Erlbaum Associates.

Bennett, N., Dunne, E. and Carré, C. (2000) *Skills Development in Higher Education and Employment*. Buckingham: Society for Research into Higher Education and Open University Press.

Bennis, W. and Townsend, R. (1996) *Reinventing Leadership*. London: Judy Piatkus.

Bercuson, D., Bothwell, R. and Granatstein, J.L. (1997) *Petrified Campus: The Crisis in Canada's Universities*. Toronto, ON: Random House.

Bereiter, C. and Scardamalia, M. (1993) *Surpassing Ourselves: An Inquiry Into the Nature and Implications of Expertise*. Chicago: Open Court.

Bernstein, B. (1975) *Class, Codes and Control* (vol. 3), *Towards a Theory of Educational Transmissions*. London: Routledge and Kegan Paul.

Bibbings, L. (2001) 'Tourism degrees and employability – creative tension in curricula', *Link*, 1, 12–13.

Biggs, J. (1999) *Teaching for Quality Learning at University*. Buckingham: Society for Research in Higher Education and Open University Press.

Biggs, J. (2003) *Teaching for Quality Learning at University*, 2nd edition. Maidenhead: Society for Research into Higher Education and Open University Press.

Black, P. and Wiliam, D. (1998) 'Assessment and classroom learning', *Assessment in Education*, 5(1), 7–74.

Blackwell, A. and Harvey, L. (1999) *Destinations and Reflections: Careers of Art, Craft and Design Graduates*. Birmingham, Centre for Research into Quality.

Blackwell, A., Bowes, L., Harvey, L., Hesketh, A. and Knight, P.T. (2001) 'Transforming work experience in higher education', *British Educational Research Journal*, 26(3), 269–86.

Blackwell, R. and Preece, D. (2002) *Changing Higher Education*. Report CHA004 Online at http://www.ltsn.ac.uk/embedded_object.asp?id=18091&prompt=yes&filename= CHA004 (accessed 4 May 2003).

Bloom, B.S. (1956) *Taxonomy of Educational Objectives, Handbook 1: Cognitive Domain*. London: Longman.

Blunkett, D. (2001) 'The hubs and spokes of UK economic takeoff', *Times Higher Education Supplement*, 16 February, 14.

Boekaerts, M. and Niemivirta, M. (2000) 'Self-regulated learning: finding a balance between learning goals and ego-protecting goals', in M. Boekaerts, P. Pintrich and M. Zeidner (eds) *Handbook of Self-regulation*. London: Academic Press, 417–50.

Booth, M. (2002) *Minority Ethnic Recruitment, Information, Training and Support (MERITS) Project. Final report prepared for submission to the Innovations Team and HEFCE/DfES*. Leicester: Association of Graduate Careers Advisory Services.

Boud, D. (1995) 'Assessment and learning: contradictory or complementary?', in P. Knight (ed.) *Assessment for Learning in Higher Education*. London: Kogan Page, 35–48.

Boud, D. and Feletti, G. (eds) (1997) *The Challenge of Problem-based Learning*, 2nd edition. London: Kogan Page.

Boud, D. and Solomon, N. (eds) (2001) *Work-based Learning: A New Higher Education.* Buckingham: The Society for Research into Higher Education and the Open University Press.

Bourdieu, P. and Passeron, J.-C. (1977) *Reproduction in Education, Society and Culture.* London: Sage Publications.

Bourgeois, E. (2002) *Higher Education and Research for the ERA: Current Trends and Challenges for the Future.* Luxembourg: Office for Official Publications of the European Communities.

Bourgeois, E., Duke, C., Guyot, J.-L. and Merrill, B. (1999) *The Adult University.* Buckingham: Society for Research into Higher Education and the Open University Press.

Brennan, J. (1999) 'Higher education and employment in the UK', *Higher Education Digest*, 34, Summer, supplement.

Brennan, J. (2003) *Graduate Employability: 10 Issues for Debate and Inquiry.* Mimeo. London: The Centre for Higher Education Research and Information (mimeo).

Brennan, J. and Little, B. (1996) *A Review of Work Based Learning in Higher Education.* London: Quality Support Centre, Open University.

Brennan, J. and Shah, T. (2002) *Access to What? How to Convert Educational Opportunity into Employment Opportunity for Groups from Disadvantaged Backgrounds. Interim Report on Phase 2.* London: The Centre for Higher Education Research and Information.

Brennan, J. and Williams, R. (2003) *The English Degree and Graduate Careers.* Egham: LTSN English Subject Centre.

Brennan, J., Johnstone, B., Little, B., Shah, T. and Woodley, A. (2001) *The Employment of UK Graduates: Comparisons with Europe and Japan.* Bristol: The Higher Education Funding Council for England. Online at www.hefce.ac.uk/Pubs/hefce/2001/01_38.htm (accessed 12 May 2003).

Bridges, D. (1993) 'Transferable skills: a philosophical perspective', *Studies in Higher Education*, 18(1), 43–52.

Bridges, P., Cooper, A., Evanson, P., Haines, C., Jenkins, D., Woolf, H. and Yorke, M. (2002) 'Coursework marks high, examination marks low: discuss', *Assessment and Evaluation in Higher Education*, 27(1), 36–48.

Brown, G. (1999) 'Foreword', in D.A. Heylings and V.N. Tariq (eds) *Employer-linked Project-based Learning.* Belfast: Enterprise QEB, 4.

Brown, G., Bull, J. and Pendlebury, M. (1997) *Assessing Student Learning in Higher Education.* London: Routledge.

Brown, J.S. and Duguid, P. (2000) *The Social Life of Information.* Cambridge, MA: Harvard University Press.

Brown, P. and R. Scase (1994) *Higher Education and Corporate Realities: Class, Culture and the Decline of Graduate Careers.* London: UCL Press Limited.

Brown, P., Hesketh, A. and Williams, S. (2002) 'Employability in a knowledge-driven economy', in P. Knight (ed.) *Innovations in Education for Employability. Notes from 13th June 2002 Skills plus Conference.* Online at http://www.open.ac.uk/cobe/pdfDocs/docs-skill%2B/ProjPaper5.pdf (accessed 12 May 2003).

Brown, R. and Puddick, R. (2002) 'Experiencing entrepreneurship at Cambridge', *Industry and Higher Education*, February, 49–53.

Brown, S. and Knight, P. (1994) *Assessing Learners in Higher Education.* London: Kogan Page.

Bruner, J. (1985) 'Vygotsky: a historical and conceptual perspective', in J.V. Wertsch (ed.) *Culture, Communication and Cognition: Vygotskian Perspectives*. Cambridge: Cambridge University Press, 21–34.

BSA (British Sociological Association) (2002) *Opportunities for Sociologists*. Online at http://www.britsoc.co.uk/index.php?link_id=7&area=item1 (accessed 12 May 2003).

Buchanan, D. and Badham, R. (1999) *Power, Politics and Organisational Change: Winning the Turf Game*. London: Sage.

Burnes, B. (1992) *Managing Change: A Strategic Approach to Organisational Development*. London: Pitman.

Cambridge, B.L. (2001) 'Electronic portfolios as knowledge builders', in B.L. Cambridge, (ed.) *Electronic Portfolios: Emerging Practices in Student, Faculty and Instructional Learning*. Washington DC: The American Association for Higher Education, 1–11.

Cannon, D. (2002) 'Learning to fail: learning to recover', in M. Peelo and T. Wareham (eds) *Failing Students in Higher Education*. Buckingham: Society for Research into Higher Education and the Open University Press, 73–84.

Cappelli, P. (1995) 'Is the "skills gap" really about attitudes?', *Californian Management Review*, 37(4), 108–24.

Charles, D. and Benneworth, P. (2001) *The Regional Mission: The Regional Contribution of Higher Education*. London: Universities UK.

CHERI (Centre for Higher Education Research and Information) (2002) *Access to What? How to Convert Educational Opportunity into Employment Opportunity for Groups from Disadvantaged Backgrounds. Executive Summary*. London: The Centre for Higher Education Research and Information.

Cherniss, C. and Caplan, R.D. (2001) 'Implementing emotional intelligence programs in organizations', in C. Cherniss and D. Goleman (eds) *The Emotionally Intelligent Workplace: How to Select for, Measure and Improve Emotional Intelligence in Individuals, Groups and Organizations*. San Francisco, CA: Jossey-Bass, 286–304.

Chisholm, C. (2002) 'A postgraduate framework for work-based learning', *Exchange*, 2, 13–14.

CIOB (1995) *CIOB Educational Framework*. Ascot: Chartered Institute of Building. Online at http://www.ciob.org.uk/membership/education_framework.jsp (accessed 11 May 2003).

CIOB (2002) *Accreditation Procedures and Policy*. Ascot: Chartered Institute of Building. Online at http://www.ciob.org.uk/membership/educational_requirements.jsp (accessed 11 May 2003).

CIOB (2003) *Constructing our Future: The Way Forward for Higher Education in Construction*. Ascot: Chartered Institute of Building. Online at http://www.ciob.org.uk/media/constructing_our_future.pdf (accessed 6 May 2003).

Claxton, G. (1998) *Hare Brain, Tortoise Mind*. London: Fourth Estate.

Coleman, S. and Keep, E. (2001) *Background Literature Review for PIU Project on Workforce Development*. London: Cabinet Office Performance and Innovation Unit.

Coulter, E. (2003, forthcoming) *Accelerating Change in Built Environment Education: Shared Problems – Shared Solutions*. (To be online at http://www.cebe.ltsn.ac.uk/.)

Council for Industry and Higher Education (2002) *Employer Perceptions of Subject Benchmark Statements*. London: CIHE. Online at http://www.cihe-uk.com/employability.htm (accessed 12 May 2003).

Darrah, C. (1997) 'Complicating the concept of skill requirements: scenes from a workplace', in G. Hall (ed.) *Changing Work, Changing Workers*. Albany, NY: State University of New York Press, 249–72.

De Corte, E. (2000) 'Marrying theory building and the improvement of school practice', *Learning and Instruction*, 10, 249–66.

Department of Health (1997) *The New NHS: Modern, Dependable*. London: HMSO.

Department of Health (1999) *Making a Difference: Strengthening the Nursing, Midwifery and Health Visiting Contribution to Health and Healthcare*. London: HMSO.

DfEE (Department for Education and Employment) (2001) *Developing Modern Higher Education Careers Services*. London: DfEE. Online at www.dfes.gov.uk/hecareers servicereview/index/shtml (accessed 11 May 2003).

DfES (Department for Education and Skills) (2003) *The Future of Higher Education* (Cm. 5753). Norwich: The Stationery Office.

Dickerson, A. and Green, F. (2002) *The Growth and Valuation of Generic Skills*. Warwick: Skills, Knowledge and Organisational Performance Project.

Dochy, F., Segers, M. and Sluijsmans, D. (1999) 'The use of self-, peer and co-assessment in higher education: a review', *Studies in Higher Education*, 24(3), 331–50.

Dolan, T.G. (2003) 'Are universities and colleges delivering what they promised?', *Hispanic Outlook*, 2 October, 24–5.

Donnelly, J.F. (1999) 'Schooling Heidegger: on being in teaching', *Teaching and Teacher Education*, 15, 933–49.

Donnelly, R.D. (2003) 'Teaching enterprise – can it be done in large groups?', *Industry and Higher Education*, February, 37–44.

Donovan, M., Bransford, J. and Pellegrino, J. (eds) (2000) *How People Learn: Bridging Research and Practice*. Washington, DC: National Academy Press.

Doyle, W. (1983) 'Academic work', *Review of Educational Research*, 53(2), 159–99.

Dreyfus, H. and Dreyfus, S. (1986) *Mind Over Machine*. Oxford: Blackwell.

DTI (Department of Trade and Industry) (2000) *UK Competitiveness Indicators*, 2nd edition. London: DTI.

Dweck, C.S. (1999) *Self-theories: their role in motivation, personality and development*. Philadelphia, PA: Psychology Press.

Dweck, C.S., Chiu, C. and Hong, Y. (1995) 'Implicit theories and their role in judgments and reactions', *Psychological Inquiry*, 6(4), 267–85.

Elton, L. (2003) *Dissemination: A Change Theory Approach*. Report CHA001. Online at http://www.ltsn.ac.uk/embedded_object.asp?id=17888&prompt=yes&filename= CHA001 (accessed 12 May 2003).

EMTA (2000) *Graduate Apprenticeship Project in Engineering. Final Report*. Watford: EMTA.

Engineering Professors Council (2000) *The EPC Engineering Graduate Output Standard Interim Report of the EPC Output Standards Project*. Coventry: Engineering Professors Council.

Entwistle, N. (1996) 'Recent research on student learning', in J. Tait and P. Knight (eds) *The Management of Independent Learning*. London: Kogan Page, 97–112.

Fischer, K. (2002) 'Learning and self-organization as motivations that shape development'. Paper presented to the Development and Motivation Conference, Windermere, UK, 17 April.

Flavell, J.H. (1979) 'Metacognition and cognitive monitoring: a new area of cognitive-developmental inquiry', *American Psychologist*, 34, 906–11.

Frost, M. (1996) 'An analysis of the scope and value of problem-based learning in the education of health care professionals', *Journal of Advanced Nursing*, 24, 1,047–53.

Fullan, M. (1999) *Change Forces: The Sequel*. London: Falmer.

Fullan, M. (2001). *The New Meaning of Educational Change*, 3rd edition. New York: Teachers' College Press.

Gaff, J.G. and Ratcliff, J.L. (eds) (1996) *Handbook of the Undergraduate Curriculum*. San Francisco: Jossey-Bass.

Ganesan, R., Edmonds, G. and Spector, M. (2002) 'The changing nature of instructional design for networked learning', in C. Steeples and C. Jones (eds) *Networked Learning: Perspectives and Issues*. London: Springer-Verlag, 93–110.

Gibb, A. (2002) 'Creating conducive environments for learning and entrepreneurship', *Industry and Higher Education*, June, 135–48.

Gibbs. G. (1999) 'Using assessment strategically to change the way students learn', in S. Brown and A. Glasner (eds) *Assessment Matters in Higher Education: Choosing and Using Diverse Approaches*. Buckingham: Society for Research into Higher Education and Open University Press, 41–53.

Glen, S. and Clark, A. (1999) 'Nurse education: a skill mix for the future', *Nurse Education Today*, 19(1), 12–19.

Goleman, D. (1996). *Emotional Intelligence*. London: Bloomsbury.

Goodyear, P. (2002) 'Psychological foundations for networked learning', in C. Steeples and C. Jones (eds) *Networked Learning: Perspectives and Issues*. London: Springer-Verlag, 49–76.

Guile, D. (2002) 'Skill and work experience in the European knowledge economy', *Journal of Education and Work*, 15(3), 251–76

Hannan, A. and Silver, H. (2000) *Innovating in Higher Education: Teaching, Learning and Institutional Cultures*. Buckingham: Society for Research into Higher Education and Open University Press.

Hargreaves, A. (1994) *Changing Teachers, Changing Times*. London: Cassell.

Hartley, J.L. and Smith, B.W. (2000) 'Strengthening academic ties by assessment of learning outcomes', *Journal of Co-operative Education*, 35(1), 41–7.

Harvey, L. (1999) *Employability Audit Toolkit*. Birmingham: Centre for Research into Quality, University of Central England.

Harvey, L. (2001) 'Defining and measuring employability', *Quality in Higher Education*, 7(2), 97–109.

Harvey, L. (2003) *Transitions from Higher Education to Work*. York: The Learning and Teaching Support Network. Online at www.ltsn.ac.uk/ESECT (accessed 11 July 2003).

Harvey, L. and Knight, P.T. (1996) *Transforming Higher Education*. Buckingham: Society for Research into Higher Education and Open University Press.

Harvey, L., Locke, W. and Morey, A. (2002) *Enhancing Employability, Recognising Diversity*. London: Universities UK.

Harvey, L., Moon, S., Geall, V. and Bower, R. (1997) *Graduates' Work: Organizational Change and Students' Attributes*. Birmingham: Centre for Research into Quality, University of Central England.

Hawkins, P. and Winter J. (1995) *Skills for Graduates in the 21st Century*, Cambridge: AGR.

Hedlund, J. and Sternberg, R. (2000) 'Too many intelligences?', in R. Bar-On and J. Parker (eds) *The Handbook of Emotional Intelligence*. San Francisco: Jossey-Bass, 136–67.

HEFCE (Higher Education Funding Council for England) (2001) *Strategies for Widening Participation in Higher Education. A Guide to Good Practice* (Report 01/36). Bristol, Higher Education Funding Council for England.

HEFCE (Higher Education Funding Council for England) (2002) *Performance Indicators in Higher Education in the UK, 1999–2000, 2000–1* (Report 02/52). Bristol: Higher Education Funding Council for England.

HEQC (Higher Education Quality Council ) (1997) *Graduate Standards Programme: Final Report* (2 vols). London: Higher Education Quality Council.

Heywood, J. (2000) *Assessment in Higher Education.* London: Jessica Kingsley Publishers.

Hillage, J. and Pollard, E. (1998) *Employability: Developing a Framework for Policy Analysis.* London: Department for Education and Employment.

HM Treasury (2000) *Productivity in the UK: The Evidence and the Government's Approach.* London: UK Treasury.

Hodkinson, P. and Bloomer, M. (2003) 'Cultural capital and young people's career progression', Part 2, *Career Research and Development*, 8, 3–8.

Holmes, L. (2001) 'Reconsidering graduate employability: the graduate identity approach', *Quality in Higher Education*, 7(2), 111–19.

Honeybone, A. (2002) 'Skills are dead! Long live skills', *Educational Developer*, 3(4), 7–9.

Hopkiss, I. (2001) *Graduate Employability Award: Scheme Handbook.* Exeter: College of St Mark and St John.

Hornby, W. (2003) 'Assessing using grade-related criteria: a single currency for universities?', *Assessment and Evaluation in Higher Education*, 28(4), 437–56.

Hörning, K., Gerhard, A. and Michailow, M. (1995) *Time Pioneers: Flexible Working Time and New Lifestyles.* Cambridge: Polity Press.

Hounsell, D., McCulloch, M. and Scott, M. (eds) (1996) *The ASSHE Inventory.* Edinburgh: University of Edinburgh and Napier University.

Human Resources Development Canada (2002) *Essential Skills Database.* Online at http://www15.hrdc-drhc.gc.ca/english/readers_guide.asp (accessed 12 May 2003).

Jobbins, D. (2003) 'Figures hide true graduate jobs picture', *Times Higher Educational Supplement*, No. 1588, 9 May, 1.

Keep, E. (2002) 'The English vocational education and training policy debate', *Journal of Education and Work*, 15(4), 457–79.

Keep, E. (2003) 'The learning and skills sector – a theoretical introduction'. Paper presented to The Learning and Skills Sector Conference, Westminster, 24 April.

Kelly, J. (2002) 'New recruits must be keen to keep on learning, say top employers', *The Financial Times*, 11 May: 13.

Keynote Project (2002) *The Keynote Project – External Audit.* Nottingham: Nottingham Trent University School of Art and Design.

King, P.M. and Kitchener, K.S. (1994) *Developing Reflective Judgment: Understanding and Promoting Intellectual Growth and Critical Thinking in Adolescents and Young Adults.* San Francisco: Jossey-Bass.

Klein, K.J. and Sorra, JS. (1996) 'The challenge of innovation implementation', *Academy of Management Review*, 21(4): 1,055–80.

Klenowski, V. (2002) *Developing Portfolios for Learning and Assessment.* London: RoutledgeFalmer.

Kneale, P.E. (1997) 'Encouraging student responsibility for learning through developing skills, profiling and records of achievement', in A. Jenkins and A. Ward (eds) *Developing Skill-based Curricula Through the Disciplines.* Birmingham: Staff and Educational Development Association (SEDA) paper 89, 121–6.

Knight, P.T. (1989) 'Children's concepts, the curriculum and change', *Curriculum*, 10(1), 5–12.

Knight, P.T. (2002a) *Being a Teacher in Higher Education*. Buckingham: Society for Research in Higher Education and the Open University Press.

Knight, P.T. (2002b) 'Employability in the first graduate job'. Paper presented to the Skills *plus* Conference, 13 June, Manchester. Online at http://www.open.ac.uk/cobe/pdfDocs/ docs-skill%2B/ProjPaper5.pdf (accessed 11 May 2003).

Knight, P.T. (2002c) 'Summative assessment in higher education: practices in disarray', *Studies in Higher Education*, 27(3), 275–86.

Knight, P.T. and Saunders, M. (1999) 'Understanding teachers' professional cultures through interview: a constructivist approach', *Evaluation and Research in Education*, 13(2), 61–72.

Knight, P.T. and Trowler, P.R. (2000) 'Academic work and quality', *Quality in Higher Education*, 6(2), 109–14.

Knight, P.T. and Trowler, P.R. (2001) *Departmental Leadership in Higher Education*. Buckingham: Society for Research into Higher Education and Open University Press.

Knight, P.T. and Yorke, M. (2002) *Skills plus: Tuning the Undergraduate Curriculum*. June 2002 edition. Online at http://www.open.ac.uk/cobe/pdfDocs/docs-skill%2B/ ANewIntroSkills.pdf (accessed 11 May 2003).

Knight, P.T. and Yorke, M. (2003a) 'Employability and good learning in higher education', *Teaching in Higher Education*, 8(1), 3–16.

Knight, P.T. and Yorke, M. (2003b) *Assessment, Learning and Employability*. Maidenhead: Society for Research into Higher Education and the Open University Press.

Knight, T.T. and Knight, P.T. (2002) *A Pilot Study of 'Employability' as Seen by Unemployed Recent Graduates*. Online at http://www.open.ac.uk/cobe/pdfDocs/PilotStudy- employability.pdf. (accessed 11 May 2003).

Knowledge House (2000) *Key Certification Program*. Halifax, NS: Knowledge House.

Kohlberg, L. (1964) *The Philosophy of Moral Development: Moral Stages and the Idea of Justice*. San Francisco: Harper and Row.

Kotter, J. (1996) *Leading Change*. Boston, MA: Harvard Business School Press.

KPMG (2000) *KPMG Graduate Selection: First Interview Guide*. London: KPMG.

Lathbury, D. (2003) Personal communication.

Lawton, D. (1983) *Curriculum Studies and Educational Planning*. London: Hodder and Stoughton.

Lazarus, F.C. (1992) 'Learning in the academic workplace: perspectives of a co-operative education director', *Journal of Co-operative Education*, 28(1), 67–76.

Leadbeater, C. (2000) *Living on Thin Air*. London: Penguin.

Lechner, F.J. and Boli, J. (eds) (2000) *The Globalization Reader*. Oxford: Blackwell Publishers.

Leinhardt, G., McCarthy-Young, K. and Merriman, J. (1995) 'Integrating professional knowledge: the theory of practice and the practice of theory', *Learning and Instruction*, 5, 401–8.

Lent, R., Brown, S. and Hackett, G. (1994) 'Toward a unifying social cognitive theory of career and academic interest, choice and performance', *Journal of Vocational Behavior*, 45, 79–122.

Leon, P. (2002) 'Graduates say degrees leave them short of skills', *The Times Higher Education Supplement*, No. 1565, 22 November, 6.

Light, R. and Pillemer, D. (1982) 'Numbers and narrative: combining their strengths in research reviews', *Harvard Educational Review*, 52(1), 1–26.

Linke, R. (Chair) (1991) *Performance Indicators in Higher Education*. Report of a trial evaluation study commissioned by the Commonwealth Department of Employment, Education and Training (2 vols). Canberra: Australian Government Publishing Service.

Little, B. (2000) 'Undergraduates' work based learning and skills development', *Tertiary Education and Management*, 6(2) 119–35.

Little, B. (2001) 'Reading between the lines of graduate employment', *Quality in Higher Education*, 7(2), 121–9.

Locke, E. (1997) 'The motivation to work: what we know', in M. Maehr and P. Pintrich (eds) *Advances in Motivation and Achievement*, vol. 10. Greenwich, CT: JAI Press, 375–412.

Maddocks, A. and Sher, W. (2003) 'Transferring the "RAPID Progress File" – a personal development planning tool – between disciplines and continents', *Proceedings of CIB W89 International Conference on Building Education and Research* (BEAR 2003: 9–11 April), vol. 2. Salford: Salford University, 840–51.

Maharasoa, M. and Hay, D. (2001) 'Higher education and graduate employment in South Africa', *Quality in Higher Education*, 7(2), 139–47.

Marzano, R.J. (1998) *A Theory-based Meta-analysis of Research on Instruction*. Aurora, CO: Mid-continent Regional Educational Laboratory.

Marzano, R.J., Gaddy, B.B. and Dean, C. (2000) *What Works in Classroom Instruction*, Aurora, CO: Mid-continent Research for Education and Learning.

Mason, G. (2002) 'High skills utilisation under mass higher education: graduate employment in service industries in Britain', *Journal of Education and Work*, 15(4), 427–56.

Mayer, J.D., Salovey, P. and Caruso, D.R. (2000) 'Emotional intelligence as zeitgeist, as personality and as a mental ability', in R. Bar-On, and J. Parker (eds) *The Handbook of Emotional Intelligence*. San Francisco: Jossey-Bass, 92–117.

McGoldrick, C. (2001) *Social Science at Work: A Study of Employability Issues*. Liverpool: Liverpool John Moores University.

McKnight, A. (2003) *Employability and Performance Indicators*. Online at http://www.prospects.ac.uk (accessed 12 July 2003).

Mentkowski, M. *et al.* (2000) *Learning that Lasts: Integrating Learning Development and Performance in College and Beyond*. San Fancisco: Jossey-Bass.

Minder, R. (2003) 'Do grades help or hinder?', *The Financial Times*, 31 March, 16.

Morgan, G. (1997) *Images of Organization*, 2nd edition. Thousand Oaks, CA: Sage.

Morley, L. (2001) 'Producing new workers: quality, equality and employability in higher education', *Quality in Higher Education*, 7(2), 131–8.

Mortimore, P., Sammons, P., Stoll, L., Lewis, D. and Ecob, R. (1988) *School Matters*. Wells: Open Books.

Murphy, J. (1995) 'A degree of waste', *Oxford Review of Education*, 19(1), 9–31.

Naylor, R. and Smith, J. (2002) *Schooling Effects on Subsequent University Performance: Evidence for the UK University Population*, Warwick Economic Research Papers No. 657. Coventry: Department of Economics, Warwick University.

NCIHE (1997) *Higher Education in the Learning Society*. Report of the National Committee of Inquiry into Higher Education, chaired by Ronald Dearing. Main Report. Norwich: HMSO.

Noble, M. (1999) 'Teaching and learning for employability', in H. Fry, S. Ketteridge and S. Marshall (eds) *A Handbook for Teaching and Learning in Higher Education*. London: Kogan Page, 120–33.

Noble, M. and Paulucy, B. (2002) 'Think through the implications of work-based learning', *Exchange*, 2, 26–9.

Nove, A., Snape, D. and Chetwynd, M. (1997) *Advancing by Degrees: A Study of Graduate Recruitment and Skills Utilisation*, Research Report RR33. Norwich: DfEE/HMSO.

Oakland, R. (2002) *Directory of Employability Resources.* York: The LTSN Generic Centre. Also at www.ltsn.ac.uk/ESECT (accessed 11 July 2003).

O'Neill, J. (1999) 'Project-based learning: an employer's perspective', in D.A. Heylings and V.N. Tariq (eds) *Employer-linked Project-based Learning*. Belfast: Enterprise QEB, 75–6.

Pascarella, E.T. and Terenzini, P.T. (1991) *How College Affects Students*. San Francisco: Jossey-Bass.

Perkins, D. and Saloman, G. (1989) 'Are cognitive skills context bound?', *Educational Researcher*, 19(1), 16–25.

Perry, R. (1997). 'Perceived control in college students: implications for instruction', in R. Perry and J. Smart (eds) *Effective Teaching in Higher Education*. New York: Agathon Press.

Perry, W.G. (1970/1998) *Forms of Ethical and Intellectual Development in the College Years*, reprint of 1970 text, with a new introduction by L.L. Knefelkamp. San Francisco: Jossey-Bass.

Peterson, C., Maier, S. and Seligman, M. (1993) *Learned Helplessness: A Theory for an Age of Personal Control*. New York: Oxford University Press.

Pintrich, P.R. (2000) 'The role of goal orientation in self-regulated learning', in M. Boekaerts, P. Pintrich and Zeidner. M. (eds) *Handbook of Self-regulation*. New York: Academic Press, 451–502.

Pintrich, P.R. and Schunk, D.H. (1996) *Motivation in Education*. Englewood Cliffs, NJ: Prentice-Hall.

Piper, W. (1946) *The Little Engine that Could*. London and Glasgow: Collins.

PIU (Performance and Innovation Unit) (2001) *In Demand: Adult Skills in the 21st Century.* London: The Cabinet Office.

Platten, A. (2003) 'A review of CIOB accreditation procedures and future perspectives', *Proceedings of CIB W89 International Conference on Building Education and Research* (BEAR 2003: 9–11 April), vol. 3. Salford: Salford University, 1,427–36.

Polanyi, M. (1967) *The Tacit Dimension*. London: Routledge and Kegan Paul.

Pownall, H. and Rimmer, J. (2002) 'Employability and the curriculum: keys to success', in *Integrating Work and Learning in Europe: ASET Annual Conference Proceedings*. Sheffield: Association for Sandwich Education and Training, 15–17.

Prospects (2002) *A Review of the Latest Graduate Employment Research*, http://www.prospects.ac.uk (accessed 22 October 2002).

Prosser, M. and Trigwell, K. (1999) *Understanding Learning and Teaching*. Buckingham: Society for Research in Higher Education and Open University Press.

Purcell, K. and Elias, P. (2002) 'Seven years on', *Graduate Recruiter*, Autumn, 22–3.

QAA (Quality Assurance Agency) (2001a) *Guidelines for HE Progress Files*. Gloucester: The Quality Assurance Agency for Higher Education.

QAA (Quality Assurance Agency) (2001b) *Nursing Benchmark Statements.* Gloucester: The Quality Assurance Agency for Higher Education.

QAA (Quality Assurance Agency) (2001c) *Sociology Benchmark Statements.* Gloucester: The Quality Assurance Agency for Higher Education.

QAA (Quality Assurance Agency) (2001d) *Code of Practice for the Assurance of Academic Quality and Standards in Higher Education: Section 9: placement learning.* Gloucester: The Quality Assurance Agency for Higher Education.

QAA (Quality Assurance Agency) (2001e) *Framework for Higher Education Qualifications.* Gloucester: The Quality Assurance Agency for Higher Education.

Reich R.B. (1991) *The Work of Nations.* London: Simon and Schuster.

Reich R.B. (2002) *The Future of Success.* London: Vintage

Rhem, J. (1998) 'Social class and student learning', *The National Teaching and Learning Forum*, 7(5), 1–4.

RICS (2001) *Policy and Guidance on UK University Partnerships: Education and Practice Qualifications 2001.* London: The Royal Institution of Chartered Surveyors.

Rogers, C. (2002) 'Developing a positive approach to failure', in M. Peelo and T. Wareham (eds) *Failing Students in Higher Education.* Buckingham: Society for Research into Higher Education and the Open University Press, 113–23.

Rotter, J.B. (1966) 'Generalized expectancies for internal versus external control of reinforcement', *Psychological Monographs*, 80, 1–28.

Rowley, G. and Purcell, K. (2001) 'Up to the job? Graduates' perceptions of the UK higher education careers service', *Higher Education Quarterly*, 55(4), 416–35.

Salovey, P. and Mayer, J.D. (1990) 'Emotional intelligence', *Imagination, Cognition, and Personality*, 9, 185–211.

School of Geography, Leeds (2003a) *What are Context Materials?* Leeds: School of Geography. http://www.geog.leeds.ac.uk/courses/other/casestudies/what.html (accessed 11 May 2003).

School of Geography, Leeds (2003b) *Why Enterprising Entrepreneurship?* Leeds: School of Geography. Online at http://www.geog.leeds.ac.uk/courses/other/casestudies/intra/why.html (accessed 11 May 2003).

Seligman, M. (1998) *Learned Optimism.* New York: Pocket Books.

Senge, P. (1992) *The Fifth Discipline: The Art and Practice of the Learning Organization.* London: Century Business.

Sidhu, B. (2000) *Improving the Quantity and Quality of Work Experience in Higher Education.* Wolverhampton: Graduate Link, University of Wolverhampton.

Slavin, R. (1996) *Education for All.* Lisse, Netherlands: Swets and Zeitlinger.

Speakman, Z., Drake, K. and Hawkins, P. (2001) *The Art of Crazy Paving.* London: Student Volunteering UK.

Spouse, J. (2001) 'Bridging theory and practice in the supervisory relationship: a sociocultural perspective', *Journal of Advanced Nursing*, 4, 512–22.

Stenhouse, L. (1975) *An Introduction to Curriculum Research and Development.* London: Heinemann.

Stephenson, J. (1998) 'The concept of capability and its importance in higher education', in J. Stephenson and M. Yorke (eds) *Capability and Quality in Higher Education.* London: Kogan Page, 1–13.

Sternberg, R.J. (1997) *Successful Intelligence.* New York: Plume.

Sternberg, R.J. and Grigorenko, E.L. (2000a) 'Practical intelligence and its development', in R. Bar-On and J. Parker (eds) *The Handbook of Emotional Intelligence.* San Francisco: Jossey-Bass, 215–43.

Sternberg, R.J. and Grigorenko, E.L. (2000b) *Teaching for Successful Intelligence.* Arlington Heights, IL: SkyLight Professional Development.

Sternberg, R.J., Forsythe, G., Hedlund, J., Horvath, J., Wagner, R., Williams, W., Snook,

S. and Grigorenko, E. (2000) *Practical Intelligence in Everyday Life.* Cambridge: Cambridge University Press.

Stigler, J.W. and Hiebert, J. (1999) *The Teaching Gap.* New York: The Free Press.

Taylor, A. (1998) 'Employability skills: from corporate wish list to government policy', *Journal of Curriculum Studies*, 30(2), 143–64.

Taylor, P.G. (1998) 'Institutional change in uncertain times: *lone ranging* is not enough', *Studies in Higher Education*, 23(3), 269–79.

Teichler, U. (2000) 'New perspectives of the relationships between higher education and employment', *Tertiary Education and Management*, 6(2), 79–92.

TimeBank (2001) *British Firms Rate Voluntary Work.* Online at http://www.timebank. org.uk/media/releases/britishfirms.htm (accessed 11 May 2003).

Torrance, H. and Pryor, J. (1998) *Investigative Formative Assessment: Teaching, Learning and Assessment in the Classroom.* Buckingham: Open University Press.

Trowler, P. (1998) *Academics Responding to Change: New Higher Education Frameworks and Academic Cultures.* Buckingham: Society for Research into Higher Education and the Open University Press.

Trowler, P., Saunders, M. and Knight, P. (2003) *Change Thinking, Change Practices: A Guide to Change for Heads of Department, Programme Leaders and other Change Agents in Higher Education.* York: Learning and Teaching Support Centre. Online at http://www.ltsn.ac.uk/embedded_object.asp?id=18740&prompt=yes&filename= CHA005 (accessed 4 May 2003).

Turiel, E. (2002) *The Culture of Morality.* Cambridge: Cambridge University Press..

UKCC (1999) *Fitness for Practice* (The Peach Report). London: United Kingdom Central Council for Nursing, Midwifery and Health Visiting.

UKCC (2001) *Requirements for Pre-Registration Nursing Programmes.* London: United Kingdom Central Council for Nursing, Midwifery and Health Visiting. Online at http://www.nmc-uk.org/cms/content/quality%20assurance/QA%20Regulations%20 and%20guidelines.pdf (accessed 11 May 2003).

Universities UK (2002) *University Chancellors Voice Fears on Higher Education Funding Crisis.* London: UUK. Online at www.universitiesuk.ac.uk (accessed 26 October 2002).

Universities UK and Standing Conference of Principals (2002) *Modernising HE Careers Education: A Framework for Good Practice.* London: UUK/SCOP.

University of Cambridge Programme for Industry (2000) *Frameworks for Effective Work-related Learning.* Cambridge: University of Cambridge Programme for Industry.

Utley, A. (2002) 'Whatever you learn, learn about yourself', *The Times Higher Education Supplement*, No. 1568, 13 December, 10.

Utley, A. (2003) 'Industry hits out at diluted degree trend', *The Times Higher Education Supplement*, No. 1583, 4 April, 1.

Valentin, E.M.M. and Sanchez, J.J.N. (2002) 'University–industry partnerships, 1990– 2000', *Industry and Higher Education*, February, 55–61.

van Geert, P. (1994) *Dynamic Systems of Development: Change Between Complexity and Chaos.* Hemel Hempstead: Harvester Wheatsheaf.

Vieira, F. (2002) Pedagogic quality at university: what teachers and students think, *Quality in Higher Education*, 8(3), 255–72.

Volkwein, J.F. (ed.) (1999) *What is Institutional Research All About?* San Francisco: Jossey-Bass.

Walker, I. and Zhu, Y. (2003) 'Education, earnings and productivity, recent UK evidence', *Labour Market Trends*, 111(3), 145. Also at http://www.statistics.gov.uk/STATBASE/ Product. asp?vlnk=550 (accessed 11 July 2003).

Walvoord, B.E. and Anderson, V.J. (1998) *Effective Grading: A Tool for Learning and Assessment*. San Francisco: Jossey-Bass.

Ward, R. and Pierce, D. (2003) *Employability and Transitions from Higher Education to Work*. York: Learning and Teaching Support Network. Also at www.ltsn.ac.uk/ESECT (accessed 11 July 2003).

Watton, P. and Collings, J. (2002) 'Developing a framework for independent work experience', in P. Watton, J. Collings and J. Moon (eds) *Independent Work Experience: An Evolving Picture*, SEDA Paper 114. Birmingham: Staff and Educational Development Association, 25–34.

Weick, K. (1976) 'Educational institutions as loosely coupled systems', *Administrative Science Quarterly*, 21(1), 1–19.

Wenger, E. (1998) *Communities of Practice: Learning, Meaning and Identity*. Cambridge: Cambridge University Press.

Wilkie, K. and Burns, I. (2003) *Problem-Based Learning: A Handbook for Nurses*. Basingstoke: Palgrave Macmillan.

Wolf, A. (1995) *Competence-based Assessment*. Buckingham: Open University Press.

Wolf, A. (2002) *Does Education Matter? Myths About Education and Economic Growth*. London: Penguin Books.

Wood, D., Bruner, J.S. and Ross, G. (1976) 'The role of tutoring in problem-solving', *Journal of Child Psychology and Psychiatry*, 17(2), 89–100.

Work Experience Group (2002) *Work Related Learning Report*. London: Department for Education and Skills.

Wright, W.A. (2002) *Foundations for Change: Final Report of the Skills plus Project's External Evaluator*. Unpublished: http://www.open.ac.uk/vqportal/skills-plus/publications.html (accessed 11 July 2003).

Yorke, M. (2002a) 'Degree classifications in English, Welsh and Northern Irish Universities: trends, 1994–95 to 1998–99', *Higher Education Quarterly*, 56(1), 92–108.

Yorke, M. (2002b) 'Subject benchmarking and the assessment of student learning', *Quality Assurance in Education*, 10(3), 155–71.

Yorke, M. (2003a) *Transition into Higher Education: Some Implications for the 'Employability' Agenda*. York: Learning and Teaching Support Network. Also at www.ltsn.ac.uk/ESECT (accessed 11 July 2003).

Yorke, M. (2003b) 'Going with the flow: first-cycle higher education in a lifelong learning context', *Tertiary Education and Management*, 9(2), 117–30.

Yorke, M. *et al.*, (2002) 'Does grading method influence honours degree classification?', *Assessment and Evaluation in Higher Education*, 27(3), 269–79.

Yorke, M. and Knight, P.T. (2003) *The Undergraduate Curriculum and Employability*. York: Learning and Teaching Support Network. Also at www.ltsn.ac.uk/ESECT (accessed 11 July 2003).

Yorke, M., Bridges, P. and Woolf, H. (2000) 'Mark distributions and marking practices in UK higher education', *Active Learning in Higher Education*, 1(1), 7–27.

# Index

eBooks – at www.eBookstore.tandf.co.uk

# A library at your fingertips!

eBooks are electronic versions of printed books. You can store them on your PC/laptop or browse them online.

They have advantages for anyone needing rapid access to a wide variety of published, copyright information.

eBooks can help your research by enabling you to bookmark chapters, annotate text and use instant searches to find specific words or phrases. Several eBook files would fit on even a small laptop or PDA.

**NEW:** Save money by eSubscribing: cheap, online access to any eBook for as long as you need it.

## Annual subscription packages

We now offer special low-cost bulk subscriptions to packages of eBooks in certain subject areas. These are available to libraries or to individuals.

For more information please contact webmaster.ebooks@tandf.co.uk

We're continually developing the eBook concept, so keep up to date by visiting the website.

# www.eBookstore.tandf.co.uk